eat *up*

slim

down

Tried-and-true
recipes and
tips from real
weight-loss
winners

Jane Kirby, RD, and David Joachim

RODALE

Notice

This book is intended as a reference volume only, not as a medical manual. It is not intended as a substitute for any treatment that may have been prescribed by your doctor. If you suspect that you have a medical problem, we urge you to seek competent medical help. Keep in mind that nutritional needs vary from person to person, depending upon age, sex, health status, and total diet. The foods discussed and recipes given here are designed to help you make informed decisions about your diet and health.

Cover and Interior Designer: Carol Angstadt
Cover Photographer: Mitch Mandel/Rodale Images, Will Yurman/Liaison Agency
Interior photography credits for this book are on page 321.

Front Cover Recipes: Slow-Cooked Pork Stew (page 142), Chicken Fajitas (page 132), Peanut Butter
    Cake with Chocolate Frosting (page 254), and Chicken Fettuccine (page 166)

ISBN 1-57954-641-2

2   4   6 ‾8   10   9   7   5   3   1   hardcover

Visit us on the Web at www.rodalecookbooks.com.

RODALE

WE **INSPIRE** AND **ENABLE** PEOPLE TO IMPROVE
THEIR LIVES AND THE WORLD AROUND THEM

Acknowledgments

Books don't just happen. They develop from a tiny germ of an idea and take shape as they grow and mature. That kind of alchemy is hardly the result of a single person. Rather, it's an evolution that stems from the input of many contributors. It is here that we want to acknowledge these people. Our sincere thanks to all the following individuals and organizations

The staff at Rodale Books, particularly Anne Egan, the project's director, without whom the germ would not have sprouted.

Kristen O'Brien, who effortlessly contacted, cajoled, and co-ordinated the contributions of our esteemed experts.

Catherine Collins, BSc (Hons), SRD, for her impeccable nutrition analysis.

Mitch Mandel, for his beautiful photographs.

Carol Angstadt, for her inventive and inviting design.

All the health experts and spas that shared their weight-loss advice and recipes:

Dean Ornish, MD; Deepak Chopra, MD; Deirdra Price, PhD; Howard Rankin, PhD, of the Carolina Wellness Retreat; Don Mauer; Kathie Graham, RD, of the Spa at Doral; Joan Lunden; Marsha Hudnall, RD, of the Green Mountain Program at Fox Run in Vermont; Richard Simmons; Jeanne Jones for Canyon Ranch Health Resorts; Michel Stroot of the Golden Door; and Bill Wavrin of Rancho la Puerta.

The generous supporters of *Prevention*'s Recipe Sweepstakes: Mary Rodgers from Cuisinart; Julia Stambules from All-Clad; Jack Saunders at LamsonSharp; and Beverly Kastell at Hamilton Beach.

The loyal readers of *Prevention* magazine who so enthusiastically shared their weight-loss success stories, tips, and recipes with us.

And to everyone who has ever struggled to reach a healthier weight. It is your tenacity and success that encourages us all.

—*Jane Kirby, RD, and David Joachim*

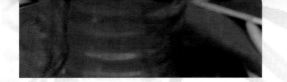

Contents

Weight Loss That Works

The people who share their advice in this book lost a combined total of more than 54,000 kg/8,500 st. And they've kept that weight off for an average of six years. Some have kept it off for 10 years or more. That's true weight-loss success.

To find these weight-loss winners, we set up a web site in conjunction with *Prevention* magazine. We also got in touch with the American National Weight Control Registry, a unique database of people who have lost at least 13 kg/2 st and kept it off for at least a year. Then we went to the telephone and talked with these people.

Our goal in writing this book was to bring these weight-loss winners directly to you – to bring you their stories, their strategies, and their wonderful recipes.

For expert advice, we also talked to top weight-loss professionals, including Kelly Brownell, PhD; Dean Ornish, MD; and Deepak Chopra, MD; and tapped into the perspective of weight-loss spas.

This book contains the combined wisdom of trained professionals and ordinary people who found out what really works. We have organized everything into an easy-to-follow plan. Charts and tables simplify the process of figuring out whether you need to lose weight and, if so, how much to lose, how to do it safely, what's good to eat, and how much to exercise. We know there isn't a one-size-fits-all method for everybody, so we have made the book as flexible as possible. You can customize the plan to meet your individual needs and to suit your own lifestyle.

Proven weight-control strategies are the core of this book, but if you ask us, the recipes are the best part. This is the food that successful dieters eat to lose weight and maintain their slimness. We were amazed at how good these recipes are. They range from simple breakfasts and salads to more indulgent main dishes. Yes, indulgent. Don't be alarmed by some of the higher-fat meals. We included 'Splurge Meal' menu suggestions with these recipes for those times when you want to indulge. And when you don't want to overdo it, look for the 'Slimming Meal' menus.

Either way, you'll never feel deprived. This is easy-to-make, great-tasting food from people just like you. How do Double Chocolate Chip Fudge Brownies sound? How about Blueberry-Pecan Pancakes? Hot Black Bean Dip? Grilled Pork Chops? Roast Sirloin Steak? Every recipe gets our hearty seal of approval, especially the Peanut Butter Cake with Chocolate Frosting. Yummy!

What's the point of rattling off these recipe names? The point is to enjoy eating. That's what this book is about. Whether you want to lose a little weight or a lot, you can't do it if you have to eat food that you don't like. This book shows you how to eat well and enjoy the experience of eating while losing or maintaining weight.

Wisdom from the Winners

You've heard the heartbreaking statistics: 'Ninety-five per cent of people who lose weight will gain it back.' It's enough to make you exchange your scales for a store card at the outsize shop.

Don't believe it. Plenty of people lose weight and keep it off. And you can, too. That's worth repeating.

Plenty of people lose weight and keep it off. And you can, too.

But what about that 95 per cent failure rate? That's a widely quoted statistic that comes from a study of only 100 people at a single nutrition clinic in the 1950s. It does not represent the real world of today, where lots of people lose weight and keep it off on their own. Our evidence: thousands of weight-loss winners are coming out and speaking up. The National Weight Control Registry at the University of Pittsburgh School of Medicine in the United States has identified the largest group of weight-loss winners ever recorded, and they have lots of good advice to share. We've interviewed dozens of successful dieters. They're people just like you. Some lost weight on their own; some joined weight-loss programmes. Some had to lose weight for health reasons; others wanted to make a better impression at their school reunions. And a few had simply had enough of being overweight.

Break the Rules

The patterns of success that we saw in our interviews were the same as those at the National Weight Control Registry. And they weren't what you might expect. The registry has tracked more than 2,000 people who have lost at least 13 kg/2 st and kept it off for at least one year. Amazingly, the average loss of those in the registry is about 130 kg/4½ st, and they have maintained it for more than six years. What these people told us flies in the face of conventional weight-loss wisdom. Consider these myth-busting truths.

1

It Worked for Me!

Connie Bissonnette

VITAL STATS

Weight lost: 20 kg/3 st

Time kept it off: 7 years

Weight-loss strategies:
Strength training, low-fat diet

Weight-maintenance strategies:
Exercise, healthy eating

Connie went from feeling old and achy to 20 kg/3 st trimmer and feeling younger with weight training. Now she teaches others to do the same.

'My knees hurt and I was always tired. I found myself napping whenever I could. At 53, it didn't occur to me that my sluggishness could be caused by anything else than simply getting old.

'I was a full-time university laboratory instructor and was about 13 kg (2 st) overweight. My blood pressure began to creep up. My son Jeff, who was working on his master's degree in human performance, told me that I'd feel better if I exercised. But excuses came easy. "Are you kidding? With my knees? Where am I supposed to find the time? I'm not spending all that money on shoes and going to a gym. I barely have enough energy to get through the day."'

'Jeff persisted and planned a simple 10-minute workout for me. Just three days a week of seated leg lifts, wall push-ups, and lifts with milk jugs half filled with water. It was so easy that I had no trouble sticking to it. After a few months, my knees were feeling better, so Jeff toughened up my programme and challenged me to a single diet change: stop using butter on my morning toast.

'After about six months, my jeans were looser. But what impressed me most was how good I started to feel. I had more energy and my knees didn't bother me anymore. I began to do more exercises and started walking for about 30 minutes two or three times a week. Soon, I could run with our dogs and lift an 18-kg (40-lb) bag of dog food easily.

'I was hooked. I wanted to learn all I could about exercise and diet. My son even suggested that I become a personal trainer. At first, I thought he was joking. But then, he said, "You already know this stuff and you're a good teacher." Because I was ready to retire and wanted to find a part-time job close to home, I considered what he said. Two months later I became a certified personal trainer. Today, most of the clients I have are 40, 50, and 60. I have a contract that if they are not happy after three to six sessions, they can have a full refund. I haven't refunded a single penny.

'Even at 58 I am still adding muscle. I enjoy weight lifting, and I want to see how far I can go.' ▪

It's never too late. Being heavy as a child doesn't sentence you to life as an overweight adult. At the registry, 46 per cent of the participants said that they were overweight as children at age 11 or younger. Twenty-five per cent first became heavy between ages 12 and 18. Only 28 per cent became overweight as adults. That means most of these weight-loss winners overcame a lifetime of being overweight.

Forget your 'ideal' weight. Ideal weight is just that: an ideal. Most people who consider themselves successful at maintaining a weight loss drop only about half the amount that they'd hoped to. Weight-loss researcher Dr Thomas Wadden proved the point. He and his colleagues asked 60 overweight women (their average weight was about 99 kg/15½ st) to write down three numbers: their ideal 'goal' weight, weight loss that they considered 'acceptable', and weight loss that they saw as 'disappointing'. Most set their ideal weights about 32 kg/5 st less than their current weights – an average ideal of 66 kg/10½ st. The average 'acceptable' weight loss was about 25 kg/4 st, which would put them at an average weight of 74 kg/11½ st. A loss of only 17 kg/2 st 10 lb was considered 'disappointing' – an average weight of 82 kg/13 st.

After six months of dieting, exercising, and behaviour modification, plus six months of maintenance, these women lost an average of only 16 kg/2½ st, 1 kg/2 lb *less* than their 'disappointing' weight loss. The good news? All were absolutely thrilled with their new weight. Even though they hadn't reached the loss that they initially called 'disappointing', they felt better physically and emotionally than they had ever expected.

A weight loss of only 10 per cent of your current weight is enough to bring down high blood pressure, lower cholesterol and triglycerides (substances that can put you at risk for heart disease), and improve your overall medical health. And that translates into feeling better instantly. So reach for a reasonable goal weight, not an ideal. That's exactly what Susan Cursi did. Susan is 165 cm/5 ft 5 in. tall and now weighs 59 kg/9 st 4 lb. She lost 22.5 kg/3½ st and has kept it off for five years. But she had to get real first. 'I realized that I may never be as skinny as I was in school. But when I lost just 13 kg (2 st), I felt so much better.'

Keep trying. Contrary to rumours, yo-yo dieting (or continually losing weight and gaining it back) does not lower your chances of ever losing weight permanently. The research that started that rumour was done on rats, not humans. Even so, it caused some weight-loss 'experts' to think that it might be healthier to stay heavy than to continue trying to lose weight. Nothing could be further from the truth. In America a national task force was organized to do a comprehensive survey of 43 human studies on the subject (known among doctors as 'weight cycling'). Guess what they concluded? Repeat dieting does not increase body fat, make future weight-loss attempts more difficult, or permanently lower metabolic rate (the rate at which your body burns calories).

Proof positive. Nearly all the weight-loss winners (91 per cent) in the National Weight Control Registry are veteran dieters. They lost an average of 27 kg/4 st and kept it off for 10 years. The people we interviewed had similar dieting patterns. What triggered the lasting success? Among other things, they all said that this time they were going to make long-term behaviour changes. They watched what they ate more closely, and they exercised more.

Adrienne Jacobson dieted for years. She tried everything: weight-loss pills, liquid diet products, even starvation. Finally, she found a registered dietitian who designed an eating plan based on her lifestyle – a diet that she could stick with for the long term. Initially, Adrienne saw her dietitian once a week for positive reinforcement and fine tuning. She has maintained a loss of 16 kg/2½ st for 3½ years.

Mark Ballard dropped an amazing 57 kg/9 st – but not the first time he tried. 'My first weight-loss attempt was a fast that I did in secondary school. From there, I moved on: Weight Watchers, the Cambridge System, Slim Fast, Nutri/System, Cabbage Soup.' Mark eventually found that a sensible low-fat eating plan and exercise worked for him. If you've tried before, it couldn't hurt to try again. This time could be different.

Ignore your family's weight history. Genetics tell you only that you have a tendency to be overweight. Your genes do not predict your ability to lose weight. 'I saw pictures of my grandmothers, great-grandmothers, and great-great-grandmothers, and they were all overweight and short like I am. My mother was only about 150 cm (5 ft) tall, and she was also overweight,' says Jean Ross. Despite her family's weight history, Jean dropped 16 kg/2½ st and went from a size 22 to a size 12. How about the weight-loss winners at the registry? Forty-six per cent reported having at least one parent who was overweight.

Trust your instincts. People told us that one of the keys to permanent weight loss was getting triggered by something deep inside, coming to a turning point, an incident or time in their lives that made them say, 'This is it. This time will be different.' For Richard Daly, it was his overall health. 'I looked down at the floor beside my easy chair and counted eight soft-drink cans that I'd emptied in less than an hour. The next thing I knew, I was in the hospital, diagnosed with diabetes and learning how to give myself insulin to bring down my sky-high blood sugar.' Right then, Richard knew that he had to make a change for good.

More than three-quarters (77 per cent) of the men and women in the registry said that there was a trigger or a turning point that motivated them. Thirty-two per cent said that their triggers were either medical conditions like back pain, breathing trouble, or fatigue, or emotional events such as divorce. 'I had asthma, poor circulation, chronic constipation, and heartburn,' says Lynne Watson. But poor health wasn't enough. Lynne went on and off diets for years until her powerful emotions finally moved her. 'I sat alone on Christmas Day 1985 and realized that I had two choices: end my life or take control of it. I decided to grab control; I didn't want to die.' For Lynne, the trigger had to come from deep within. Once she found her motivation, she lost 47 kg/7½ st.

Be honest with yourself. Not everyone has to be hit with an earth-shattering event. For more than 11 per cent of the people at the registry, the trigger was simply seeing themselves in a mirror or a photograph. That's all it took for Matt Salmon. 'I was rummaging through some snapshots of my formerly athletic self. I realized that I now looked like a walrus. I couldn't believe I'd let myself get so bloated. I was ashamed and embarrassed.' Matt started a basic eating and exercise strategy and lost 32 kg/5 st.

Luanne Barrett had a similar experience. 'I looked at a photo. My heart sank. My weight had crept up to more than 77 kg (12 st). It was time to do something about my weight – and my lifestyle.' Luanne took control and lost 12 kg/2 st.

How Much Should You Weigh?

Most people want to know what the 'right' weight is. The answer is that there is no ideal weight that applies to every person. Everybody is a little different. Nevertheless, there are ways to tell whether your body shape and weight are putting your health at risk and what weight range is considered healthy for you.

Do the maths. Two simple formulas will tell you whether your weight is healthy or unhealthy: body mass index (BMI) and waist circumference. As your BMI goes up, so does your risk of high blood pressure and increased blood cholesterol levels. Likewise, the more weight you have around your middle, the greater your chances of developing diseases like adult-onset diabetes, heart disease, and some forms of cancer. See pages 6–7 to check your BMI and see where you stand.

Measure your middle. It's important to check your waist circumference even if you're not overweight on the BMI chart. A large waist measurement means that you're shaped more like an apple than a pear and could have increased risk for ailments such as diabetes and heart disease. Waist circumference is particularly useful for older people whose weight has altered with age. Their risk for major diseases goes up not because of weight gain but because their weight has collected around their middle. Older men are often aware of their changing shapes because their trousers are sized by waist measurement. Women's clothing is not sized this way, so women may be less aware of increased waist size as they age.

To check your waist circumference, place a tape measure just above your tummy button at your natural waistline. Pull the tape snug but not tight. Jot down your waist size. World Health Organization guidelines state that a circumference of more than 100 cm/40 in. for a man and 88 cm/35 in. for a woman puts your health at risk. A circumference of more than 94 cm/37 in. for a man and 80 cm/32 in. for a woman means your health could be at risk. Losing some weight now will make a difference.

Find your healthy weight range. Your best weight is not a particular number on the scales. In fact, making a single number your goal always keeps you 1 kilogram or 1 pound away from failure. Instead, think of your target weight as a range. This strategy gives you leeway for your body's natural monthly and seasonal weight fluctuations. To find your range, see 'Find Your Target Weight Range' on page 10.

Follow Your Own Plan

Knowing that weight loss is different for everybody, we designed this book to be flexible. You can personalize your own weight-loss strategy. If you like the

(continued on page 10)

IS YOUR CURRENT WEIGHT HEALTHY? 1

Body mass index (BMI) is a tool health professionals use to determine how healthy a person's weight is. Generally, the higher BMIs are associated with unhealthy amounts of body fat, not just total weight.

To determine your BMI, find your height on the left, then move across until you find your weight. Your BMI is the number on the bottom of that column. See pages 8–9 for imperial measurements.

Height (m)	Weight (kg)										
1.50	41	43	45	47	50	52	54	56	59	61	63
1.52	42	44	46	49	51	53	56	58	60	62	65
1.54	43	45	47	50	52	55	57	59	62	64	66
1.56	44	46	49	51	54	56	58	61	63	66	68
1.58	45	47	50	52	55	57	60	62	65	67	70
1.60	46	49	51	54	56	59	61	64	67	69	72
1.62	47	50	53	55	58	60	63	66	68	71	74
1.64	48	51	54	57	60	62	65	67	70	73	75
1.66	50	52	55	58	61	63	66	69	72	74	77
1.68	51	54	56	59	62	65	68	71	73	76	79
1.70	52	55	58	61	64	67	69	72	75	78	81
1.72	53	56	59	62	65	68	71	74	77	80	83
1.74	55	58	61	64	67	70	73	76	79	82	85
1.76	56	59	62	65	68	71	73	77	80	84	87
1.78	57	60	63	67	70	73	76	79	82	86	89
1.80	58	62	65	68	71	75	78	81	84	88	91
1.82	60	63	66	70	73	76	80	83	86	89	93
1.84	91	64	68	71	75	78	81	85	88	91	95
1.86	62	66	69	73	76	80	83	87	90	93	97
BMI	18	19	20	21	22	23	24	25	26	27	28

Underweight: Less than 18
Normal: 18–24
Overweight: 25–29

Obese: 30–34
Very obese: 35–39
Extremely obese: 40 and above

29	30	31	32	33	34	35	36	37	38	39	40
65	68	70	72	74	77	79	81	83	86	88	90
67	69	72	74	76	79	81	83	86	88	90	92
69	71	74	76	78	81	83	85	88	90	93	95
71	73	75	78	80	83	85	88	90	93	95	97
72	75	77	80	83	85	88	90	93	95	97	100
74	77	79	82	85	87	90	92	95	97	100	102
77	80	82	85	87	90	92	95	97	100	102	105
78	81	83	86	89	91	94	97	100	102	105	108
80	83	85	88	91	94	97	99	102	105	108	110
82	85	88	90	93	96	99	102	104	107	110	113
84	87	90	93	95	98	101	104	107	110	113	116
86	89	92	95	98	101	104	107	109	112	115	118
88	91	94	97	100	103	106	109	112	115	118	121
90	93	96	99	102	105	108	112	115	118	121	124
92	95	98	101	105	108	111	114	117	120	124	127
94	97	100	104	107	110	113	117	120	123	126	130
96	100	103	106	109	113	116	119	123	126	129	133
98	102	105	108	112	115	119	122	125	129	132	135
100	104	107	111	114	118	121	125	128	131	135	138
29	**30**	**31**	**32**	**33**	**34**	**35**	**36**	**37**	**38**	**39**	**40**

IS YOUR CURRENT WEIGHT HEALTHY? 2

This table of body mass index (BMI) is presented in the imperial system of measurements. First work out your weight in pounds (14 lb = 1 st). To determine your BMI, find your height in the column at the left, then move across until you find your weight. Your BMI is the number at the bottom of that column. See pages 6–7 for metric measurements and an explanation of BMI.

Height (ft)	Weight (lb)										
4'10"	86	91	96	100	105	110	115	119	124	129	134
4'11"	89	94	99	104	109	114	119	124	128	133	138
5'	92	97	102	107	112	118	123	128	133	138	143
5'1"	96	100	106	111	116	122	127	132	137	143	148
5'2"	99	104	109	115	120	126	131	136	142	147	153
5'3"	102	107	113	118	124	130	135	141	146	152	158
5'4"	105	110	116	122	128	134	140	145	151	157	163
5'5"	109	114	120	126	132	138	144	150	156	162	168
5'6"	112	118	124	130	136	142	148	155	161	167	173
5'7"	116	121	127	134	140	146	153	159	166	172	178
5'8"	120	125	131	138	144	151	158	164	171	177	184
5'9"	123	128	135	142	149	155	162	169	176	182	189
5'10"	126	132	139	146	153	160	167	174	181	188	195
5'11"	130	136	143	150	157	165	172	179	186	193	200
6'	134	140	147	154	162	169	177	184	191	199	206
6'1"	138	144	151	159	166	174	182	189	197	204	212
6'2"	141	148	155	163	171	179	186	194	202	210	218
6'3"	145	152	160	168	176	184	192	200	208	216	224
6'4"	149	156	164	172	180	189	197	205	213	221	230
BMI	18	19	20	21	22	23	24	25	26	27	28

Underweight: Less than 18	**Obese:** 30–34
Normal: 18–24	**Very obese:** 35–39
Overweight: 25–29	**Extremely obese:** 40 and above

29	30	31	32	33	34	35	36	37	38	39	40
138	143	148	153	158	162	167	172	177	181	186	191
143	148	153	158	163	168	173	178	183	188	193	198
148	153	158	163	168	174	179	184	189	194	199	204
153	158	164	169	174	180	185	190	195	201	206	211
158	164	169	175	180	186	191	196	202	207	213	218
163	169	175	180	186	191	197	203	208	214	220	225
169	174	180	186	192	197	204	209	215	221	227	232
174	180	186	192	198	204	210	216	222	228	234	240
179	186	192	198	204	210	216	223	229	235	241	247
185	191	198	204	211	217	223	230	236	242	249	255
190	197	203	210	216	223	230	236	243	249	256	262
196	203	209	216	223	230	236	243	250	257	263	270
202	209	216	222	229	236	243	250	257	264	271	278
208	215	222	229	236	243	250	257	265	272	279	286
213	221	228	235	242	250	258	265	272	279	287	294
219	227	235	242	250	257	265	272	280	288	295	302
225	233	241	249	256	264	272	280	287	295	303	311
232	240	248	256	264	272	279	287	295	303	311	319
238	246	254	263	271	279	287	295	304	312	320	328

FIND YOUR TARGET WEIGHT RANGE

Your body mass index (see pages 6–7 for metric tables, pages 8–9 for imperial tables) will tell you if your health is at risk. Use this chart to determine your weight goals. Remember that these numbers represent a range that is appropriate at various heights. They are not absolutes, so use them only as a guide. The chart on the left shows height and weight in metric measurements; the chart on the right gives imperial measurements (to find the weight in stones, divide pounds by 14).

	Metric				Imperial			
m	kg	m	kg	ft	lb	ft	lb
1.50	45–56	1.70	58–72	5'	99–125	5'10"	137–172
1.52	46–58	1.72	59–74	5'1"	104–130	5'11"	141–176
1.54	47–59	1.74	61–76	5'2"	108–137	6'	145–183
1.56	49–61	1.76	62–77	5'3"	110–139	6'1"	148–185
1.58	50–62	1.78	63–79	5'4"	115–143	6'2"	152–192
1.60	51–64	1.80	65–81	5'5"	117–148	6'3"	156–196
1.62	53–66	1.82	66–83	5'6"	121–154	6'8"	161–203
1.64	54–67	1.84	68–85	5'7"	126–156	6'5"	165–209
1.66	55–69	1.86	69–87	5'8"	130–163	6'6"	170–214
1.68	57–70			5'9"	132–165		

psychological approach, see 'What's Your Weight-Loss Personality?' on pages 12–15. Knowing your general response to life might help you figure out the weight-loss strategy that suits you best. If you just want some healthier recipes in your diet, look through the recipes until you find a few that you like. (For tips on making your own recipes more healthy, see 'What Works in the Kitchen', starting on page 29.) If you want to exercise more, see 'Burn, Baby, Burn' on page 25. Or, if structured meal plans are for you, pick a calorie level (see how on page 17), then follow the simple two-week slimming plan starting on page 284.

Play the numbers. The most surefire method of losing weight is to take in fewer calories than you use. That's what this book is based on. If you are overweight, you are simply taking in more calories than you need. The solution is to take in fewer calories (by altering your diet gradually) or use up more (by gradually getting more active).

Lose weight gradually. Here's the science behind the principle of calorie balance: 500 g/1 lb of fat is equivalent to

3,500 calories. For every 3,500 calories you cut, your weight will drop 500 g/1 lb.

However, cut too many calories too quickly and you may not lose any weight at all. It's too sharp a change for your body. Studies show that on fewer than 800 to 1,000 calories a day (by eating less, exercising strenuously, or a combination of the two), your body will turn down its thermostat to conserve every calorie it gets. Your body goes into survival mode and doesn't know if you're a prisoner of war suffering from starvation or a prisoner of your own head. That's why rapid weight-loss diets don't work.

Barbara Miltenberger knows this principle. 'As soon as I saw the weight coming off, I thought, "If it's working at this rate, I'll eat less so that I'll lose more," she admits. 'Then I stalled and put on even more weight because I was undereating. And my metabolism slowed down. I'd start losing again when I'd eat a little bit more.' In the end, Barbara lost 18 kg/3 st the safe, reliable way: slowly.

Drop a little weight a week. Safe, effective weight loss is considered to be 0.5–1 kg/1–2 lb a week. That's not as slow as you might think. In just two months, you could be 9 kg/1 st 6 lb slimmer.

To lose 500 g/1 lb a week, you need to reduce your calories by 500 each day (500 × 7 = 3,500 calories). To lose 1 kg/2 lb a week, reduce your calories by 1,000 a day (1,000 × 7 = 7,000 calories). Reducing calories means eating fewer of them and burning off more.

See how many calories you eat now. Before changing the way you eat, it helps to know how many calories you eat to maintain your current weight. Some people keep a food journal and average out the number of calories they eat using a fat-and-calorie-count book (these are available in many bookshops). 'It took a few extra minutes a day, but keeping a food journal helped me become aware of how much I was eating', says Alan Mathis, who lost 59 kg/9 st.

A journal will yield a wealth of information about your eating habits. If you're not very aware of your diet, give it a try. Keep a small notebook in your pocket or handbag for just three days, including at least one weekend day. Jot down what you eat, when you eat, how much, and how you felt when you ate. Write down every last bit of food and drink. Then review it to see the average number of calories that you eat in a day. You'll also discover your snacking patterns and the emotions that prompt you to eat.

This method may be too time-consuming for many people. If you are generally aware of what and how much you eat, see 'How Many Calories Do You Eat Now?' on pages 18–19 to figure out the average number of calories that you eat to maintain your current weight.

Make a reasonable calorie budget. Once you know how many calories you eat each day to maintain your current weight, it's easy to plan a diet to lose weight. You can cut 150 calories simply by choosing a glass of diet cola instead of a can of standard cola (most colas have about 150 calories).

Get Balance

After you pick a daily calorie level, you could eat a day's worth of calories in chocolate or in steamed broccoli. It really doesn't matter for weight loss. But if you want to keep the weight off long-term and stay healthy, a

(continued on page 16)

WHAT'S YOUR WEIGHT-LOSS PERSONALITY?

Knowing your general approach to life can help you choose the weight-loss method that suits you best. Here's a list of questions that will help you pinpoint your weight-loss personality. Every question has four statements that may or may not apply to you. Rank each statement 1, 2, 3, or 4, where 1 describes you least and 4 describes you best.

Transfer your scores to the Scoring Table on page 14, then add them up. Your highest score will reveal your weight-loss personality. Read the corresponding description to find out the most effective approach for you to lose weight and keep it off.

1 Least like me

2 Hardly like me

3 Somewhat like me

4 Most like me

1. When it comes to new health information, I:
   a. read several sources to make sure that they are giving the same advice.
   b. like to see statistics and how the information was compiled before believing it.
   c. don't have time to read the news.
   d. like to try new things, especially if they've worked for someone else.

2. When I dress in the morning, I:
   a. wear what makes me feel good that day.
   b. dress after hearing the day's weather forecast.
   c. wear what I planned for that day at the beginning of the week.
   d. wear what fits my mood.

3. I shop for food:
   a. when we're out of food, and I buy what looks good.
   b. by buying only what's on the list that I compiled for my weekly menu.
   c. by compiling a list of what's on sale.
   d. without a list and buy what seems good for my body.

4. When I pass my favourite fast-food restaurant, I:
   a. stop if it's mealtime, but check nutritional information first.
   b. almost always stop to get my favourite food, even if I'm not hungry.
   c. stop if it's mealtime and get my favourite food.
   d. stop only if I've planned it into my weekly meals.

5. When contemplating my weekend activities, I prefer:
   - a. to plan several days in advance.
   - b. intellectually stimulating activities.
   - c. to keep my options open until Friday.
   - d. activities that help my personal growth.

6. The activity I like best is:
   - a. choosing catalogue items for my family.
   - b. organizing kitchen and bathroom cupboards.
   - c. finding activities to help everyone in my family grow personally.
   - d. decorating the house so it's an enjoyable, fun place to live.

7. In relationships with others, I:
   - a. am sometimes late because I get involved in something fun and forget the time.
   - b. am known to get impatient when I'm not understood.
   - c. am considered idealistic.
   - d. often have expectations of how others should behave.

8. Those who know me well say that I am:
   - a. reliable and dependable.
   - b. empathetic and inspirational.
   - c. fun to have around when things become dull.
   - d. intelligent and clever.

9. If I'm trying to lose weight, I will:
   - a. plan my meals in the morning, following my guidelines.
   - b. ignore my food plan if I'm busy or if it doesn't sound good to me.
   - c. plan meals weekly and eat what's on my plan even if it doesn't sound good to me that day.
   - d. fix something in the healthy category, but not necessarily follow a meal plan.

10. When it comes to sending Christmas cards, I:
   - a. don't get to it until the very last minute.
   - b. buy the cards early and write a few every night so that I can send them all by the recommended posting date.
   - c. compile a special mailing list on my computer and then use it to print the envelopes.
   - d. would rather hire someone to do it.

(continued)

WHAT'S YOUR WEIGHT-LOSS PERSONALITY?

SCORING TABLE AND PERSONALITIES

Transfer your answers to the table below. (Note that the spaces are not always in a-b-c-d order.) Total your points in each column. Match the symbol underneath the column with the highest score to the personality types. If your two highest totals are nearly equal, read the descriptions for both types to see which fits you best.

1.	a__	b__	c__	d__
2.	c__	b__	d__	a__
3.	b__	c__	a__	d__
4.	d__	a__	b__	c__
5.	a__	b__	c__	d__
6.	b__	a__	d__	c__
7.	d__	b__	a__	c__
8.	a__	d__	c__	b__
9.	c__	a__	b__	d__
10.	b__	c__	a__	d__
Total	__	__	__	__
	O	**A**	**S**	**I**

O = Organized

You thrive on routines and schedules. Your kitchen cupboards are likely to be highly organized and everything has its place in your home. You're usually prepared for anything. Your weight-loss strategy:

• Calculate your current daily calorie intake on page 18. Subtract 500 or 1,000 from that number so that you can lose 500 g–1 kg/1–2 lb a week. Match your calorie level to the menu plan starting on page 286 and follow the menus.
• Chart your progress. Use a checklist to record what you eat and how much you exercise every day.
• Plan a week or two of menus at a time.
• Try to be flexible. Structure and organization might feel so comfortable that you get stuck in a pattern that isn't working.

A = Analytical

You're an information gatherer. You enjoy complexity and the challenges of problem solving. Your weight-loss strategy:

• Design your own programme.
• Use the tables on page 18–19 to calculate the number of calories you are eating

now. Subtract 500 per day to lose 500 g/ 1 lb a week. Keeping a food journal and using a calorie-counter book may help you chart the calories that you eat daily.

- Turn to 'What to Eat' on page 17 to read about the building blocks of a balanced lower-calorie diet. Use the information to make your daily food choices.
- You may benefit from seeing a dietitian, who can help you analyse how you're eating now and make suggestions for changes. Ask your GP to refer you, look at the British Dietetic Association web site (www.bda.uk.com), or send an s.a.e. marked 'Private Practice' to BDA, 5th Floor, Charles House, 148/9 Great Charles Street, Queensway, Birmingham B3 3HT, to get a list of state-registered dietitians in your area.

S = Spontaneous

You live life as it comes, expanding each moment to overflowing. You look for variety and maximum flexibility. You hate schedules and have a crisis approach to life. Your weight-loss strategy:

- Skip rigid food plans. If they don't fit into your lifestyle, you'll just ignore them.
- Stock up on a selection of healthy, low-calorie, and low-fat foods to eat when you're hungry. Keep problem foods out of the house.

- Read through the recipes that begin on page 49 and flag the ones that sound appetizing and are low in calories and fat.
- Eat at least five fruits and five vegetables each day.
- Eat only from salad-size plates. Drink from juice glasses. Stock up on pre-portioned foods such as low-calorie frozen meals and individually packaged healthy snacks.

I = Inspirational

You're always interested in improving yourself, mentally and physically. People often confide in you because you're a great listener – and you have a wonderfully kind, effective way of inspiring others. Your weight-loss strategy:

- Join a weight-loss group. You like people, so group settings work extremely well. Read the profiles of weight-loss winners throughout this book. Just look for the logo 'It Worked for Me!'
- Keep tempting foods out of the house, but don't rule out your favourite foods entirely. Deprivation leads you to overeat, so be sure to plan occasional desserts.
- You're likely to enjoy an extra scoop of a food you love, so serve only a single portion. Don't eat out of the bag. At meals avoid putting the food on the table for everyone to help themselves. Instead, put food on each dish and then serve.

balanced diet is the way to go. Here are two ways to get balance.

Eat from the plate. The Food Standards Agency divides food into five groups. It uses a plate as a model to show the approximate proportions of each group we should consume to maintain a well-balanced, healthy diet:

- 5 or more servings of bread, cereals, or potatoes

- 5 or more servings of fruit and vegetables

- 2–3 servings of milk and other dairy

- 2–4 servings of meat, fish, and alternatives

- 2 servings of food containing fats, and 2 servings of foods containing fats and sugar

Notice that a range of servings is given in each food group. If you eat the lower number of servings a day, you'll get about 1,600 calories. If you eat the larger number of servings, your calorie total will be about 2,700. Either way, you'll get a good balance of vitamins, minerals, and fibre.

Try the exchange programme. A similar food-grouping system is the Dietary Exchange System. The advantage of this system is its greater level of detail, so it's easier to keep track of what you eat if you're trying to lose weight. To use the exchange system, choose the calorie level you need to lose 500 g–1 kg/1–2 lb a week. Then see 'What to Eat' to determine how many servings of the various food groups you should eat each day. The recipes in this book include dietary exchanges to make meal planning simpler.

Make servings count. Knowing serving sizes is crucial to making any meal plan work. Unfortunately, because many of us are eating in restaurants more often and their portions are large, we've become used to eating more than we should. The average take-away muffin is about five times the size it should be. Even healthy foods like potatoes are nearly three times the size that health experts recommend. When in doubt about what makes a serving, minimize, don't super-size, and find a smaller plate to serve your food on. You'll find more specifics on the pages that follow.

Bread. Sometimes called starches, the bread group encompasses all carbohydrate-rich foods like cereals, grains, pastas, breads, savoury biscuits and crackers, and snacks; and starchy vegetables like plantains, potatoes, winter squash, and yams. In general, one serving is:

- 30 g/1 oz breakfast cereal

- 2 tablespoons cooked rice, pasta, or starchy vegetable

- 1 slice of bread or toast or $\frac{1}{2}$ a small bread roll

- 1 egg-sized potato

- 30 g/1 oz of most snack foods (see 'Counting treats' on page 20 for a list)

Fruit and vegetables. This includes all vegetables except the starchy ones mentioned above. Go for the richest colours you can find. Dark green and dark yellow vegetables – such as spinach, broccoli, romaine lettuce, carrots, and peppers – are the most nutritious. Fruits and vegetables can be fresh, frozen, canned, and fruit can also be dried or juice. One serving equals:

- 1 medium piece fresh fruit

- 2 small fruits, such as satsumas

WHAT TO EAT

In the chart below, pick the daily calorie level that is closest to the one you have chosen to reach your weight goals. Then scan the food groups to see how many servings of each food to eat in a day. Of course, these numbers are meant only as a guide. Some days, you may end up eating more or less in any given food category.

Food Group	Daily Calorie Level				
	1,200	1,500	1,800	2,000	2,500
Bread	5	6	8	9	10
Vegetable	2	5	5	4	5
Fruit	3	3	5	5	6
Milk	1½	2	2	2	4
Meat	5	6	6	8	10
Fat	3	4	5	5	6

- 2 tablespoons canned fruit (with a small amount of juice)
- 200 ml/7 fl oz fruit juice
- a small salad
- 2 tablespoons vegetables

Milk. Skimmed milk and fat-free yogurt are included here. Cream and other dairy fats are counted in the fat group. One serving of milk equals:

- 200 ml/7 fl oz skimmed milk
- Small pot fat-free or low-fat yogurt or low-fat fromage frais
- 40 g 1½ oz cheese

Meat. When buying meats, choose ones labelled 'lean' or 'very lean'. Look for 'minced steak' or 'extra-lean' mince or ground beef rather than standard mince because the latter may contain more fat. This group includes meats and other protein-based foods like cheese, eggs, and beans. Remember that there may be several portions of meat in any one meal you eat. Bacon is counted in the fat group. Generally, one serving of meat equals:

- 60–85 g/2–3 oz cooked lean meat, skinless poultry, oily fish, or shellfish
- 115–150 g/4–5 oz white fish
- 40 g/1½ oz cheese
- 2–3 tablespoons cooked dried beans, peas, or lentils
- 1–2 eggs (maximum 6 a week)

Fat. Most fats have the same number of calories per serving, but some are better for

(continued on page 20

HOW MANY CALORIES DO YOU EAT NOW?

Here's a quick way to estimate the number of calories that you currently eat to maintain your weight. First, determine your activity level using the descriptions on the right. Then, find your weight on the left in kilograms or pounds (multiply your weight in stones by 14).

Follow across the row until you find the column that matches your activity level. The corresponding number is approximately how many calories you now take in each day. Remember, to lose 500 g/1 lb a week, drop that number by 500. To lose 1 kg/2 lb a week, drop the number by 1,000.

WOMEN

Current Weight		Activity Level		
kg	lb	Light	Moderate	Heavy
58	128	1,698	1,819	1,940
60	132	1,730,	1,853	1,977
62	137	1,756	1,881	2,006
64	141	1,782	1,909	2,036
66	146	1,807	1,936	2,065
68	150	1,833	1,964	2,095
70	154	1,859	1,992	2,214
72	159	1,884	2,019	2,154
74	163	1,910	2,047	2,183
76	168	1,936	2,074	2,213
78	172	1,962	2,102	2,242
80	176	1,988	2,130	2,272
82	181	2,013	2,157	2,300
84	185	2,039	2,185	2,330
86	190	2,065	2,212	2,360
88	194	2,090	2,240	2,389
90	198	2,116	2,267	2,418
92	203	2,142	2,295	2,448
94	207	2,168	2,323	2,477
96	212	2,193	2,350	2,507
98	216	2,219	2,378	2,536
100	220	2,245	2,405	2,565

Light: Reading, playing cards, playing piano, typing, cooking, sewing, dusting, making beds, showering, bowling, playing snooker or cricket, walking slowly
Moderate: Painting and decorating, gardening, cleaning windows, carpentry, golf, moderate swimming, slow jogging
Heavy: Labouring, climbing stairs, cross-country walking, football, cycling, average jogging, tennis, skiing

MEN

Current Weight		Activity Level		
kg	lb	Light	Moderate	Heavy
86	190	2,407	2,579	2,751
88	194	2,440	2,615	2,789
90	198	2,474	2,650	2,827
92	202	2,507	2,686	2,865
94	207	2,540	2,722	2,903
96	212	2,573	2,757	2,941
98	216	2,607	2,793	2,979
100	220	2,640	2,829	3,017
102	225	2,673	2,864	3,055
104	230	2,707	2,900	3,093
106	234	2,740	2,936	3,131
108	238	2,773	2,971	3,169
110	243	2,806	3,007	3,207
112	247	2,840	3,042	3,245
114	251	2,873	3,078	3,283
116	256	2,906	3,114	3,321
118	260	2,939	3,149	3,359
120	265	2,973	3,185	3,397
122	269	3,006	3,221	3,435
124	273	3,039	3,256	3,473
126	278	3,072	3,292	3,511
128	282	3,106	3,328	3,549
130	285	3,139	3,363	3,587

you than others. The good monounsaturated and polyunsaturated fats are generally found in plant foods like olive oil and nuts, and in some seafood. Generally, one serving of fat equals:

- 5 g butter or regular margarine (80 per cent fat), or 10 g low-fat margarine (40 per cent fat)
- 1 teaspoon vegetable oil, ghee, or lard
- 2 tablespoons soured cream
- 2 teaspoons mayonnaise or oily salad dressing
- 8–10 olives
- 2 teaspoons peanut butter
- 2 teaspoons double cream

Counting treats. You've probably become used to many of the foods that you consider treats. If a little bit of these foods helps you stick to a healthy eating plan, there's no reason to stop eating them. Just eat moderate amounts. Here's how to count them using the dietary exchange system. Foods like sorbet and jam are included in the bread group because they are mostly carbohydrates, but don't let them account for more than one bread portion a day: they contain few essential nutrients, unlike other starchy foods that count as more bread exchanges.

- Brownie, unfrosted (5 cm/2 in. square) = 1 bread, 1 fat
- Doughnut, plain (1) = 1 bread, 2 fat
- Cream-filled biscuit (2) = 1½ bread, 1 fat
- Jam (1 tablespoon) = 1 bread
- Fruit juice bars (20 g/¾-oz bar) = 1 fruit

- Ice cream (1 scoop) = 1 bread, 3 fat
- Fruit pie with 2 crusts (⅙ of pie) = 3 bread, 2 fat
- Potato crisps or tortilla chips (30 g/1 oz) = 1 bread, 2 fat
- Whipped dessert made with skimmed milk (8 tablespoons) = 2 bread
- Sorbet (1 scoop) = 1 bread, 1 fat

Eat Smart

Food-grouping systems like the Plate Model and the Dietary Exchanges may help you eat a more balanced diet, but they're not the whole picture. We uncovered some other key principles to eating wisely and losing weight. Once you have balance in your diet, here's what weight-loss winners recommend to keep the weight off for good.

Eat when you're hungry. The people in the National Weight Control Registry eat an average of five meals a day. The truth is that most people need to eat every two to four hours. Otherwise, we over-ride our built-in mechanism that tells us when we're hungry and when we've had enough. We're 'starved', so then we overeat. Learn to recognize your hunger cues – grumbly tummy, energy crash, irritability – and eat in response to them.

'Naturally slim' people eat differently from the rest of us, according to Vicki Hansen, author of *The Seven Secrets of Slim People*. These lucky people eat only when they are really hungry. All of us were born with this ability, but we let appetite, cravings, and years of conditioning to finish all the food on our plates short-circuit our natural hunger-control mechanism. Then we try to compensate. The fact is that denying hunger and skipping meals always backfire: you'll overeat when you do allow yourself food.

Stop when you're full. Your body tells you when it has had enough to eat, but the signs are subtle and you may need to relearn how to recognize them. One way is to eat slowly. It takes your body about 20 minutes to feel the food you eat. If you eat too quickly, you'll eat right past the point of being satisfied and eat too much. Another trick is to wear clothing with non-elastic waistbands. Elasticized skirts and trousers are very forgiving, but something snug around your waist will signal you to stop eating as it tightens up.

Eat a good breakfast. Breakfast helps you avoid overeating later in the day. Choose foods that have some protein and a little fat in addition to carbohydrates and sugar. They will give you the energy you need to make it through the morning. Good choices include whole-grain cereal with skimmed milk, eggs and toast, or a fruity breakfast smoothie. Beware of sugary breakfast foods like children's cereals and Danish pastries. While initially satisfying, these are out of your system in about 30 minutes, leaving you hungry for more.

Count calories, not just fat. Sure, fat has more calories than protein or carbohydrate foods (9 calories per gram versus 4 calories per gram for protein and carbohydrate foods). However, that doesn't mean that eating only low-fat foods will help you lose weight. Research done at the University of Vermont in the United States showed that there's more to weight loss than counting fat grams. One group of dieters was asked to restrict their fat consumption to 22–26 grams a day but not to count calories. Another group was asked to count calories but not fat. After six months the calorie counters had lost more than twice as much weight as those who had focused on restricting fat. Why? One reason is the incredible number of low-fat products on the market that are not low in calories. By counting only fat grams, you could be taking in more calories than you need.

Don't pass on pasta. Every few years a new diet promising the secret formula for easy and permanent weight loss hits the market. One formula that has come in and out of style severely limits, or even bans, carbohydrate foods. That means bread, pasta, cereal, and starchy vegetables like potatoes and beans.

Revolutionary? Hardly. In the 1960s the plan was promoted by Dr Irwin Stillman. It was also called the Drinking Man's Diet. It has resurfaced as The Zone, Protein Power, Carbohydrate Addict's Diet, and a retooling of the old Atkins Diet, among others. The difference today is how the diets are packaged. Knowledge about nutrition has come a long way since 1960, and the recent crop of books uses lots of scientific-sounding jargon to sell the plans. It's very convincing until you analyse the diets and realize that, regardless of the promises and premises, all the plans are basically low in calories. And that is why people lose weight on them. Don't be fooled. Breads, pasta, and grains are the basis of a healthy diet.

Fill up on fibre. Combined with a good supply of water, fibre-rich foods are a dieter's dream. They're filling and come packaged with lots of vitamins, minerals, and other helpful plant nutrients. What are the best sources of fibre? Whole grains such as cereals, whole-meal bread, and brown rice; watery vegetables such as salad greens, tomatoes, courgettes, green beans, and broccoli; and fruits such as apples and oranges.

Look at portion sizes. We're used to seeing our plates full, but if you're eating from a dinner plate, it's probably too much food. Try using smaller plates and try to visualize portion size. For example, a serving of pasta is about the size of a tennis ball, and a portion of meat or fish is about the size of a deck of cards. See 'Eyes on the Size' on page 150 for other visual cues to healthy portion sizes.

If you're going out for fast food, choose a kid's meal instead of the 'Super Combo'. You'll save about 438 calories per meal at most restaurants. Having a salad? Eat as much as you want – but be sparing with what goes on top.

'I usually misjudge portions of salad dressing and mayonnaise', says Theresa Revitt, who lost 36 kg/6 st. 'They're really high in fat and calories (100 calories per tablespoon), so I still measure them.'

Make Peace with Yourself

Losing weight may be mostly about reducing calories, but it's also about your relationship to food: how you look at the food you eat and at yourself. Many successful dieters told us that they had to make peace with their relationship to food and their bodies before they kept the weight off for longer than a month or two. Here's what they recommend.

Accept your cravings. The faster you give in and have a small portion of the food that you're craving, the better off you'll be. You can pack in plenty of calories trying to eat around the one thing you truly want. So go for it. Have a small serving of the food you crave and get over it.

Alternatively, use the 90-10 principle that Verona Mucci-Hurlburt used to go from a size 20 to a size 10. 'If you watch what you eat 90 per cent of the time, the other 10 per cent is not a problem.'

Eat cake! Eat all the foods you love, says weight-loss expert Dr Deidra Price, who wrote *Healing the Hungry Self*. She says that you won't gain weight when you eat chocolate, biscuits, sweets, cake, and crisps, as long as you eat them in moderate amounts *after* (not instead of) a meal. What's a moderate amount of these foods? Whatever you can fit in the palm of your hand is a moderate serving for you.

Love who you are. A positive body image is central to lasting weight loss. It's so important that the programme at Green Mountain at Fox Run, a weight-loss centre, specializes in it.

'If people accept their bodies, they will have an easier time losing and maintaining weight,' says nutrition director Marsha Hudnall. 'If you have a negative attitude and hate your body, it's more difficult to eat healthy and exercise.'

Don't go it alone. More than half of the people at the registry finally lost weight when they joined some kind of formal programme. 'Programmes provide structure, a supportive group setting, and follow-up,' says Dr Kelly D. Brownell, professor of psychology at Yale University.

A group can help you feel safe. 'It's like

an extended family,' says Susan Cursi, who joined a programme to help keep her focused. 'You can call someone and say, "I'm having a hard day. I need your help".'

Of course, many people lose weight without going to formal programmes. Some people can motivate themselves, and others use informal support systems. Debra Mazda lost 60 kg/9½ st after starting her own group. 'It was just a group of women who got together once a week, and we would compare notes.'

Gloria McVeigh lost 16 kg/2½ st and her friend lost 22 kg/3½ st when they dieted together. 'We spoke daily on the phone. We talked about our personal lives, swapped recipe ideas, and compared exercise routines. We always motivated each other to keep going.'

Move It to Lose It

Weight loss doesn't have to be about what you give up or cut out. The most successful dieters we spoke to were focused on what they *added*. Some said, 'I now put more vegetables on my plate.' Some said, 'I'm more aware of what I eat.' Exercise falls into the same category. It's an add-in, something you can do. Of course, it may be hard at first if you've been inactive for a while, but the payoffs are incredible: more energy, better

MOOD FOODS

It's always best to deal with your emotions before you eat, says Cheryl Hartsough, a nutritionist at a heath resort. However, sometimes you may be anxious or depressed, and feel that nothing but food will help. When that happens, it's important to know that there are some foods you should avoid because they'll actually make you feel even worse. And it's equally important to know which foods you can eat that may improve your mood. Follow this chart that Hartsough developed to satisfy your cravings without busting your weight-loss plan.

If You Feel . . .	Avoid These . . .	And Try These . . .
Anxious	Cake, chocolate, ice cream	Fresh fruit, dried fruit, pasta, whole-grain bread, potatoes, rice
Depressed	Cake, ice cream, pastries	Whole-grain foods like cereal, pasta, rice, beans
Sleepy and lethargic	High-fat foods, sweets, pizza	Low-fat, high-protein foods like fish, chicken, turkey, non-fat or low-fat cheese

looks, better physical health, even better mental health.

Yes, better mental health. We're not talking simply about 'runner's high' or an 'endorphin buzz'. Each time you get physically active, you send a message to yourself that you are doing something positive. Some psychologists even prescribe exercise for depressed patients to improve their moods. In some cases the results are about as effective as taking prescription antidepressant drugs. The bottom line is that, when you feel good about yourself, it is a lot easier to stay with your weight-loss commitment.

Start slowly. There's no need to run out and buy exercise equipment. If you're among the large majority of people who do not exercise at all, just going for a walk or playing with the children will get you moving again. Do some kind of activity for just 10 minutes a day. Then, slowly work up to a total of 30 minutes of moderate-intensity activity. 'Moderate' means things like brisk walking and swimming.

Another way to look at it is to expend a minimum of 1,000 calories a week. For increased weight loss, try expending 1,500– 2,000 calories a week. That equals 200–300 calories a day or 60 minutes of moderate-intensity activity. To step up your weight loss to this level, try walking more often, walking faster, and walking longer. See 'Burn, Baby, Burn' to check the number of calories you can expect to burn by doing your favourite activities.

Sneak it in. Exercise doesn't have to be done all at once. Finding a continuous 60 minutes is difficult for just about everyone. What counts most is the day's total amount of activity. Three 20-minute periods of exercise burn the same number of calories as one continuous 1-hour workout. Even 10 minutes here and there can add up to sufficient exercise. 'I could never find the time for long walks and aerobic exercise classes,' says Lorraine Stevens, who eventually reached her goal weight. 'But I can always find 10 minutes. I can climb stairs at work for 10 minutes. I can walk around the car park for 10 minutes on my lunch hour. I can even jog in place in a hotel room for 10 minutes.' Lorraine is 172 cm/5 ft 8 in. tall and has kept her weight at 66–67 kg/10 st 5 lb–10 st 8 lb for years.

Walk, walk, walk. Don't worry about counting your pulse or getting into your 'target heart zone' as you walk. It's not important. Research shows that, for calorie burning, a greater amount of exercise at a lower intensity is better than small amounts of high-intensity exercise. You'll know you're walking at the right pace if you can talk but can't sing.

Muscle up. Studies have demonstrated that, when a person diets, the weight that is lost is 75 per cent fat and 25 per cent muscle. That's not good. As muscle is lost, so is your ability to burn and use calories efficiently. That's one of the reasons why so many dieters who don't exercise reach a plateau and stop losing weight, even though they are still eating a very calorie-restricted diet. For every 500 g/1 lb of muscle that you build, your resting metabolic rate increases by 60 calories a day. In other words, for every 500 g/1 lb of muscle you build, you will burn more calories and lose more weight. 'It wasn't until I put on more muscle through resistance training that I was able to keep the

BURN, BABY, BURN

Almost every activity burns calories. Even sitting quietly. Of course, moderate-intensity activities like swimming or aerobic dancing will burn more. The important thing is to choose activities that you enjoy. That's the only way you will stay active. Below are more than 20 activities and the calories they burn after 20 minutes

Activity	Calories Burned in 20 Minutes	
	63 kg/10 st person	86 kg/13 st 5 lb person
Sitting quietly	27	36
Raking leaves	68	92
Cleaning	78	106
Weeding	92	124
Walking (normal pace on pavement	102	138
Golf	108	146
Stacking firewood	112	152
Weight training	120	148
Bicycling leisurely 15 km/h (9.4 mph)	127	172
Dancing the Twist	131	178
Scrubbing floors	139	188
Tennis	139	188
Aerobic dancing	141	178
Mowing	142	192
Skiing (moderate speed)	151	204
Football	168	228
Hockey	170	230
Basketball	176	238
Boxing (sparring)	176	238
Swimming	183	278
Skipping rope (80 per min)	209	282
Running 14 min/km (9 min/mile)	245	332

weight off – almost effortlessly,' says Mucci-Hurlburt.

Prioritize. Lack of time is the main reason most people give for not exercising. Amy Reed, who lost 36 kg/5½ st, lets the beds go unmade to make time for exercise. 'I have to schedule it in and let go of other things, like a perfectly clean house.' Here are some other solutions to the time problem: get your partner to watch the children; make family time a time to walk together; get up half an hour early; use your lunch hour to walk.

Get a friend. Better yet, get several friends and make a commitment to them. Chances are, one of you will want to keep moving, even when the others don't. Chris Koehler lost 17 kg/2½ st with the help of his daughter, Katie. 'Her enthusiasm was contagious. We'd walk 5 km (3 miles) a day through the park. It only took about 35 minutes. All of a sudden, those walks that had been so easy to forget became an essential part of my day.'

Make it fun. Look at the items people are advertising for sale in the local paper and you might see ads for rowing machines, exercise bikes, and stair climbers. Did the owners of this expensive equipment reach their weight-loss and fitness goals? We doubt it. It's more likely that they got bored with these machines because they simply are not fun to use.

Anne Geren lost 25 kg/3 st 9 lb and kept it off for 13 years without any exercise equipment. She tuned in to her love of dancing and discovered Jazzercize. 'If somebody told me that I had to go out and run 5 days a week, I'd still weigh 84 kg/13 st.' Pick an activity that you love.

Get centred. Very large people who are not used to exercising may feel clumsy at first. It takes a little time for your body to adjust. Comfortable footwear that has a wide sole and good support will help. So will walking on a flat, paved surface rather than a bumpy path. And if you've never weight trained before, you'll be surprised at how quickly your body responds. Lisa Getz, who had never weight trained before, lost 2 kg/ 4 lb and 6.5 cm/2½ in. in just three weeks. She was having trouble balancing while doing lunges at first. 'Now, I'm much more in control,' she says. 'It feels like my legs have come out of hibernation and are alive again.'

Fear not. Fear stops us from doing all kinds of things. The best antidote to fear is action. You might think that you can't start exercising because you're not in good shape or you weigh too much. 'I call that the cleaning-up-for-the-maid syndrome,' says Karen Andes, a personal trainer. You don't need to join a gym. You don't need a special outfit. We're talking about walking, jogging, or running. You can saunter, meander, or stroll. Take it at your own pace. You don't have to go to a special place, although you may find it motivating to go to the local sports track, the shopping centre, the woods, or some other walker-friendly environment. If you don't like walking, you can take the stairs instead of the lift whenever possible, get off the bus a little earlier and walk the rest of the way, park at the far end of the car park, or pace while waiting for the train instead of sitting. Be sure to give yourself credit for every bit of exercise you do – even if some days you don't achieve your goal. Some activity is always better than none.

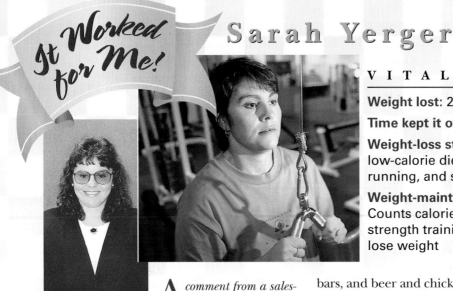

It Worked for Me!

Sarah Yerger

VITAL STATS

Weight lost: 25 kg/4 st

Time kept it off: 5 years

Weight-loss strategies: Low-fat, low-calorie diet; aerobics, running, and strength training

Weight-maintenance strategies: Counts calories, runs and does strength training, helps others lose weight

A comment from a saleswoman motivated Sarah. She dropped 25 kg/4 st and has kept it off for five years. Now she has more energy than ever.

'At 162 cm (5 ft 4 in.) and over 90 kg (14 st), I knew that if I didn't make some changes to my lifestyle, I would die of an early heart attack. Both of my parents died by age 50.

'After examining my mother, the doctor warned us. He told us that she could die of a heart attack within months. She did. And it scared me into action. I joined a health club and began low-impact aerobics classes.

'My new friends at the gym kept me going. But it was a nasty comment from a saleswoman that really pushed me to lose weight. A friend asked me to be her bridesmaid. I could barely squeeze into a size 20 dress, and the saleswoman insisted that I buy the size 22. Hurt and determined, I ordered an 18. Suddenly, I had a goal and a point to prove.

'To lose the weight, I took stock of how I was eating and made changes. My chocolate bars, and beer and chicken-wing dinners were replaced by smaller, healthier meals. Once I began measuring food, I realized that I'd been eating three times the desired amount.

'Breakfast, which I used to skip, became a piece of fruit and dry toast. For protein, I added a small pot of low-fat yogurt. Lunch was often water-packed tuna and raw vegetables. For dinner, I ate fish or pasta and salad. I also started drinking lots of water, which helped me feel full and cut my nine-cups-a-day coffee habit down to just two.

'I lost about 1 kg (2 lb) a week. In just six months my weight dropped to 68 kg (10 st 10 lb). The bridesmaid gown didn't need to be altered one stitch. I had achieved my goal – but I didn't stop there. I felt so good, I started running three times a week. Now I also lift weights for half an hour twice a week.

'I've started helping others to make the commitment to health. It helps me stay committed to my choice. Every time I lace my running shoes or choose a celery stick over a chocolate bar, I'm reminded that nothing is inevitable. Life is about choices, and I've chosen health.' ■

Seven Habits of Highly Effective Winners

People who lose weight have the most useful tips because they've done it. Of all the advice shared by the weight-loss winners in this book, here are the techniques mentioned most often.

1. Stop dieting. Get out of deprivation mode and back into enjoying the food you love. All of the successful weight losers told us that they never felt deprived. Only about 40 per cent of them thought that losing weight was hard, and more than 25 per cent said that it was easy. They said that to lose weight once and for all, they had to be stricter with themselves than they had been in the past, but most didn't call it dieting. The food choices they made (more fruits, vegetables, and grains) and the lifestyle changes they made (regular mealtimes and exercise) didn't feel like being 'on a diet'.

2. Exercise daily. The registry shows that just about everyone did some form of exercise. On average, they burned 2,800 calories a week by walking and weight training. That's a lot! You don't have to commit to that much, but try to stick with daily activity of some kind, even if it's only 10 minutes of brisk walking at first.

3. Drink more water. The brain is about 75 per cent water. It's the first organ to be affected by dehydration, clouding your thinking and making you feel fatigued and irritable. Dehydration-related fatigue is what may be behind most people's hunger cravings. Next time you think you're hungry, have a drink of water instead. 'Drinking lots of water keeps me from snacking when I'm not hungry, and it gives me more energy',

says Theresa Revitt. 'It also stopped what I thought were hunger headaches, which were probably due to dehydration.'

4. Eat every 2–4 hours. If four hours go by and you haven't eaten, you're setting yourself up for the starvation–binge scenario – a calorie and fat disaster for anyone. Eating every 2–4 hours avoids it. When you eat small meals regularly, you're never too hungry or too full. And you'll more easily find your natural hunger and satiety clues.

5. Limit fat. Current advice from health experts recommends limiting fat to no more than 35 per cent of total calories. The people at the registry did even better. On average, they limited daily fat to about 24 per cent of total calories. Why cut back on fat? Because it's so calorie-dense. Fat has more than twice as many calories per gram as carbohydrates or proteins.

6. Eat more vegetables. Concentrate on what you *can* eat and what you can add to your diet. If you're like most people, you should be eating more fruit and vegetables. People who eat lots of fruit and vegetables naturally eat fewer calories and fat than people who don't.

7. Watch portion sizes. You can eat anything you want and still lose weight. No food is too fattening. But size does matter. It could spell the difference between a good-for-you meal and a fattening one. If you need to, at least in the early stages of your weight-loss plan, measure your food, or see 'Eyes on the Size' on page 152. Soon, you'll instinctively know what a teaspoon of mayonnaise looks like on your sandwich or a tablespoon of dressing on a salad, 1 portion of spaghetti on your plate, 85 g/3 oz of chicken … . You get the idea.

What Works in the Kitchen

Healthy cooking starts when you shop for food. Long before you get to the kitchen, your shopping habits determine the foods you'll have at hand to cook with – and to snack on. If you stock bags of potato crisps in the cupboard, they'll get eaten. If you have lots of butter and cream in the refrigerator, you'll use it. Likewise, if you keep fresh red peppers in the refrigerator, you'll eat those, too. Before you rush off to the recipe chapters, read about how you can shop faster, cook more quickly, reduce the calories in your favourite recipes, and stock the healthiest foods available.

Shop Smart

Food retailing is marketing at its best. Many products in the supermarket are deliberately packaged to entice you to buy more. Even a food's location is calculated to keep you in the store longer in the hope that you'll spend more money. Take milk and eggs, for example. These frequently purchased foods are often located farthest from the main entrance, which means that you have to pass by many, many temptations to get what you need. Some in-store bakeries and delicatessen counters send aromas throughout the store to tickle your nose and coax you to buy. And many food stores have sweets displayed near the checkout till to tempt you while you queue.

Even pricing policies are designed to prod you to shell out a few more pounds. Coupons often require that you buy two items to take advantage of their discount deals. Simply putting a number on an item's price sign such as '2 for £1.00' rather than selling the item for 50 pence each encourages us to buy more. The perception is that you're getting a greater value, despite the fact that you are spending more money.

Here's what weight-loss veterans recommend to keep your slim-down strategy from getting sabotaged before you even make it back home.

Have a plan. Knowing exactly what you need when you go to the shops helps to minimize excessive and impulsive purchases.

And don't forget to check your cupboards, freezer, and refrigerator before you shop to avoid duplicating purchases. Research has shown that the more of a product we have in the cupboards, the more willing we are to eat it. 'I stopped shopping for an army, even for low-fat foods like chicken breasts,' says Victoria Bennett, who lost 27 kg/4 st 4 lb and kept it off for five years. 'I used to think that everybody had to have two or three chicken breasts. Now, I just make sure that everyone has one.'

FOOD LABELS FOR WAIST WATCHERS

We know you can find the calories and fat grams on a food label. They're as easy to find as the nose on your face. But here are a few numbers that you might not always check and what they mean.

Serving size. That's the first thing to look at (even before fat and calories) because the information is given per 100 g/100 ml of product and per serving size suggested by the manufacturer. Compare the food manufacturer's serving size to the size that you'll actually eat. For instance, do you usually eat about two scoops of ice cream? That's twice the standard serving, which means doubling all the figures. 'Servings per container' can also help. To see how much fat and calories are in an entire container of food, multiply the figures by the 'servings per container' number. You'll be amazed at some foods.

For example, the average bag of corn chips contains more than 1,000 calories and 50 grams of fat.

Calories and fat. Focus on the absolute numbers here: calories and grams of fat per serving. The recommended daily allowance (RDA) percentages are based on 2,000 calories a day, which is probably more than you'll be eating if you're trying to lose weight. For the true numbers on packaged foods that require additional ingredients, read the 'As prepared' column. Many mixes need fats or eggs added in preparation.

Fibre. Choose foods with the most fibre. Research shows that people who eat lots of fibre also eat fewer calories. Fibre-rich foods help you feel full so that you don't overeat. Try to get at least 18 grams of fibre a day.

LOOKEE HERE! 'FAT-FREE!'

Health claims on the front of a label can be very misleading. Don't buy the product before checking the nutrition facts on the back of the label. Often, fat-free products are loaded with calories. And it's the total number of calories that you really need to watch. Here are some other labelling terms and what they mean.

If the Label Says . . .	The Food Contains . . .
Fat-free	Less than 0.15 g of fat per 100 g/100 ml
Low-fat	Less than 3 g of fat per 100 g/100 ml
Lean	Less than 10 g of fat per serving, with less than 4 g of saturated fat and 95 mg of cholesterol
Extra-lean	Less than 5 g of fat per serving, with less than 2 g of saturated fat and 95 mg of cholesterol
Less	25 per cent less of a nutrient than the food it is compared with
Reduced	25 per cent fewer calories, fat, sugar, or sodium than the standard version
Light/lite	This term is not governed by any legislation and can mean different things to different manufacturers. Check the label to see if the dietary content is suitable for you
Cholesterol-free	Less than 5 mg of cholesterol and 1 mg of saturated fat per 100 g/100 ml

Make a list when you're hungry. Try planning meals when your tummy is growling. It will make your menus more interesting.

But don't shop when you're hungry. Have a roll or some fruit before you go out. You'll have more control. Don't forget to feed the children, too. Hunger makes controlled shopping difficult for adults and nearly impossible for children. 'Grocery shopping after school is always a disaster – unless we have a snack before we head to the shops,' says Liza Arnow. 'My daughters' hunger alarms go off at 3.30 in the afternoon. If we have a snack first, then shop, we're all less likely to be drawn to unhealthy foods.' A pre-shopping snack also helps you resist the temptation of high-fat free samples.

Plan the plate model in your trolley. For a balanced and varied diet, your filled shopping trolley should match the proportions in the plate model. Bread, cereal, rice, and pasta should occupy the largest space. Fruits and vegetables come next. Then meat and dairy. Fats, oils, and sugary foods should take up very little room.

Grab a basket for fill-in shopping. Don't automatically reach for a huge trolley every time you enter a supermarket. It's too easy to fill it up with foods that you don't need, says Dr Michael Hamilton, an obesity expert. 'I sometimes recommend that people shop frequently – every day if possible – instead of loading up the trolley and refrigerator once a week.'

Wise Buys, Aisle by Aisle

Balance, variety, and moderation. These are the keys to any healthy diet, especially a weight-loss or weight-maintenance eating plan. Sure, cutting calories will drop weight. But balance and variety with occasional indulgences will help keep you satisfied and therefore keep the weight off long-term. It will also provide the nutrients that you need for more energy.

Load up on cereal, bread, pasta, and rice. These foods are the foundation of a long-term weight-loss strategy, and they keep in your cupboards the longest. Just don't overdo the refined grains such as white bread and white rice. Whole grains are higher in fibre and essential nutrients than refined grains. That makes them more filling and more satisfying, too.

- When buying breads and cereals, look to see that the first ingredient is a whole grain, such as wheat or oats.

- Items from the bakery usually don't have labelling. If there isn't an ingredients list, ask for items made with wholemeal flour.

- Pass up those giant muffins, biscuits, and scones. They're loaded with fat. If you can't resist, look for a smaller size.

- Most bakery bagels are the equivalent of three servings of bread. Frozen bagels are usually two servings worth.

- Baked goods should have 3 grams of fat or less per serving.

- Cereal should have 2 grams of fibre or more per serving.

- Seeded crackers have virtually the same calories as plain ones, but they have more fibre and are a good choice for this reason.

- Brown rice has almost three times the fibre of white rice. It also has a pleasant, nutty flavour.

- Like pasta? Keep a supply of brown (wholegrain) pasta or pasta verde (green pasta, made with spinach) in preference to white varieties.

Get sweet on produce. For the best buy and best flavour, choose what's fresh and in season. When buying canned and frozen fruits and vegetables, choose those not in sweet syrups and sauces. Some waist watchers reduce calories by giving sugar-packed frozen fruits a quick rinse before using. Nutrition experts also say:

- Reach for richly coloured fruit and vegetables. They have more nutrients than the pale ones. Dark greens like spinach, watercress, and rocket are healthier than iceberg lettuce. Deep orange or red-fleshed fruit like oranges, melons, and mangoes are richer in vitamins than pears, apples, and bananas.
- Most fresh and frozen fruit and vegetables are fat-free and have fewer than 40 calories per serving – as long as they're not packed in cream sauce, butter, or added sugar. The exceptions are avocado and coconut. Both of these foods are high in fat and calories.
- Shop at the salad bar when you need ingredients for a recipe but don't want to purchase too much, or when you need pre-cut produce for a quick meal.
- If you don't eat salad because you can't bear to make it, try pre-bagged salad mixes. Buy the ones without dressing packets or garnishes, or give these to someone who isn't counting calories. Also, see 'Dressings to Live By' on page 232 for quick, easy, and really tasty, low-calorie salad dressings.

- Although 100 per cent fruit and vegetable juices count as a serving of fruits or vegetables, they lack fibre, so they're not as filling or satisfying as a whole fruit or vegetable. Similarly, unfortified fruit drinks are mostly water, sugars, and flavourings. Try to keep your consumption of these to a minimum since they're really just empty calories.
- Dried fruits have most of the water removed from them, which concentrates the flavour and nutrients but also increases the calories. Keep an eye on portion size (40 g/1½ oz, or a handful, is one serving).

Dive in for dairy. This is one area of the store where low-fat really is a guarantee of fewer calories.

- Buy semi-skimmed or skimmed milk. Even though semi-skimmed milk contains some fat, the nutritional benefits of milk make this tiny amount irrelevant.
- Look for low-fat and fat-free yogurt. If you prefer flavoured yogurt, choose the 'diet' varieties, low in fat, sugar, and calories.
- Choose cheeses labelled 'reduced-fat', 'low-fat', or 'fat-free'. Don't forget strong-flavoured cheeses like Parmesan and the various blue cheeses. A little of these grated goes a long way.
- All butters and most margarines are 80 per cent fat and provide 100 calories per 15 g/ ½ oz. Choose low-fat (40–60 per cent) spreads to reduce fat and calorie intake.

Make meat lean. Meat is definitely on the menu. The leanest cuts of beef are flank, sirloin, and tenderloin. The leanest varieties of pork are fresh, canned, cured, and boiled ham, pork tenderloin, rib chops, and roast. Lean lamb includes roasts, chops, and legs. Be realistic about portion size when stocking meats. 'If you can't pass on some high-fat favourites, stick to the most flavourful ones,' says Helen Fitzgerald, who lost 23 kg/ 3 st 9 lb. 'A single slice of bacon is enough to flavour eggs or a potato.'

- Reach for meat labelled with low-fat percentages. Standard mince, for example, contains 20 per cent fat, but you can buy ground beef or ground steak with only 10 per cent or 5 per cent fat.

- Look for 'minced turkey breast' for a low-fat treat. Check the label to make sure it doesn't contain the skin, which would make it very high in fat and calories.

- Avoid self-basting turkeys. They have fat injected into the meat. Buy a plain turkey and baste it with your favourite stock instead.

- Buy fresh seafood. Its taste is beyond compare. If you stock frozen seafood, choose varieties without high-calorie breading.

- Tuna packed in water or brine has less fat and fewer calories than tuna packed in oil.

- Check the labels of packaged sliced ham, salami and other sandwich fillers carefully. Ones made from turkey or chicken don't always have fewer calories and less fat than the ones made from beef and pork.

Get the Right Tools

You don't need to completely restock your kitchen for low-calorie cooking. In fact, you probably already own most of the really useful fat-fighting and time-saving gadgets.

Sharp knives. One of the greatest deterrents to cooking, low-cal or otherwise, is not being able to cut and chop quickly and safely. The basics: a serrated-edge bread knife (great for tomatoes, too), a paring knife (about 7.5 cm/3 in.), and a chef's knife (20–25 cm/8–10 in.) for chopping.

Food processor. It speeds up chopping, grating, and blending – jobs that otherwise may seem too daunting done by hand. A mini chopper is good for small jobs like finely chopping parsley or chopping an onion or garlic.

Non-stick frying pans. Non-stick coatings have come a long way since the early days of scratch-and-peel Teflon. Today's non-stick pans are chip-resistant and durable. Invest in top quality if you can. Look for pans with a tough, textured coating and a heavy weight so that they're less likely to warp. These also deliver more even, high heat without hot spots. Of course, the best advantage of non-stick pans is that they require less cooking fat. 'I've found a way to make home fries without any fat,' says Kara Kelly. 'I use chicken stock and a non-stick pan instead of lots of butter or bacon fat.' A bonus is that non-stick pans clean up faster.

Microwave oven. If you use it for nothing else than zapping leftovers or 'steaming' vegetables and fish without added fats, it's worth it.

Gravy strainer. Even if you don't make gravy, this jug with a pouring spout that starts at its base is handy to have round. Instead of skimming away the fat from the top of soups, for example, you pour away the fat-free stock

MEAT BEATS CHEESE FOR PROTEIN

Many dieters cut out meat because it's high in calories and fat. Instead, they eat cheese and peanut butter for protein. It is a good idea to eat less meat and to make it lean. But replacing meat with dairy and nut products won't save you any calories. In fact, it'll cost you. For instance, to match the protein in 115 g/4 oz of roast lean pork tenderloin, you'd have to eat nearly130 g/ 4½ oz of peanut butter, which piles on an additional 550 calories. For vegetarians who want to lose weight, better protein choices are eggs (especially the whites), low-fat tofu or tempeh, beans, and grains. If you're a meat lover, here are a few protein comparisons that demonstrate why a little meat isn't such a bad idea, even when you're slimming down.

To match the protein in 115 g/4 oz of . . .		You'd need this much Cheddar cheese . . .	Or this much peanut butter . . .
Well-done hamburger		**125 g/4.5 oz**	**125 g/4.5 oz**
Protein	32 g	32 g	32 g
Calories	301	521	740
Fat	18 g	41 g	64 g
Grilled beef tenderloin		**125 g/4.5 oz**	**125 g/4.5 oz**
Protein	32 g	32 g	32 g
Calories	239	521	740
Fat	11 g	41 g	64 g
Roast lean pork tenderloin		**125 g/4.5 oz**	**125 g/4.5 oz**
Protein	32 g	32 g	32 g
Calories	186	521	740
Fat	5 g	41 g	64 g
Roast boneless, skinless chicken breast		**140 g/5 oz**	**145 g/4.8 oz**
Protein	35 g	35 g	35 g
Calories	187	570	807
Fat	4 g	45 g	64 g
Baked or grilled salmon		**125 g/4.5 oz**	**120 g/4.3 oz**
Protein	31 g	31 g	31 g
Calories	245	502	723
Fat	12 g	40 g	62 g

from the bottom and leave the high-calorie fat behind.

Measuring spoons and scales. No, you don't need to portion out every ingredient or serving of food with exact gram accuracy before it passes your lips. But watching portions is the easiest way to cut calories. This is especially true of the little things like salad dressing and oil. The difference between a teaspoonful of olive oil and a casual splash is about 100 calories. Just ask Theresa Revitt. 'I usually misjudge portions of salad dressing, mayonnaise, and ice cream,' she says. 'They're really high in fat and calories, and cause the most damage if overdone. So I still measure them.' Until you're comfortable visually determining a teaspoon, tablespoon, 30 g/1oz, and 85 g/ 3 oz, you might want to use measuring spoons and scales. You could also simply tie an attractive measuring teaspoon to your olive oil bottle and a tablespoon to your salad dressing. Also, see 'Eyes on the Size' on page 150.

Plastic bags. Use them to store cut-up vegetables and fruit so that they're ready to cook or to take along for snacks. Resealable bags also make marinating easier and less messy.

Plastic spray bottles. A refillable spray bottle is less expensive than can after can of chlorofluorocarbon-filled cooking spray. Just fill a bottle with olive or sunflower oil. Use it to lightly coat frying pans and baking tins or to spray a shimmer of oil over foods before roasting. Squeeze bottles (like the ones used for ketchup in cafés) can shave calories, too. They allow you to dribble a tiny bit of high-fat sauces or gravies only where you need it.

Popcorn popper. If you like popcorn (it makes a great snack), invest in an air popper or one that can be used in the microwave without added oil. Once popped, coat the popcorn with a light mist of water or oil spray before adding salt or herbs (avoid sugar). The seasonings will stick better.

Cupboard Clues

When you're really hungry and trying to lose weight, staring into a cupboard full of only fattening foods is a nightmare. Don't be caught off guard. Keep low-calorie, low-fat foods and ingredients at hand. When you have them at the ready, you'll be less tempted to pop a frozen deluxe pizza in the oven. Below are basic ingredients to stock for healthy cooking. For a list of the best snacks to keep around, see '50 Low-Calorie Snacks' on page 110.

Beans. You can buy them dried, cook them, and freeze them, or stock lots of different kinds in cans. 'I like to add beans to whatever other vegetables I have on hand,' suggests Lorraine Stevens, who lost 16 kg/ 2½ st. 'I stir-fry them for about 5 minutes, then add a fat-free barbecue sauce.' Beans are also great puréed into sandwich spreads and dips, added to soups and pastas, and sprinkled on salads.

Extra-virgin olive oil. Keep a small bottle on hand to make uncooked dishes like salad dressings and dips. It's pronounced flavour allows you to use less. Olive oil spoils easily, so keep it in a cool place, even in the fridge. It will thicken and turn cloudy, but a few minutes at room temperature will return it to a golden liquid without damage to the quality or flavour. You might want to

(continued on page 40)

It Worked for Me!

Teresa Tomeo

VITAL STATS

Weight lost: 27 kg/4 st 4 lb

Time kept it off: 12 years

Weight-loss strategy: Low-fat, low-calorie diet

Weight-maintenance strategies: Low-fat, low-calorie diet with occasional splurges; walking

The only thing keeping Teresa Tomeo from a career in TV journalism was her weight. Teresa got motivated and dropped 27 kg/4 st 4 lb.

'You're a good reporter, but if you want to make it on TV, you have to lose weight.'

'Believe it or not, a friend and mentor spoke those words. And, believe it or not, I needed to hear them. I was 25 and a successful newswoman for a local radio station, but I was ready to try on-camera work. My friend, a producer, summed up my situation with a journalist's stone-cold objectivity: I was too fat.

'The words stung, but he wasn't telling me anything that the scales hadn't already. At 167 cm (5 ft 6 in.), I weighed 86 kg (13½ st) and wore a size 20. In the image-conscious world of TV, my look would never be acceptable. So I took action: I went to a medically supervised clinic. I wanted real-world foods, healthy recipes, and sensible amounts. The clinic gave me a calorie chart and balanced eating plan. I recorded my calories and weighed in once a week.

'For six months, I ate fish and chicken and lots of fruits and vegetables. At work, I ignored the pastries, sweets, and cheese trays sent by fans. And I drank water like a camel – nearly 2 litres (3½ pints) a day – since the nutritionists at the clinic kept telling me how water makes you feel full.

'At first, the weight came off quickly – about 2 kg (4 lb) the first week, a bit less the next. In three months, I'd lost 13 kg (2 st)! Then the weight came off more slowly, but with every bit I lost, I had more energy and confidence. After seven months, I'd lost 27 kg (4 st 4 lb) and felt great. What's more, I looked great, and in 1988 I landed a job on TV.

'Now, at 40, I adhere to the same eating principles as I did then, but with an occasional treat. I'm more disciplined if I can indulge in my mother's lasagne once in a while. And I still have my on-camera figure; I weigh about 61 kg (9 st 10 lb) and wear a size 10.

'I still struggle with exercise. I wish that when I was re-learning how to eat, I'd also learned how to exercise regularly. If I had, I could be less rigid about my diet.' ■

CALORIE-SAVING SWAPS IN THE KITCHEN

Sometimes a simple switch is all it takes to make a low-calorie meal. For instance, tuna in water has 80 fewer calories than tuna in oil. Experiment with the calorie shavers below. You may not like a sweet potato more than a white potato, but you won't notice the difference in taste in the bakery swaps. Unless indicated, the foods and their alternatives have the same serving size.

Instead of Using . . .	Try . . .	And Save This Many Calories . . .
Soups and stews		
Back bacon rasher (40 g/1½-oz)	Back bacon rasher trimmed of fat	32
Condensed chicken soup (220 ml/8 fl oz)	Low-cal chicken soup	70
Green peas (100 g/3½ oz)	Broccoli	26
Pork steak, grilled (100 gl/3½ oz)	Pork steak trimmed of fat	120
White potato	Sweet potato	100
Entrées		
Standard mince (180 g/6 oz)	Lean mince	81
Salmon (120 g/4 oz)	Cod	86
T-bone steak (4 oz)	Flank steak	116
Tuna in oil (100 g/3½ oz)	Tuna in brine	57
Chicken nuggets (100 g/3½ g)	Chicken breast	128
Sardines in oil (100 g/3½ oz)	Sardines in tomato sauce	36

Instead of Using . . .	Try . . .	And Save This Many Calories . . .
Baking		
Butter (115 g/4 oz)	100 g/3½ oz puréed apple plus 30 g/1 oz butter	594
Chocolate (30 g/1 oz)	Cocoa (3 tbsp)	119
Biscuit crumb crust made with eggs (30 cm/12 in.)	Crust made with egg whites	360
Thick double cream (1 tbsp)	Thick single cream	87
Cream cheese (30 g/1 oz)	Ricotta cheese	57
Whole egg	2 egg whites	49
Whole milk (200 ml/7 fl oz)	Skimmed milk	56
Crunch-corner yogurt (150 g/5 oz)	Diet yogurt	165
Salad dressings		
French dressing (1 tbsp)	Low-fat French dressing	35
Soured cream (100 g/3½ oz)	50 g/1¾ oz low-fat yogurt plus 50 g/1¾ oz double cream	91
In casseroles		
Cheddar cheese (30 g/1 oz)	Reduced-fat Cheddar	23
Flour tortilla (50 g/1¾ oz)	Corn tortilla	21
Minced beef (340g/12 oz)	90 g/3 oz soaked bulgur plus 170 g/6 oz minced beef	103
Minced beef (500 g/1 lb)	Chopped mushrooms (280 g/10 oz)	810
Ground steak (115 g/4 oz)	Minced turkey breast	100
Whole milk (225 ml/8 fl oz)	Skimmed milk	100

stock a less expensive olive oil for cooking and sautéing.

Fresh produce. With a microwave oven, you can cook fresh vegetables as quickly as frozen or canned ones. Fresh vegetables are a lot less caloric than ones packed in sauce or butter. 'I've been known to eat a whole bag of vegetables,' says Verona Mucci-Hurlburt, who went from a size 20 to 10. 'And with 60 ml (2 fl oz) of homemade sauce, it's only about 3 grams of fat.'

But don't you hate it when your fresh vegetables spoil before you can get to them? Here's what stays freshest longest: green beans, broccoli, cabbages, carrots, potatoes, peppers, bananas, apples, and citrus fruit. Keep a supply of canned and frozen sweetcorn and peas on hand, too, since the

---

TWO FAT FAUX PAS

Some low-fat cooking techniques were not meant to be. Here are two methods that many people use in the hopes of cutting calories. Avoid them. They don't save calories, and they may cost you flavour.

Skinny chickens. You don't have to cook chicken without the skin to save calories. Very little of the fat from the skin gets into the meat – just enough to keep it moist. Leave the skin on during cooking so that the bird doesn't dry out. You will save about 30 calories per chicken breast, though, if you don't eat the skin *after* it's cooked.

Extra-lean burgers. The leanest ground beef is not always the tastiest (or least expensive) choice for burgers. The calorie and fat difference between a fried or grilled burger made with 20-per-cent-fat mince and one made with 5-per-cent-fat ground beef is slim. Here's why: during cooking, the leanest beef loses water and only a little fat. That makes extra-lean burgers extra-dry, too. The fattier beef loses mostly fat, but remains moist. This principle applies only to burgers that are grilled on a rack so that the fat drips away. If you're pan-frying the burgers (or using the meat for something like meat loaf), stick with the leanest beef you can find. Here are the numbers for grilled burgers made with 115 g/4 oz raw mince or ground beef.

	Raw		Well-Done	
Ground beef	**Calories**	**Fat (g)**	**Calories**	**Fat (g)**
Extra-lean (5% fat)	264	19	186	11
Lean (10% fat)	298	23	196	12
Standard (20% fat)	350	30	198	13

season for fresh is so short. Many people prefer canned sweetcorn because it is sweeter and more tender than frozen. As for peas, the frozen kind are far tastier than canned.

As a general rule, wash produce only just before you use it, and store it in the right place for maximum flavour and freshness. Below are the foods that keep best *out* of the fridge and why.

- Tomatoes: taste better at room temperature

- Winter squash: shells protect them without refrigeration

- Potatoes: get too green if kept too cold

- Onions: moisture collects under their skins and spoils them

- Basil: cold blackens tender leaves

- Unripe fruit: refrigeration stops the ripening processes

Keep all your other produce in the vegetable drawer in unsealed plastic bags to allow air to circulate.

Herbs and spices. Flavour is the name of the game when you're cooking low-calorie. Herbs and spices are an easy way to boost any food's flavour. To get the most taste, add fresh or frozen herbs just at the end of cooking. Dried herbs, on the other hand, should go in towards the beginning to coax out their 'sleeping' aromas while the food cooks. (Crushing dried herbs helps release their flavours, too.) Generally, you can substitute a third of any dried herb for fresh.

A good stock. Use it in salad dressings to replace some of the oil, instead of water to cook vegetables and enhance their flavour, to start a homemade soup, or to replace butter or oil for sautéing. The taste of homemade stocks is far better than that of store-bought ones. If you can, store homemade stocks frozen in ice-cube trays to punch out 2 tablespoons whenever needed.

Vinegars. Sherry, rice, raspberry, wine, and balsamic vinegars are all more flavourful and mild than pungent and acidic malt vinegar or cider vinegar. Use them for dressings and marinades, to sauté chicken breasts, or to splash over grilled fish.

Aged cheese. The stronger the flavour, the less you'll need. Intensely flavoured cheeses like extra-sharp aged Cheddar, Asiago, and Parmesan, and smoked cheeses like Gouda can really add a shot of flavour to soups, salads, pastas, and casseroles. Grate the cheese on top of a dish, where you can see it, so that it's the first thing you'll taste.

Whole grains. Here they are again – we can't recommend them enough. Whole grains don't have fewer calories than refined ones, but they do have extra fibre, which helps fill you up and keep you satisfied. Store them in the refrigerator, since whole grains go rancid more quickly. Oats are a good breakfast staple for sprinkling over cereal or tossing into baked goods. Wholemeal flour can replace half the white flour in just about any baking recipe. Here are some other whole grains to try:

- Quinoa (KEEN-wa), an ancient grain, is one of the best grain sources of protein. It cooks up like rice (even faster) and can be used in casseroles, salads, or desserts.

- Brown rice takes a little longer to cook than white (35 versus 20 minutes), but it has three times the fibre.

- Bulgur (cracked wheat) can be used to make salads and to toss into chilli.

CALORIE-SAVING SWAPS AWAY FROM HOME

Eating out is fast, easy, and fun. But the temptation to eat (and eat) is everywhere. Here are some healthy options to consider whenever you face a meal, food store, or any food choice. Keep these in mind as you plan your menus and write your shopping list. Unless indicated, the foods and their alternatives have the same serving size.

Instead of Choosing...	Try...	And Save This Many Calories...
Vegetables		
Chips (60 g/2 oz)	Coleslaw	60
French fries (100 g/3½ oz)	Potato wedges	173
Mashed potatoes (120 g/4 oz)	Medium baked potato	35
Potato salad (85 g/3 ox)	French bread/roll	144
Potato salad (60 g/2 oz)	Corn on the cob, no butter	104
Meat, poultry, and fish		
Cheeseburger (170 g/6 oz)	Plain hamburger	122
Chicken breast with skin (100g/3½ oz)	Chicken breast without skin	50
Chicken nuggets (6)	Grilled skinless chicken breast (100 g/3½ oz)	116
Chicken parmigiana	Chicken piccata	40
Sausage and pepperoni pizza slice	Vegetable pizza slice	120
Ham and cheese sandwich with mayonnaise	Ham, cheese, and pickle sandwich	140
Slice of salami (30 g/1 oz)	Slice of turkey breast	50

Instead of Choosing . . .	Try . . .	And Save This Many Calories . . .
Snacks and treats		
Apple pie slice	Stewed apples (8 tbsp)	300
Cherry pie slice	Fruit salad (8 tbsp)	424
Pecan pie slice (115 g/4 oz)	Lemon meringue slice	190
1 naan	2 fried poppadums	442
1 naan	1 large chappati	336
Fried tortilla chips (30 g/1 oz)	Baked tortilla chips	20
Potato crisps (60 g/2 oz)	Baby carrots (60 g/2 oz)	280
Guacamole (1 tbsp)	Salsa	58
Onion dip (1 tbsp)	Salsa	22
Peanuts (30 g/1 oz)	Popcorn (20 g/^{3}/$_4$ oz, small bowl)	80
Premium ice cream (1 scoop)	Standard ice cream	100
Ice cream (1 scoop)	Sorbet	140
Thick-chocolate-coated ice cream lolly	Frozen chocolate bar-type ice cream	172
Beverages		
Fast-food milkshake (300 ml/^{1}/$_2$ pt)	Semi-skimmed milk	140
Single cream (2 tbsp) in coffee	Skimmed milk	30
Irish coffee (200 ml/7 fl oz)	200 ml/7 fl oz coffee wih 25 ml/1 fl oz whole milk	171
Standard cola (330 ml/^{1}/$_2$ pint)	Diet cola	99
Jumbo soft drink (500ml/18 fl oz)	Small soft drink (330 ml/^{1}/$_2$ pint)	68
Wine (2 glasses)	Wine (1 glass)	120

Experiment with different cooking liquids. The Herb Rice recipe on page 218 is a great place to start. 'For variety, I cook rice in tomato juice, apple juice, or stock,' says Helen Fitzgerald. 'Rice cooked in pineapple juice is especially good for Chinese dishes.'

De-Calorize Your Favourite Recipes

Any dish tastes great with lots of butter, cheese, and other fats thrown in, but you don't have to give up taste and flavour for weight-wise cooking. The people we talked with found lots of ways to cut calories in their favourite recipes without severely sacrificing flavour. Of course, your tastebuds need a little time to adjust, so make changes gradually.

Toss that yolk. Whenever a recipe calls for two eggs, throw out one yolk, and you'll save about 45 calories and 5 grams of fat. This trick works with baking, casseroles, scrambled eggs, egg salad, you name it!

Swap fruit for most of the fat in baked goods. You can't take out all the oil or butter in baked goods and still have something worth eating. But you can reduce the fat to about one-quarter of the original amount. Replace the rest with prune pie

(continued on page 46)

THREE CHEERS FOR CHEESE

Low-fat cheeses have come a long way since they were first introduced. Although they're not the same as full-fat versions, today's low-fat varieties taste a lot better than they used to. Manufacturers have figured out how to make them melt better, too. Here are a few tips to help get that gooey, stretchy texture that makes melted cheese such a pleasure.

Grate it cold. Low-fat cheese grates easiest when it's well-chilled.

Grate it finely. Big chunks don't melt well. The key is grating it as finely as possible, then distributing it evenly throughout the food you're using it with.

Add moisture. Low-fat cheese is low in moisture (because fat is moist and there's less of it). For the best results, use it with foods high in moisture, such as soups, sauces, lasagne, and casseroles. It doesn't work as well in low-moisture foods such as pizza.

Turn down the heat. High heat tends to make low-fat cheese dry and gluey. Think 'low-fat, low heat'. When adding cheese to a soup or sauce, reduce the heat, then gradually stir in the cheese until it melts.

Cover it. To create a creamier texture, cover foods to keep in the moisture. When microwaving with low-fat cheese, use a low setting, cover the food, rotate it often, and stir it frequently.

It Worked for Me!

Lea Richards

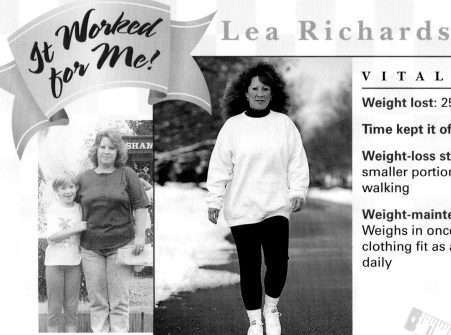

VITAL STATS

Weight lost: 25 kg/4 st

Time kept it off: 7 years

Weight-loss strategies: Eating smaller portions, low-fat diet, walking

Weight-maintenance strategies: Weighs in once a year, uses clothing fit as a gauge, walks daily

Lea walked every day to reduce the stress in her life. After five years, she was calmer and a lot leaner.

'One particularly stressful night, I just had to get out of the house. So I went for a walk. I was gone only 10–15 minutes, but that little bit of exercise helped me vent my emotions and calm me down. It didn't take long before that little evening walk became a habit. I walked every day, in all kinds of weather. My walk was my time, my chance to shed the day's stresses.

'Soon, I started walking farther, increasing my distance by nearly 1 km (½ mile) every six months. Within three years, I was walking 6 km (4 miles) an hour every night. De-stressing wasn't the only benefit. In a few months, I had also dropped a dress size!

'As I became a more dedicated walker, I also became a more conscientious eater. I started paying attention to portion sizes by measuring my servings. What an eye-opener. I'd been eating two, three, even four times the recommended amounts of foods like pasta and meats. I also cut back on rich ingredients like cream, butter, and cheese. I still allow myself treats, but always in moderation.

'Now, I use my clothing as a gauge of how well I'm keeping my weight in check. I don't concentrate on the scales. Instead, I weigh in just once a year. And I walk every day. At this point, my exercise and eating habits have become second nature. Now, I'm addicted to walking. It sure beats living in a too-large body clothed in stress.' ■

filling, apple sauce, mashed bananas, or puréed canned pears. Reconstituted and puréed dried fruits like apricots and apples also work. The trick is to pair the fruit with the other flavours in the bread, muffins, or cake. For instance, prunes and chocolate work well. If you don't like prunes, apple sauce works with chocolate, too. Apple sauce is also a better choice when you want the finished product to remain light in colour. For the best results, drain apple sauce in a colander for 10 minutes to remove excess liquid. If you're using bananas, keep in mind that they will darken when baked.

Switch from chocolate to cocoa powder. In baking, 3 tablespoons of cocoa has the same chocolaty flavour as 30 g/1 oz of solid chocolate, but 100 fewer calories. This is an easy switch for chocolate cakes, biscuits, brownies, and sauces. Depending on the liquid in the recipe, you might want to add a little extra moisture in the form of semi-skimmed milk or low-fat soft cheese.

Bake a crispy pie crust. Digestive biscuit and chocolate biscuit crusts are held together with lots of melted butter. But egg whites have the same binding properties as butter. You can substitute one lightly beaten egg white for every 60 g/2 oz of butter in pre-baked crusts. This fat saver is not recommended for unbaked crusts because of the possibility of salmonella in eggs.

Use strong tea in salad dressings. Simply reducing the amount of oil in a vinaigrette results in a very acidic dressing (because there's less oil and more vinegar). Adding strong black tea mellows the vinegar's acid without diluting the dressing.

Stretch your beef budget with bulgur. Meatballs and meat loaf come out fluffier and leaner when you substitute bulgur for part of the mince or ground beef. For every 500 g/1 lb of beef, mix in 70 g/2½ g of soaked and drained bulgur (start with 30 g/1 oz dry). Bulgur is a form of cracked wheat available in most supermarkets and health-food stores.

Beware the oil sponges. Grill or bake aubergine, but avoid sautéing or frying it in oil. Aubergines are sponges that absorb just about any amount of oil they get. In dishes that call for cooked aubergine, cut it in half or slice it, coat with a little non-stick spray, salt, and pepper, and bake at 190°C/375°F/gas 5, or until tender. You'll never miss the fat.

Sweat instead of sautéing. To really cut back on fat, when recipes call for onions and garlic to be cooked in oil, use a non-stick pan and 2 tablespoons of stock or water in place of the oil. Cook over a low heat and cover the pan to coax out the vegetable's natural juices.

Make and use yogurt cheese. Drained yogurt, often called yogurt cheese, makes a good substitute for soured cream and double cream. If you drain it well, it can even be substituted for cream cheese. Spoon 500 g/1 lb of low-fat natural yogurt into a colander lined with muslin or a coffee filter. Allow the yogurt to drain over a bowl in the refrigerator for 8–24 hours, depending on how firm you want the 'cheese' to be. For a delicious dessert topping, drain low-fat vanilla yogurt for 4–8 hours, or until just thickened, or use a diet yogurt straight from the pot. Don't try to drain yogurts containing aspartame or gelatin; they don't separate properly.

Roast garlic. When it's roasted, garlic transforms into a rich, buttery, non-biting, non-odorous spread. It makes a great substitute for some of the mayonnaise in potato, pasta, and chicken salads. It's also good spread on bread in place of butter. Cut the top off a bulb of garlic to expose the cloves, sprinkle with a couple of teaspoons of water, seal in foil, and bake at 200°C/400°F/ gas 6 for 45 minutes. Unwrap the garlic, allow it to cool until it is easy to handle, then squeeze the creamy roast garlic from its skin.

Brown butter. Browning boosts flavour so that you don't need to use as much. Heat butter in a frying pan until it becomes fragrant and begins to turn nutty brown (but not burnt). This is a great trick when making dishes such as mashed potatoes. Try drizzling it over corn on the cob, too.

Toast nuts. Like butter, a little browning pumps up the flavour of nuts so that you can use less without missing a flavourful morsel. Simply toast the nuts in a dry frying pan over medium heat for a few minutes, shaking the pan often, or until the nuts are fragrant. Then place them where you'll really taste them: on top of muffins or a casserole (not buried inside), or sprinkled over a salad.

Marinate, marinate. Lean meats, poultry, and seafood are less tender than fatty ones. Marinating does tenderize and adds flavour. Experiment with different marinades made from soy sauce, stocks, citrus juices, vinegars, and your favourite herbs and spices.

Get fired up. Barbecuing intensifies flavours like no other cooking method can. The high heat of the charcoal concentrates a food's tastes. Grilling over charcoal also imparts a smoky aroma. Instead of sautéing vegetables, chicken, meats, or fish, try marinating and barbecuing them instead. The flavour boost is remarkable.

Fry in the oven. 'I bake instead of frying,' says Jean Ross, who lost 16 kg/2½ st. Baking at high heat creates results similar to deep-frying, but without nearly as much fat. This method works especially well for oven-fried chips, homemade tortilla chips, and breaded chicken, meats, and seafood. Here is the basic method: preheat the oven to 230°C/450°F/gas 8. Place the food on a non-stick baking tray and coat it with non-stick spray. Bake until crisp, turning occasionally.

Bring on the Breakfasts and Brunches

Easy Ham and Cheese 'Soufflé'

300 Calories

Sandie Robinson

"This mock soufflé is a trimmed-down version of a one-dish brunch favourite. It's healthier than most other breakfast foods and easier, too. Just assemble in the morning and bake when you are ready."

2 eggs

4 egg whites

340 ml/12 fl oz skimmed milk

115 g/4 oz grated reduced-fat extra-sharp Cheddar cheese

6 slices wholemeal bread, cubed

115 g/4 oz canned sliced mushrooms, drained

60 g/2 oz lean smoked ham, diced

½ tsp dried Italian seasoning

Preheat the oven to 180°C/350°F/gas 4. Coat a 2-litre/3½-pint soufflé dish with non-stick spray.

In a large bowl, beat the eggs and egg whites until frothy. Stir in the milk, cheese, bread, mushrooms, ham, and Italian seasoning. Pour into the prepared soufflé dish.

Bake for 45 minutes, or until golden and a knife inserted in the centre comes out clean.

Makes 4 servings

Per serving: *300 calories, 27 g protein, 27 g carbohydrates, 10 g fat, 889 mg sodium, 4 g fibre*

Diet Exchanges: *0 milk, 0 vegetable, 0 fruit, 2 bread, 2 meat, 0 fat*

Jumbo Cinnamon– Raisin Muffins

299 Calories

Marsha and Katy Fleer

"These muffins are big on flavour but not on fat. To make smaller muffins, use a regular-size 12-cup muffin tin and reduce the cooking time to about 25 minutes."

200 g/7 oz wholemeal flour

60 g/2 oz plain flour

100 g/3½ oz packed brown sugar

2 tsp baking powder

1 tsp ground cinnamon

½ tsp salt

¼ tsp bicarbonate of soda

½ tsp ground nutmeg

125 g/4½ oz raisins

2 large egg whites

225 g/8 oz low-fat natural or
    vanilla yogurt

1 tbsp maple syrup

1 tsp vanilla extract

Preheat the oven to 180°C/350°F/ gas 4. Coat a 6-cup large muffin tin with non-stick spray.

In a large bowl, combine the flour, brown sugar, baking powder, cinnamon, salt, bicarbonate of soda, and nutmeg. Stir in the raisins.

In a small bowl, beat the egg whites slightly. Add the yogurt, maple syrup, and vanilla extract. Mix well. Stir the egg white mixture into the flour mixture just until the flour is moistened. Spoon the batter into the prepared tin until the muffin cups are about two-thirds full.

Bake for 35 minutes, or until a wooden cocktail stick inserted into the centre of a muffin comes out clean. Remove muffins from the tin immediately. Cool on racks.

Makes 6

Per muffin: *299 calories, 8 g protein, 69 g carbohydrates, 1 g fat, 400 mg sodium, 4 g fibre*

Diet Exchanges: *0 milk, 0 vegetable, 1 fruit, 3 bread, 0 meat, 0 fat*

Meatless Mexican Chorizo

138 Calories

Mary Esther Ruiz

"Chorizo is a kind of spicy sausage used in many Latin dishes. It can be very fatty. My version is fat-controlled, yet as spicy as the real thing. Use it as a filling for burritos, an addition to stews, or as an accompaniment to breakfast eggs."

500 g/1 lb vegetarian sausages

½ onion, chopped

400 ml/14 fl oz vegetable or chicken stock

25 g/1 oz chilli powder

1 tbsp ground cinnamon

2 tsp ground cumin

2 tsp dried oregano

2 tsp dried thyme

¾ tsp salt or to taste

½ tsp paprika

115 ml/4 fl oz red wine vinegar

115 ml/4 fl oz tequila or alcohol-free beer

8 peppercorns

6 garlic cloves

2 bay leaves

Cook the sausages in a large non-stick frying pan according to packet directions. Finely chop and set aside.

In the same frying pan, cook the onion in 2 tablespoons stock over medium heat for 5 minutes, or until tender. Add the chilli powder, cinnamon, cumin, oregano, thyme, salt, and paprika. Cook 1 minute. Add the cooked sausage, vinegar, tequila or beer, peppercorns, garlic, bay leaves, and remaining stock.

Heat to boiling. Reduce heat to low and simmer, uncovered, for 30 minutes. Remove the garlic and bay leaves. Refrigerate for 24 hours before using.

Makes 8 servings

Per serving: *138 calories, 10 g protein, 16 g carbohydrates, 9 g fat, 2,634 mg sodium, 2 g fibre*

Diet Exchanges: *0 milk, 0 vegetable, 0 fruit, 1 bread, 1½ meat, 0 fat*

Home Baked Chips

Karen C. Gray

"For extra-crispy, put the roasting tin in the grill for the last 5 minutes."

**4 large potatoes, cut into 15 mm/
½ in. pieces**

1 green or red pepper, chopped

1 red onion, thinly sliced

2 tsp olive oil

1½ tsp seasoned salt

1 tsp ground black pepper

½ tsp garlic powder (optional)

Preheat the oven to 220°C/425°F/gas 7.
Coat a large roasting tin with non-stick spray.

Toss the potatoes, pepper, onion, oil,
seasoned salt, black pepper, and garlic powder, if using, in the tin until well-coated.
Bake, stirring occasionally, for 35–40
minutes, or until the potatoes are fork-tender
and golden.

Makes 4 servings

Per serving: *194 calories, 5 g protein, 38 g
carbohydrates, 3 g fat, 213 mg sodium,
4 g fibre*

Diet Exchanges: *0 milk, 0 vegetable, 0 fruit,
3 bread, 0 meat, ½ fat*

Fat-Free Fried Potatoes

Mrs Kara Kelly

"I make these fried potatoes without any added fat. I use chicken stock instead of butter."

340 ml/12 fl oz chicken or vegetable stock

6 potatoes, thinly sliced

3 spring onions, chopped

½ tsp onion salt

¼ tsp garlic powder

¼ tsp ground sage

¼ tsp ground black pepper

¼ tsp paprika

In a large, heavy non-stick frying pan, heat
115 ml/4 fl oz stock to boiling. Add the
potatoes, spring onions, onion salt, garlic powder, sage, pepper, and paprika. Cover and
cook over high heat for 5 minutes, or until
the liquid is absorbed, turning potatoes
occasionally. Reduce the heat to low and cook
for 10 minutes, adding stock as needed until
the potatoes are tender and brown.

Makes 4 servings

Per serving: *237 calories, 7 g protein, 53 g
carbohydrates, 1 g fat, 442 mg sodium, 4 g fibre*

Diet Exchanges: *0 milk, 0 vegetable, 0 fruit,
4 bread, 0 meat, 0 fat*

Breakfast in a Cup

141 Calories

Dinah Burnette

'These egg "muffins" make a hearty breakfast and can be eaten on the run. Make them in advance and warm them in the microwave oven for a fast breakfast treat. Try them between crumpets, too.'

115 g/4 oz reduced-fat breakfast sausages

60 g/2 oz chopped green pepper

30 g/1 oz chopped onion

5 eggs

115 g/4 oz canned sliced mushrooms, drained

60 g/2 oz grated reduced-fat Cheddar cheese

Coat a 6-cup muffin tin with non-stick spray. Preheat the oven to 180°C/350°F/gas 4.

In a medium non-stick frying pan, cook the sausage, pepper, and onion over medium-high heat for 5 minutes, or until the sausage is browned. Spoon the mixture into a bowl and cool slightly. Stir in the eggs and mushrooms. Spoon the mixture evenly into the prepared muffin tin. Sprinkle with the cheese. Bake for 20 minutes, or until the egg is set.

Makes 6 servings

Per serving: *141 calories, 13 g protein, 3 g carbohydrates, 10 g fat, 305 mg sodium, 1 g fibre*

Diet Exchanges: *0 milk, 0 vegetable, 0 fruit, 0 bread, 1½ meat, 0 fat*

Hash-Browned Potatoes

146 Calories

Marcie Lehman.

"My secret to crispy hash browns is to cook the potatoes without peeling them. The skins give a rustic flavour and add fibre, too."

1 tbsp vegetable oil
2 baking potatoes, coarsely grated
1 small onion, coarsely grated
1 garlic clove, finely chopped
¾ tsp salt
¼ tsp ground black pepper

Warm the oil in a large non-stick frying pan over medium heat.

In a large bowl, combine the potatoes, onion, garlic, salt, and pepper.

Spread the potato mixture into the frying pan. Top with a large dinner plate or cake tin weighted down with something heavy, such as cans of soup. Cook 4 minutes, or until browned. Turn potatoes over and cook 4 minutes, or until browned.

Makes 4 servings

Per serving: *146 calories, 3 g protein, 18 g carbohydrates, 8 g fat, 302 mg sodium, 2 g fibre*

Diet Exchanges: *0 milk, 0 vegetable, 0 fruit, 1½ bread, 0 meat, 1 fat*

NINE HAND-HELD BREAKFASTS

Sometimes breakfast means rushing out the door, sitting behind the wheel of a car, or sitting at a desk and wolfing down a slice of toast and jam. Why jam instead of cream cheese? To save on fat grams, right? Well, not quite. The choice of jam may seem noble, but that choice will leave you drooping way before lunchtime. A good breakfast is based on carbohydrates (like the toast, or bread, or cereal), but it should also contain some protein and fat. Yes, some fat. Meals that contain only carbohydrate and very little protein and fat (like toast with jam or cereal with skimmed milk) won't stay with you long. Within about 45 minutes, you'll be hungry again. But a meal that contains all three nutrients will keep you satisfied throughout the morning.

So go for the reduced-fat cream cheese instead of jam, or take one of the portable breakfasts below. They make great lunches, too. The best beverage choice? A handy carton of skimmed milk or juice.

Fruit 'n' Nuts. Make a sandwich with two slices of wholemeal toast. Spread one slice with orange marmalade and the other with a thin layer of chunky peanut butter. Sprinkle with raisins.

Salmon Sandwich. Mix canned salmon with reduced-fat cream cheese. Season with dried dill and black pepper. Sandwich between two slices of cracked-wheat bread with a layer of sprouts.

More Than a Muffin. Spread a bran muffin with low-fat ricotta cheese. Drizzle with honey and sprinkle with wheat germ.

Smooth Sailing. In a blender, combine low-fat yogurt (natural, lemon, or vanilla), chopped canned peaches, orange juice, ground ginger, cinnamon, and ice cubes. Pour the smoothie into a portable mug.

Go-Go Gazpacho. In a blender, combine a tomato, half of a peeled cucumber, a little sweet onion, some olive oil, tomato juice, and ice cubes. (To wake up your taste buds, add a few drops of hot-pepper sauce.) Pulse until slightly chunky. Pour into a portable mug. Enjoy with a cheese straw.

Egg Salad on a Bagel. Mix a chopped hard-cooked egg with low-fat mayonnaise (and some Dijon mustard, if you like). Spread on a bagel.

Pizza Pick-Me-Up. There's nothing wrong with cold leftover pizza, especially if you top it with some vegetables.

Go-gurt. Grab a small container of low-fat yogurt (natural, lemon, or vanilla) and stir in a serving of all-bran cereal. Top with some apple slices or berries. Bring a spoon.

Crumpet Sandwich. Slice a crumpet in half horizontally to make two thin rounds. Toast both pieces. On one round place a slice of turkey, a slice of low-fat cheese, and some cranberry sauce. then top with the other round to make a great sandwich.

Good Morning Muffins

Christine Finnigan

198 Calories

"The apples, raisins, and nuts pack lots of flavour into these muffins. I like them on lazy weekend mornings with a cup of coffee. They keep in the refrigerator for about 5 days and in the freezer up to 4 months."

150 g/5¼ oz plain flour

2 tsp bicarbonate of soda

½ tsp salt

½ tsp ground cinnamon

¼ tsp ground nutmeg

5 tbsp sugar

2 large eggs

85 ml/3 fl oz vegetable oil

170g/6 oz grated carrots

1 small Granny Smith apple,
    grated with peel

85 g/3 oz golden raisins

85 g/3 oz chopped dates

30 g/1 oz sliced almonds

30 g/1 oz unsweetened
    coconut (optional)

Preheat the oven to 180°C/350°F/gas 4. Coat a 12-cup muffin tin with non-stick spray or line with paper liners.

In a small bowl, combine the flour, bicarbonate of soda, salt, cinnamon, and nutmeg.

In a large bowl, combine the sugar, eggs, and oil. Stir the sugar mixture into the flour mixture until just moistened. Stir in the carrots, apple, raisins, dates, almonds, and coconut, if using.

Spoon batter into the prepared pan until each muffin cup is three-quarters full. Bake for 20 minutes, or until a wooden cocktail stick inserted into the centre of a muffin comes out clean.

Makes 12

Per muffin: *198 calories, 4 g protein, 21 g carbohydrates, 12 g fat, 134 mg sodium, 2 g fibre*

Diet Exchanges: *0 milk, 0 vegetable, 1 fruit, 1 bread, 0 meat, 1½ fat*

Quick Breakfast Crumble

427 Calories

Dixie Lunderville

*"Now here's an easy breakfast dish. It doubles as a dessert or snack, too.
Use apples, pears, or peaches or a mixture of all three. This single-serve recipe cooks
in its serving dish. To make several for friends, cook each dish one at a time in a microwave
oven – it takes only a moment."*

1 apple or pear, cored and sliced

2 tbsp packed brown sugar

2 tbsp quick-cooking oats

2 tbsp plain flour

⅛ tsp ground cinnamon

15 g/½ oz reduced-fat margarine or
butter, softened

Preheat the oven to 180°C/350°F/gas 4.
Place the fruit in a small baking dish.

In a small bowl, combine the brown sugar,
oats, flour, and cinnamon. Rub in the
margarine or butter with your fingertips or a
fork until the mixture resembles coarse
crumbs. Sprinkle over the fruit. Bake for
15–20 minutes, or until the fruit is tender
when pierced.

Makes 1 serving

Per serving: *427 calories, 8 g protein, 81 g
carbohydrates, 8 g fat, 111 mg sodium,
5 g fibre*

Diet Exchanges: *0 milk, 0 vegetable, 1 fruit,
3 bread, 0 meat, 1 fat*

Blueberry-Pecan Pancakes

162 Calories

Melissa Welch

We enjoy these pancakes most in summer with fresh blueberries. But I make them with other fresh and frozen blueberries, too. There's one thing that never varies: we always eat them with real maple syrup.

125 g/4 oz plain flour
60 g/ 2 oz wholemeal flour
60 g/2 oz oat bran
60 g/1½ oz chopped pecans
1 tsp bicarbonate of soda
¼ tsp salt
4 tbsp molasses
225 ml/8 fl oz boiling water
225 g/ 8 oz fat-free vanilla yogurt
2 large eggs
1 tbsp vegetable oil
150 g/5 oz fresh or frozen blueberries, rinsed and drained

Coat a large non-stick frying pan with non-stick spray and set over medium heat.

In a small bowl, combine the plain flour, wholemeal flour, oat bran, pecans, bicarbonate of soda, and salt.

In a large bowl, combine the molasses and water. Stir in the yogurt, eggs, and oil. Pour the molasses mixture into the flour mixture. Mix just until moistened. Gently stir in the blueberries. Using a ladle, pour the batter into the frying pan to make a few pancakes at a time. Cook for 2–3 minutes, or until bubbly and the edges look dry. Turn and cook for 1 minute, or until the underside is golden. Serve immediately.

Makes 12

Per pancake: *162 calories, 5 g protein, 22 g carbohydrates, 6 g fat, 221 mg sodium, 2 g fibre*

Diet Exchanges: *0 milk, 0 vegetable, ½ fruit, 1 bread, 0 meat, 1 fat*

Lemon Wedges

Joyce Dickerman

"Most cakes are loaded with fat, but not these little wedges, which means that I can still "live it up" without putting into jeopardy the 16 kg/2½ st I've lost. I serve them with all-fruit strawberry preserves."

240 g/8½ oz plain flour

1 tbsp baking powder

1 tsp ground cardamom or coriander

½ tsp salt

3 tbsp sugar

1 tbsp vegetable oil

3 egg whites

115 g/4 oz low-fat plain or lemon yogurt

1 tbsp grated lemon peel

Preheat the oven to 200°C/400°F/gas 6. Coat a baking tray with non-stick spray.

In a large bowl, combine the flour, baking powder, cardamom or coriander, salt, and 2 tablespoons sugar. Drizzle with the oil and mix with a fork until evenly distributed.

Reserve 1 tablespoon of the egg whites.

Stir the yogurt, lemon peel, and remaining egg whites into the flour mixture. Stir gently with a fork until the mixture holds together. Turn on to a lightly floured surface and knead about 8 strokes to mix the dough thoroughly. Pat out the dough to form a 20 cm/8 in. circle. Using a sharp knife, cut it evenly into 8 wedges and arrange the wedges about 2.5 cm/1 in. apart on the prepared baking tray. Brush with the reserved egg whites and sprinkle with the remaining sugar. Bake for 15 minutes, or until golden brown.

Makes 8

Per wedge: *155 calories, 5 g protein, 31 g carbohydrates, 2 g fat, 194 mg sodium, 1 g fibre*

Diet Exchanges: *0 milk, 0 vegetable, 0 fruit, 2 bread, 0 meat, 0 fat*

Hot Banana-Wheat Cereal

341 Calories

Dawn Morrow

"This is a very satisfying breakfast that keeps me going all morning. I vary it by using apples, peaches, or berries in place of the bananas."

285 ml/½ pint water
85 g/3 oz bulgur wheat
¼ tsp ground cinnamon
2 bananas, mashed
1 tbsp packed brown sugar
2 tbsp walnuts, chopped (optional)

In a medium saucepan, heat the water to boiling. Stir in the bulgur and cinnamon. Reduce the heat to low and simmer, uncovered, for 7 minutes, stirring occasionally. Stir in the bananas. Cook for 5 minutes, stirring occasionally. Add the brown sugar and walnuts, if using. The cereal will thicken as it cools.

Makes 2 servings

Per serving: *341 calories, 7 g protein, 64 g carbohydrates, 8 g fat, 6 mg sodium, 2 g fibre*

Diet Exchanges: *0 milk, 0 vegetable, 1½ fruit, 2 bread, 0 meat, 0 fat*

Deepak Chopra, MD

This breakfast cereal is featured at the Dr Deepak Chopra's Center for Well-Being, and gives guests a healthy start to their day. Tuck a few handfuls into a plastic bag for a snack, to stir into yogurt, or to sprinkle on fruit. Ghee is a type of clarified butter used in Indian cooking. You can also use butter.

CHOPRA CEREAL

193 Calories

150 g/5 oz rolled oats
40 g/1½ oz slivered almonds
40 g/1½ oz flaked coconut
3 tbsp sunflower seeds
3 tbsp pine nuts
3 tbsp linseeds
3 tbsp sesame seeds
2 tbsp poppy seeds
1 tbsp ground cinnamon
1 tsp ground nutmeg
1 tsp ground allspice
175 g/6 oz maple syrup
60 ml/2 fl oz ghee or melted butter
2 tsp vanilla extract
70 g/2½ oz currants
30 g/1 oz dried cranberries

Preheat the oven to 180°C/350°F/gas 4.

In a large bowl, combine the oats, almonds, coconut, sunflower seeds, pine nuts, linseeds, sesame seeds, poppy seeds, cinnamon, nutmeg, and allspice.

In a medium bowl, combine the maple syrup, ghee or butter, and vanilla extract. Drizzle over the oat mixture and toss to coat. Spread on a baking tray and bake for 20 minutes, stirring occasionally. Add currants and cranberries. Bake for 15–20 minutes, being careful the cereal does not burn. Cool completely. Store in an airtight container for up to 2 months.

Makes 16 servings

Per serving: *193 calories, 4 g protein, 18 g carbohydrates, 12 g fat, 7 mg sodium, 2 g fibre*

Diet Exchanges: *0 milk, 0 vegetable, 1 fruit, 0 bread, 0 meat, 2 fat*

Blueberry Brunch Cake

275 Calories

Janice Mester

"My interest in healthy cooking goes back many years. I have raised two children, who have been high achievers at university, and I attribute much of their success to a good foundation of nutritious food."

CAKE

- 180 g/6 oz plain flour
- 1 tsp bicarbonate of soda
- ¼ tsp salt
- 115 g/4 oz sugar
- 1 large egg
- 225 g/8 oz fat-free natural yogurt
- 2 tbsp vegetable oil
- 1 tsp vanilla extract
- 150 g/5 oz fresh or frozen blueberries, rinsed and drained

TOPPING

- 60 g/2 oz plain flour
- 60 g/2 oz sugar
- 30 g/1 oz butter or margarine, softened
- 1 tsp ground cinnamon

To make the cake:

Preheat the oven to 180°C/350°F/gas 4. Coat an 20 × 20 cm/8 × 8 in. cake tin with non-stick spray.

In a large bowl, combine the flour, bicarbonate of soda, salt, and sugar.

In a medium bowl, combine the egg, yogurt, oil, and vanilla extract. Stir the egg mixture into the flour mixture, just until moist. Stir in the blueberries. Spoon the batter into the prepared cake tin.

To make the topping:

In a small bowl, use a fork to combine the flour, sugar, butter or margarine, and cinnamon until the mixture resembles coarse crumbs. Sprinkle over the cake. Bake for 40–45 minutes, or until a wooden cocktail stick inserted into the centre comes out clean.

Makes 8 servings

Per serving: *275 calories, 5 g protein, 50 g carbohydrates, 7 g fat, 252 mg sodium, 2 g fibre*

Diet Exchanges: *0 milk, 0 vegetable, 1 fruit, 2 bread, 0 meat, 1 fat*

Chocolate Chip Coffee Cake

Sandy Jee

190 Calories

"I can assemble this heavenly treat in less than 10 minutes. Then, it just cooks in the oven. Leftovers freeze well for up to 2 months."

120 g/4 oz plain flour

35 g/1 oz quick-cooking oats

60 g/2 oz wheat germ

2 tsp baking powder

½ tsp bicarbonate of soda

1 tsp instant coffee granules or vanilla extract

⅛ tsp ground cinnamon

⅛ tsp ground nutmeg

225 g/8 oz low-fat coffee or vanilla yogurt

115 g/4 oz sugar

100 g/3½ oz packed brown sugar

1 egg

1 egg white

1 tbsp skimmed milk

1 tbsp vanilla extract

85 g/3 oz semi-sweet chocolate chips

Preheat the oven to 180°C/350°F/gas 4. Coat a 1½-litre/2½-pint Bundt pan or a 25 cm/10 in. pie tin with non-stick spray.

In a large bowl, combine the flour, oats, wheat germ, baking powder, bicarbonate of soda, coffee or vanilla extract, cinnamon, and nutmeg.

In a medium bowl, combine the yogurt, sugar, brown sugar, egg, egg white, milk, and vanilla extract. Stir the yogurt mixture into the flour mixture. Mix well. Stir in the chocolate chips. Spoon the batter evenly into the prepared tin.

Bake for 45 minutes, or until a wooden cocktail stick inserted into the centre comes out clean.

Makes 12 servings

Per serving: *190 calories, 5 g protein, 36 g carbohydrates, 4 g fat, 166 mg sodium, 1 g fibre*

Diet Exchanges: *0 milk, 0 vegetable, 0 fruit, 2 bread, 0 meat, 1 fat*

TIP: To make a chocolate glaze, mix together 115 g/4 oz icing sugar, 2 tablespoons unsweetened cocoa powder, 1 teaspoon instant espresso coffee powder (optional), 1 teaspoon vanilla extract, and 1½ tablespoons hot water.

Orange-Raisin Tea Bread

102 Calories

Charles M. Paugh

"I make this quick bread using dairy-free ingredients and a sugar substitute, but you don't have to. Dairy and sugar amounts are also given, and the calories are roughly the same."

C A K E

2 tsp baking powder

½ tsp salt

120 g/4 oz plain flour

60 g/2 oz butter or margarine, softened

70 g/2½ oz sugar or 15 g/½ oz sugar substitute

70 ml/2½ fl oz orange juice

60 ml/2 fl oz cashew milk (see tip) or skimmed milk

2 tsp grated orange peel

85 g/3 oz raisins

T O P P I N G

3 tbsp sugar or sugar substitute

2 tbsp plain flour

15 g/½ oz butter or margarine, softened

To make the cake:

Preheat the oven to 180°C/350°F/gas 4. Coat a 23 × 12 cm/9 × 5 in. loaf tin with non-stick spray.

In a large bowl, combine the baking powder, salt, and flour. Set aside.

In a medium bowl, beat together the butter or margarine and sugar or sugar substitute. Add the orange juice, milk, and orange peel, and beat well. Stir in the raisins. Stir into the flour mixture until moistened. Spoon the batter into the prepared loaf tin.

To make the topping:

In a small bowl, use a fork to combine the sugar or sugar substitute, flour, and butter or margarine until the mixture resembles coarse crumbs. Sprinkle evenly over the batter. Bake for 25 minutes, or until a wooden cocktail stick inserted into the centre comes out clean. Remove from the tin and cool on a wire rack.

Makes 1 loaf (18 slices)

Per slice: *102 calories, 1 g protein, 18 g carbohydrates, 3 g fat, 135 mg sodium, 0 g fibre*

Diet Exchanges: *0 milk, 0 vegetable, 0 fruit, ½ bread, 0 meat, ½ fat*

TIP: To make cashew milk, combine 75 g/2¾ oz cashews and 115 ml/4 fl oz water in a blender. Blend until smooth. Add 340 ml/12 fl oz more water, ¾ teaspoon sugar or sugar substitute, and ⅛ teaspoon salt. Blend 30 seconds. Makes about 450 ml/¾ pint. Keeps in refrigerator for 2 weeks.

Double-Quick Lunches

Roast Vegetable Wraps

292 Calories

Janie Clark

"These were just what the doctor ordered when I was pregnant and wanted something healthy, not fattening. The wraps are full of flavour and much needed calcium."

4 large portobello mushrooms, sliced 6 mm/¼ in. thick

2 red peppers, cut into 6-mm/¼-in. strips

2 small courgettes, sliced 6-mm/¼-in. thick

2 small yellow squash, sliced 6-mm/¼-in. thick

2 carrots, sliced 6 mm/¼ in. thick

2 tbsp olive oil

2 tbsp balsamic vinegar

½ tsp salt

40 g/1½ oz dry-packed sun-dried tomatoes

225 g/8 oz fat-free natural yogurt

85 g/3 oz low-fat ricotta cheese

2 garlic cloves, finely chopped

1 tsp ground black pepper

6 flour tortillas (20 cm/8 in. diameter)

3 tbsp chopped fresh basil

Preheat the oven to 200°C/400°F/gas 6.

In a large roasting tin, combine the mushrooms, peppers, courgettes, yellow squash, carrots, oil, vinegar, and salt. Toss to coat. Bake, stirring occasionally, for 20–30 minutes, or until vegetables are tender and browned.

Meanwhile, soak the tomatoes in hot water for 10 minutes, or until soft. Drain and finely chop.

In a medium bowl, combine the tomatoes, yogurt, ricotta, garlic, and black pepper.

Warm the tortillas in a microwave oven for 15–20 seconds. Spread one-sixth of the yogurt mixture on a flour tortilla. Spoon one-sixth of the vegetable mixture along the centre of the tortilla. Sprinkle the vegetables with some basil. Fold the tortilla like an envelope to make a closed packet. Cut in half on the diagonal. Repeat with the remaining ingredients.

Makes 6

Per wrap: *292 calories, 9 g protein, 43 g carbohydrates, 10 g fat, 518 mg sodium, 4 g fibre*

Diet Exchanges: *0 milk, 3 vegetable, 0 fruit, 2 bread, 0 meat, 1 fat*

Green Salad Roll-Up

216 Calories

Marjorie Mitchell

"I call this "salad on the go". No plate, no fork, no added fat. (If you like creamy salad dressing, use fat-free ranch instead of Italian.)"

65 g/2 oz torn romaine, cos or other lettuce leaves

a handful alfalfa or mung bean sprouts

2 radishes, sliced

40 g/1½ oz canned chickpeas, rinsed and drained

2 tbsps grated carrots

1 tbsp fat-free Italian dressing

1 tsp red wine vinegar

1 large flour tortilla (30 cm/12 in. diameter)

In a medium bowl, combine the lettuce, sprouts, radishes, chickpeas, and carrots.

In a small bowl, combine the dressing and vinegar. Pour the dressing over the salad and toss to coat. Spoon the salad on to one side of the tortilla and roll it up like a cone.

Makes 1

Per roll-up: *216 calories, 7 g protein, 44 g carbohydrates, 2 g fat, 329 mg sodium, 5 g fibre*

Diet Exchanges: *0 milk, 2 vegetable, 0 fruit, 2 bread, 0 meat, 0 fat*

Vegetable Quesadillas

282 Calories

Madelynne Brown

*"I like to cut these into wedges for dipping into salsa.
For extra zip, use seasoned refried beans."*

1 small onion, chopped
1 small courgette, thinly sliced
1 small yellow squash, thinly sliced
1 garlic clove, finely chopped
310 g/11 oz canned refried beans
8 tortillas, wholemeal if available
   (20 cm/8 in. diameter)
60 g/2 oz grated reduced-fat
   Cheddar cheese
225 g/8 oz no-salt-added salsa

Coat a large frying pan with non-stick spray. Warm over medium-high heat. Add the onion, courgette, yellow squash, and garlic. Cook, stirring occasionally, for 7 minutes, or until the vegetables are tender.

Spread the beans evenly on each tortilla. Spoon the vegetables evenly on to 4 of the bean-covered tortillas. Sprinkle the cheese over the vegetables. Top with the remaining bean-covered tortillas.

Place a quesadilla in the frying pan. Cover and cook over low heat for 5 minutes,

turning once, or until heated through. Repeat with the remaining quesadillas. Cut into wedges and serve with salsa.

Makes 4

Per quesadilla: *428 calories, 19 g protein, 84 g carbohydrates, 4 g fat, 713 mg sodium, 8 g fibre*

Diet Exchanges: *0 milk, 1 vegetable, 0 fruit, 3 bread, 0 meat, 0 fat*

Splurge Meal

1 serving Vegetable Quesadillas
2 tablespoons salsa
¼ avocado with orange slices and
   balsamic vinaigrette

553 calories

Deepak Chopra, MD

At the Chopra Centre for Well Being executive chef Leanne Backer features freshly prepared natural foods made with whole grains, herbs, vegetables, and fruits. Ghee, which is similar to clarified butter, is the preferred cooking fat, but you can use melted butter instead. Tamari is a flavourful type of soy sauce. Serve these burgers with your favourite toppings.

TOFU BURGERS

247 Calories

1 tbsp ghee or melted butter

1 onion, chopped

450 g/1 lb firm tofu, drained and crumbled

1 carrot, grated

1 courgette, grated

60 g/2 oz pine nuts, or 30 g/1 oz sunflower seeds or chopped walnuts

1 tbsp tamari or soy sauce

1 tsp chopped fresh basil or $^1\!/_2$ tsp dried

1 tsp chopped fresh oregano or $^1\!/_2$ tsp dried

1 tsp chopped fresh thyme or $^1\!/_2$ tsp dried

1 tsp chopped fresh tarragon or $^1\!/_2$ tsp dried

$^1\!/_2$ tsp ground black pepper

1 small garlic clove, finely chopped

35 g/1$^1\!/_4$ oz dry breadcrumbs

4 baps

Preheat the oven to 180°C/350°F/gas 4. Warm $^1\!/_2$ teaspoon ghee or butter in a large frying pan over medium heat. Add the onion and cook for 5 minutes, or until tender. Place in a large bowl. Add the tofu, carrot, courgette, nuts or seeds, tamari or soy sauce, basil, oregano, thyme, tarragon, pepper, and garlic. Mix well. Shape into 4 patties. Coat each with breadcrumbs.

Heat the remaining ghee or butter in the frying pan. Add the burgers and cook for 8 minutes, or until golden, turning once. Place on a baking tray and bake for 10 minutes. Serve on the baps.

Makes 4

Per burger: *247 calories, 13 g protein, 12 g carbohydrates, 16 g fat, 127 mg sodium, 1 g fibre*

Diet Exchanges: *0 milk, 0 vegetable, 0 fruit, 2 bread, 2 meat, 1 fat*

Baked Black Beans with Orzo

236 Calories

Jenna Finley

*This hot lunch is ready quickly. It doubles as a dip with crisps.
If you have time, substitute cooked brown rice for the orzo.
(Orzo is ready in 8 minutes; brown rice takes about 45.)*

225 g/8 oz orzo

500 g/1 lb cooked black beans, rinsed and drained

500 g/1 lb canned tomatoes, drained and finely chopped

115 g/4 oz bottled or canned green chilli peppers, drained and chopped

1 garlic clove, finely chopped

½ tsp ground cumin

½ tsp ground black pepper

115 g/4 oz grated reduced-fat Cheddar cheese

60 g/2 oz soured cream

60 g/2 oz low-sodium salsa

1 spring onion, chopped

Preheat the oven to 160°C/325°F/gas 3. Coat a large baking dish with non-stick spray.

Cook the orzo according to packet directions. Drain, return to the pan, and stir in the beans, tomatoes, chilli peppers, garlic, cumin, and black pepper. Spoon into the prepared dish and top with the cheese.

Bake for 15 minutes, or until bubbly and the cheese is melted. Serve with the soured cream, salsa, and spring onion.

Makes 4 servings

Per serving: *236 calories, 19 g protein, 25 g carbohydrates, 7 g fat, 675 mg sodium, 8 g fibre*

Diet Exchanges: *0 milk, 1 vegetable, 0 fruit, 2 bread, 1 meat, 1 fat*

Slimming Meal

1 serving Baked Black Beans with Orzo

60 g/2 oz steamed kale with ½ teaspoon olive oil

1 serving Corn Crepes with Strawberry Sauce (page 271)

414 calories

LUNCHING LIGHT

Portion control is difficult when you're eating out and trying to lose weight. Some restaurants think that 'value' to the customer means offering big portions at low prices. We're used to buying soft drinks in 450 ml/16 fl oz 'small' cups, 340 ml/12 oz cans, and 570 ml/1 pint plastic bottles. No wonder the recommended 225 ml/8 oz serving of soft drinks looks skimpy in a glass at home. And consider a trip to the cinema. The amount of popcorn that the multiplex calls 'small' is actually four or five servings.

Add to these oversized servings the fact that piling on fat is the easiest way to pack in flavour, and you can see why we are getting fatter. Fat is an inexpensive ingredient, and deep-fat frying is a a very simple cooking technique. That's one of the reasons why fast foods are often fried and the cuisine offered at top-notch restaurants is not.

Keeping portions controlled and fat content to a minimum is especially difficult to avoid when lunching out. Unless you're treating yourself to a splurge meal, check out the best choices that follow.

In General

Most restaurants don't include nutritional analyses on their menus. But they do include words that can tip you off to the nutritional content of the food you're ordering. Here's what to look for.

Best choices: *Grilled , braised, baked, poached, roasted, pan-seared,* and *steamed* or *Starter, Hors d'oeuvres, Child Size, Kiddie Size, Lunch,* and *Salad Size*

Think twice about: *Basted, battered or batter-dipped, breaded, buttery, creamy, crisp* (except for raw produce), *crunchy* (except for raw produce), *deep-fried, pan-fried, rich,* and *sautéed* or *Combo, Feast, Grande, Jumbo, King Size,* and *Supreme*

Sandwich Shops

Outrageous portion sizes will be the biggest problem here. Choose shops that make sandwiches to order, so you can get exactly what you want. Alternatively, go to lunch with a friend and split a sandwich. You could even get an extra roll, make two sandwiches from one, and take the second one home for dinner.

Best choices: Small bagels, baked or boiled ham, beetroot salad, breads made with whole grains, carrot and raisin salad, extra veggies on sandwiches, mustard instead of mayonnaise, pickles, roasted or smoked turkey, salami, sliced chicken (not chicken salad), plain tuna

Think twice about: Saltbeef, aubergine or chicken parmigiana, extra cheese, pastrami, knockwurst, liversausage, meatballs, Reuben sandwich, or any sandwich buttered, fried or cooked on a griddle

At the Shopping Centre

Food courts in shopping centres vary greatly, although a few chains seem to be in most of them. Once you've figured out the best food choices, you can avoid traps and surprises at any of them.

Best choices: Baked potatoes, grilled chicken, skimmed or semi-skimmed milk, fat-free salad dressing, salad with dressing on the side, single burgers (regular or kid size), small chips or fries

Think twice about: Cheese sauce, chicken nuggets (breaded, deep-fried and often made with fatty skin), croissants, fish sandwich (usually fried), fried chicken, large and jumbo sizes, onion rings, salad dressing (unless it's fat-free), chilli sauce, tartar sauce

Italian Restaurants

Watch out for extras on the table – especially bread dipped in oil (each dunk adds about 40 calories). Salads with just a bit of dressing are a good way to take the edge off your appetite.

Best choices: Marinara (tomato with basil) sauce, strand pasta or shaped pasta, pasta stuffed with vegetables, clam sauce, wine sauces, piccata

Think twice about: Alfredo, alla panna, carbonara, cheese-stuffed pasta, fried aubergine, fried courgettes, frito misto, parmigiana

Mexican Food

Mexican cuisine is becoming increasingly popular, particularly in many chain restaurants. Eat as much salsa as you like but avoid fried tortillas chips. Instead, ask for baked corn chips, fresh tortilla strips or cut-up fresh vegetables. Go easy on other deep-fried foods, too. Bean dishes are a good choice if they're not slathered in cheese, soured cream, and guacamole. Even so, you can eat your way round the excess fatty toppings.

Best choices: Black bean soup, chilli, enchiladas, burritos, soft tacos, fajitas, gazpacho

Think twice about: Chimichangas, extra cheese, refried beans, soured cream, fried tortillas

Pizza Places

Pizza restaurants can be a real treat for waist watchers. Lower-fat toppings, like prawns, grilled chicken, and tuna, are cropping up everywhere, and there's also increasing variety in the vegetables. Look for interesting cheeses, too. Why settle for mild mozzarella when you can choose high-flavour feta, goat's, and blue cheeses?

Best choices: Grilled chicken, reduced-fat and strongly flavoured cheeses, prawns, tuna, vegetables

Think twice about: Bacon, extra cheese, pepperoni, sausage

Quick Chicken Pasta Salad

238 Calories

Tammy Krick

*"Remember this recipe when time is short and the cupboards are almost bare.
I serve it on lettuce leaves with some crunchy bread and call it lunch."*

115 g/4 oz farfalle (bow-tie) pasta

225 g/8 oz cooked cut-up chicken breast or canned white chunk chicken, drained

200 g/7 oz canned white beans (cannellini), rinsed and drained

115 ml/4 fl oz fat-free Italian dressing

3 plum tomatoes, chopped

2 tbsp chopped fresh basil or parsley

Cook the pasta according to packet directions. Drain and place in a large bowl. While the pasta is still warm, stir in the chicken, beans, Italian dressing, tomatoes, and basil or parsley. Chill until ready to serve.

Makes 4 servings

Per serving: *238 calories, 24 g protein, 28 g carbohydrates, 4 g fat, 53 mg sodium, 3 g fibre*

Diet Exchanges: *0 milk, 0 vegetable, 0 fruit, 3 bread, 2 meat, 0 fat*

Slimming Meal

1 serving Quick Chicken Pasta Salad

2 slices wholemeal bread dipped in 1 teaspoon olive oil

1 baked apple dusted with ground cinnamon

476 calories

Feta Farfalle Salad

199 Calories

Donna Logue

*"*Kidney beans turn this pasta salad into a protein-rich dish. I especially enjoy it in the summer, but it's good any time of year.*"*

170 g/6 oz farfalle (bow-tie) pasta

500 g/1 lb canned red kidney beans, rinsed and drained

2 small bunches spring onions, chopped

2 garlic cloves, finely chopped

35 g/1¼ oz crumbled feta cheese

35 g/1¼ oz dry-cured olives, pitted

3 tbsp olive oil

2 tbsp lemon juice

2 tbsp chopped fresh basil or parsley

½ tsp salt

¼ tsp ground black pepper

Cook the pasta according to packet directions. Drain and place in a large bowl. Add the beans, spring onions, garlic, cheese, and olives.

In a small bowl, mix the oil, lemon juice, basil or parsley, salt, and pepper. Pour over the pasta and toss. Serve at room temperature or refrigerate and serve cold.

Makes 8 servings

Per serving: *199 calories, 8 g protein, 26 g carbohydrates, 8 g fat, 482 mg sodium, 5 g fibre*

Diet Exchanges: *0 milk, 0 vegetable, 0 fruit, 3 bread, 0 meat, 1 fat*

It Worked for Me!

Debra Davies

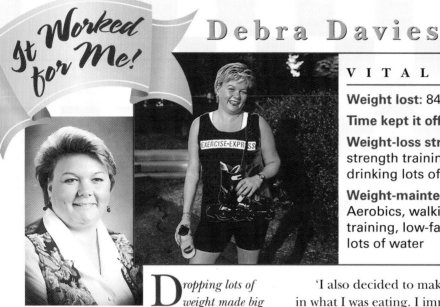

VITAL STATS

Weight lost: 84 kg/5 st 5 lb

Time kept it off: 2 years

Weight-loss strategies: Walking, strength training, low-fat diet, drinking lots of water

Weight-maintenance strategies: Aerobics, walking, strength training, low-fat diet, drinking lots of water

Dropping lots of weight made big changes in Debra Davies's body, and her spirits improved, too. That's what keeps her motivated.

'I was one of those lucky people who never worried about my weight. That is, until my first child was born. That's when I started gaining. I struggled for 15 years with diet after diet. You name it, I tried it. But the scales continued to creep up. Exercise was never a part of my diets, which I now know is why they didn't work.

'One night, something clicked. I was out with friends and looked in a mirror and didn't recognize myself because I had become so big. At that moment I wanted to look better and feel better. I was determined to stick with it.

'On the first day of my new diet, I walked 3 km (2 miles). And I kept it up. I walked rain or shine, sleet or snow. The daily commitment kept me motivated. In a year, I was walking 3 km and jogging 3 km.

'I also decided to make some changes in what I was eating. I immediately cut out fried foods. Instead, I ate lots of fish, rice, and pasta. My cooking methods changed, too. Now, I bake, grill, or steam instead of frying. Substituting water for fizzy drinks helped a lot, too. And veggies and fruits replaced sweets and crisps.

'My biggest challenges are parties and weddings. I have to stay away from the dips. In the old days I could empty a bowl by myself. It's not all nose to the grindstone, though. I do indulge occasionally, but the next day, I'm back on track or I exercise a little more.

'These days, I go to the gym 3 days a week. I love step aerobic classes and weight training. I also belong to a walking club. I feel better than I have in years. I feel better from the inside. I have a healthier attitude about myself and spend a lot of time around healthy people. Most healthy people are happy and positive. That keeps me motivated.' ■

Debra's Vegetable-Prawn Stir-Fry

224 Calories

"To keep my weight down, I stay away from fatty meats and dairy products. Seafood is one of my main protein sources."

75 ml/3 fl oz water

2 tbsp soy sauce

2 tbsp cornflour

1 tsp sugar

2 tbsp vegetable oil

½ small green cabbage, shredded

1 red pepper, cut into 5-cm/2-in. pieces

4 spring onions, cut into 2.5-cm/1-in. pieces

225 g/8 oz asparagus, cut into 5-cm/2-in. pieces

2 garlic cloves, finely chopped

500 g/1 lb peeled and deveined prawns

2 tbsp finely chopped fresh ginger

½ tsp crushed red pepper

2 tbsp dry sherry (optional)

In a small bowl, combine the water, soy sauce, cornflour, and sugar.

Warm 1 tablespoon oil in a large non-stick frying pan or wok over medium heat. Add the cabbage, chopped red pepper, onions, asparagus, and garlic. Cook, stirring frequently, for 3 minutes, or until vegetables are crisp-tender. Stir in 1 tablespoon of the soy-sauce mixture. Cook until the mixture is thickened and coats the vegetables. Spoon the vegetables on to a platter and keep warm.

Warm the remaining oil in the same frying pan. Add the prawns, ginger, and crushed red pepper. Cook, stirring frequently, for 5 minutes, or until the prawns are just opaque. Stir in the sherry, if using, and the remaining soy-sauce mixture. Cook until the mixture is thickened and coats the prawns. Spoon the prawns over the vegetables.

Makes 4 servings

Per serving: *224 calories, 23 g protein, 12 g carbohydrates, 9 g fat, 223 mg sodium, 2 g fibre*

Diet Exchanges: *0 milk, 3 vegetable, 0 fruit, ½ bread, 1½ meat, 0 fat*

Slimming Meal

1 serving Debra's Vegetable-Prawn Stir-Fry

140 g/5 oz cooked brown rice

1 Wonton Fruit Cup (page 276)

467 calories

Broccoli Soup

168 Calories

Sheri Ghaby

"This is my favourite way to cook broccoli. For Broccoli-Cheddar Soup, add 115 g/4 oz grated reduced-fat extra-sharp Cheddar cheese along with the evaporated milk."

15 g/¼ oz butter or margarine

1 onion, chopped

1 small bunch broccoli, coarsely chopped

400 ml/14 fl oz chicken or vegetable stock

1 bay leaf

60 ml/2 fl oz skimmed milk

1 tbsp plain flour

170 ml/6 fl oz semi-skimmed
    evaporated milk

⅛ tsp ground nutmeg

¼ cup grated Parmesan cheese (optional)

Warm the butter or margarine in a large saucepan over medium heat. Add the onion and cook 5 minutes, or until tender. Set aside 6–8 broccoli florets. Add the stock, bay leaf, and remaining broccoli to the saucepan. Heat to boiling. Cover, reduce heat to low, and simmer for 10 minutes.

Remove from the heat. Cool slightly and remove and discard the bay leaf. Purée the soup in a blender or food processor, and return it to the pan.

In a small bowl, combine the skimmed milk and flour. Stir this into the soup along with the evaporated milk and nutmeg. Cook over medium heat, stirring, until the soup simmers and thickens. Add the reserved broccoli florets. Cook for 2 minutes. Serve sprinkled with cheese, if using.

Makes 4 servings

Per serving: *168 calories, 12 g protein, 15 g carbohydrates, 7 g fat, 436 mg sodium, 4 g fibre*

Diet Exchanges: *½ milk, 1 vegetable, 0 fruit, 0 bread, 0 meat, ½ fat*

Slimming Meal

1 serving Broccoli Soup

3 stone-ground wheat crackers

115 g/4 oz fat-free fruit yogurt

1 pear

327 calories

Creamy Carrot-Potato Soup

192 Calories

Debbie Liban

"Pair this soup with a sandwich for large appetites. Or enjoy it alone with bread. Sometimes I add celery for more veggie power. The carrots make this soup rich in beta-carotene."

1 tbsp olive oil

½ onion, chopped

1 tsp chilli powder

2 carrots, sliced

2 potatoes, peeled and chopped small

400 ml/14 fl oz chicken stock

340 ml/12 fl oz skimmed milk

1 tsp soy sauce

2 tbsp sesame seeds

Warm the oil in a large saucepan over medium heat. Add the onion and chilli powder. Cook for 5 minutes, or until the onion is tender. Add the carrots, potatoes, and stock. Heat to boiling. Reduce the heat to low, cover, and simmer for 10 minutes, or until the vegetables are tender.

Remove from the heat and cool slightly. Purée the soup in a blender or food processor. Return it to the pan. Stir in the milk and soy sauce. Cook over medium heat just until the soup is heated through. Do not boil. Serve sprinkled with sesame seeds.

Makes 4 servings

Per serving: *192 calories, 7 g protein, 25 g carbohydrates, 8 g fat, 389 mg sodium, 3 g fibre*

Diet Exchanges: *½ milk, 1 vegetable, 0 fruit, 1 bread, 0 meat, 1 fat*

Slimming Meal

1 serving Creamy Carrot-Potato Soup

1 handful mixed salad greens with low-calorie dressing

1 wholemeal roll

¼ melon

175 calories

Garden Vegetable Soup

186 Calories

Mark Ballard

This veggie soup is chock-full of goodies, and the servings are generous. Tamari, a type of rich-tasting soy sauce, gives it a shot of big flavour. Beetroots add a pleasant rosy colour.

2 tbsp vegetable oil

1 large onion, chopped

1 litre/1¾ pints chicken stock

2 carrots, sliced

2 celery sticks, finely chopped

2 potatoes, cut into 2.5-cm/1-in. cubes

2 beetroots, peeled and cut into 2.5-cm/ 1-in. cubes

150 g/5 oz green beans, cut into 2.5-cm/ 1-in. pieces

¼ green cabbage, shredded

2 garlic cloves, finely chopped

1 bay leaf

1 tbsp tamari or soy sauce

115 g/4 oz fresh or frozen green peas

Warm the oil in a large soup pot over medium heat. Add the onion and cook for 5 minutes, or until tender. Add the stock, carrots, celery, potatoes, beetroots, beans, cabbage, garlic, bay leaf, and tamari or soy sauce. Heat to boiling. Reduce heat to low and simmer for 15 minutes. Stir in the peas and cook 10 minutes. Remove and discard the bay leaf before serving.

Makes 4 servings

Per serving: *186 calories, 6 g protein, 23 g carbohydrates, 91 g fat, 560 mg sodium, 5 g fibre*

Diet Exchanges: *0 milk, 4 vegetable, 0 fruit, 2 bread, 0 meat, 2 fat*

Salmon Chowder

267 Calories

The Rev. Aaron S. Peters

"Yogurt and buttermilk add creaminess to this chunky chowder. The salmon makes it flavourful and gives it an attractive colour."

1 large potato, peeled and cut into small cubes

1 turnip, peeled and cut into small cubes

1 small onion, chopped

1 celery stick, chopped

1 tsp dill seed

1 bay leaf

450 ml/18 fl oz water

340 g/12 oz canned pink salmon, drained

225 ml/8 fl oz buttermilk

225 g/8 oz low-fat natural yogurt

15 g/½ oz butter or margarine

2 tsp hot-pepper sauce

¼ tsp salt

½ tsp ground black pepper

¼ tsp dried tarragon

In a large saucepan, combine the potato, turnip, onion, celery, dill seed, bay leaf, and water. Heat to boiling over high heat. Reduce the heat to medium. Simmer, uncovered, for 12 minutes, or until the vegetables are tender.

Reduce the heat to low. Stir in the salmon, buttermilk, yogurt, butter or margarine, hot-pepper sauce, salt, black pepper, and tarragon. Cook for 5 minutes, or just until heated through. Remove and discard the bay leaf before serving.

Makes 4 servings

Per serving: *267 calories, 26 g protein, 19 g carbohydrates, 10 g fat, 681 mg sodium, 2 g fibre*

Diet Exchanges: *0 milk, 1 vegetable, 0 fruit, 1 bread, 2 meat, 0 fat*

FROM THE PROS

Canyon Ranch Health Resorts

You probably don't need a recipe to learn how to grill burgers. But this recipe from Canyon Ranch Health Resorts in the USA demonstrates that calorie-wise portion control goes hand in hand with great taste.

CANYON RANCH BURGERS

231 Calories

500 g/1 lb extra-lean ground steak

8 small wholemeal baps

75 g/2¾ oz low-fat Thousand
  Island dressing

8 tomato slices

8 onion slices

8 lettuce leaves

Coat a grill rack with non-stick spray and preheat the grill. Form the meat into 8 burgers and place on the prepared rack. Grill over coals or in the grill until a thermometer inserted in centre registers 70°C/160°F and the meat is no longer pink.

Spread each bap with 2 teaspoons dressing. Place 1 burger on each bap and garnish with tomato, onion, and lettuce.

Makes 8

Per burger: *231 calories, 18 g protein, 30 g carbohydrates, 5 g fat, 438 mg sodium, 5 g fibre*

Diet Exchanges: *0 milk, 0 vegetable, 0 fruit, 2 bread, 2 meat, 0 fat*

Sweet Potato and Leek Soup

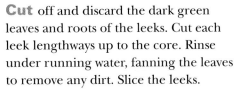
160 Calories

S. D. Freedman

"White potatoes are the classic choice for this soup, but I like the flavour and colour of sweet potatoes."

3 leeks

30 g/1 oz unsalted butter

1 tbsp olive oil

1 large onion, chopped

680 g/1½ lb sweet potatoes or yams, peeled and diced

1.25 litre/2¼ pints chicken stock

¼ tsp ground red pepper

Cut off and discard the dark green leaves and roots of the leeks. Cut each leek lengthways up to the core. Rinse under running water, fanning the leaves to remove any dirt. Slice the leeks.

In a large soup pot, melt the butter with the oil over medium heat. Add the onion and leeks. Cover and cook, stirring occasionally, for 7 minutes, or until soft. Add the sweet potatoes or yams and stock. Heat to boiling. Reduce the heat to low, cover, and simmer, stirring occasionally, for 20–25 minutes, or until the potatoes are fork-tender. Cool slightly. Purée the soup in a blender or food processor. Blend in the pepper.

Makes 8 servings

Per serving: *160 calories, 2 g protein, 27 g carbohydrates, 5 g fat, 216 mg sodium, 2 g fibre*

Diet Exchanges: *0 milk, 1 vegetable, 0 fruit, 1 bread, 0 meat, 1 fat*

Snacks, Nibbles, and Mini-Meals

Spicy Dipper Rolls

266 Calories

Stacey Carpenter

"I use this recipe whenever I need party food. It doubles easily to handle a crowd and it keeps in the refrigerator for up to a week."

225 g/8 oz reduced-fat cream
  cheese, softened

225 g/8 oz reduced-fat soured cream

6 spring onions, finely chopped

115 g/4 oz bottled or canned green chile
  peppers, drained and chopped

6 flour tortillas (30-cm/12-in. diameter)

500 g/1 lb salsa

In a large bowl combine the cream cheese, soured cream, spring onions, and peppers.

Spread one-sixth of the mixture on 1 side of a tortilla. Roll up the tortilla, like a Swiss roll, and wrap it with cling film. Repeat with the remaining tortillas.

Refrigerate the rolls overnight. To serve, remove the cling film. With a sharp knife, cut the rolls into 2.5-cm/1-in. slices on the diagonal. Serve with salsa.

Makes 6 servings (about 72 slices)

Per serving (about 12 slices): *266 calories, 9 g protein, 32 g carbohydrates, 9 g fat, 194 mg sodium,2 g fibre*

Diet Exchanges: *0 milk, 0 vegetable, 0 fruit, 2 bread, 0 meat, 1½ fat*

Spinach Squares

137 Calories

Lisa Keys

"With two children who love sports, getting enough exercise is no problem for me. But I still have to be extra careful about following a low-fat diet. These spinach squares are one of my favourite ways to do it. I sometimes serve this as a main dish for four."

1 tbsp olive oil

1 onion, chopped

85 g/3 oz chopped mushrooms

1 red pepper, chopped

140 g/5 oz chopped fresh spinach

115 g/4 oz reduced-fat cream cheese

4 eggs

35 g/1 oz seasoned dried breadcrumbs

2 tbsp sesame seeds

2 tbsp grated Parmesan cheese

¼ tsp salt

Preheat the oven to 190°C/350°F/gas 4. Coat a 23 × 23 cm/9 × 9 in. ovenproof dish with non-stick spray.

Warm the oil in a large frying pan over medium-high heat. Add the onion, mushrooms, and pepper. Cook for 5 minutes, or until the pepper is tender. Add the spinach and cook for 1–2 minutes, or until wilted. Remove from the heat. Cool slightly.

In a large bowl, beat the cream cheese until smooth. Stir in the eggs, bread crumbs, 1 tablespoon sesame seeds, 1 tablespoon Parmesan, and salt. Stir in the spinach mixture. Spoon into the prepared dish. Sprinkle with the remaining sesame seeds and Parmesan. Bake 30 minutes, or until the edges are golden brown.

Makes 8 servings

Per serving: *137 calories, 7 g protein, 5 g carbohydrates, 10 g fat, 231 mg sodium, 1 g fibre*

Diet Exchanges: *0 milk, 2 vegetable, 0 fruit, 0 bread, 1 meat, 0 fat*

Portobellos and Goat's Cheese

94 Calories

Janet Fry

"I'll dig into this mini-meal almost any time of day. For a summer lunch or supper, serve it with a fresh green salad and crusty bread."

225 g/8 oz prepared tomato and basil sauce

4 large portobello mushroom caps

115 g/4 oz mild goat's cheese (chèvre or Montrachet), cut into 4 pieces

2 tbsp finely chopped pitted black olives

1 tbsp chopped parsley

Preheat the oven to 180°C/375°F/gas 5.

Spread the sauce in the bottom of a 23 × 23 cm/9 × 9 in. ovenproof dish. Arrange the mushroom caps gill side up on top. Place a piece of goat's cheese on each mushroom. Sprinkle evenly with olives. Bake for 30 minutes, or until hot and bubbly.

Makes 4 servings

Per serving: *94 calories, 5 g protein, 4 g carbohydrates, 6 g fat, 290 mg sodium, 1 g fibre*

Diet Exchanges: *0 milk, 3 vegetable, 0 fruit, 0 bread, 0 meat, 2 fat*

It Worked for Me!

Richard Simmons

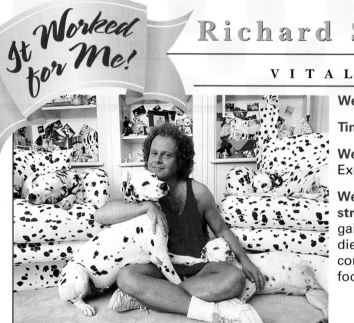

VITAL STATS

Weight lost: 62 kg/9 st 11 lb

Time kept it off: 25 years

Weight-loss strategies:
Exercise, low-calorie diet

Weight-maintenance strategies: Has a 2 kg/5 lb gain/loss window, low-calorie diet, daily exercise, finds comfort in things other than food, helps others lose weight

The Prince of Weight Loss is so successful at encouraging others to shed weight because he constantly battles with his own.

'I've been on diets since I was 8,' says Richard Simmons. He tried scores of magazine reducing plans, counting and juggling calories, all the way to a liquid diet. He even admits that he had his own subscription to *Cosmopolitan* magazine because, at the time, they ran a different diet each month. By age 12, he went on a liquid diet and lost 34 kg/5 st 5 lb. It was a short-lived loss. By the time he was 14, Richard had reached his highest weight: 121 kg/19 st. Then he tried starvation, having nothing but water for 2½ months. It worked. Richard lost 58 kg/9 st; but it landed him in hospital.

'In 1974, when I opened my exercise studio, I made up my mind that I had to stay on a strict eating plan. I also realized that I have to exercise every day. I have to do it in the morning. Later in the day, I'll make excuses and put it off.

'I eat 1,600 to 1,800 calories a day and no more than 30 grams of fat. I divide those calories among three meals a day. I often make breakfast and lunch fat-free so that I can have the fat to play with for dinner.

'Now, it's a way of life for me,' he says. His diet and exercise habits have become automatic. He has also become realistic about his weight. 'I've been obese. I've been bone thin. I've settled on a weight of about 68 kg (10 st). I had to starve to stay 5 kg/10 lb lighter, but at 68 kg I feel just right.' ▪

Pitta Pizza

288 Calories

Rachel Povse

"This is an update of the bread roll mini-pizzas of the 1950s. Nothing is easier or tastier."

4 small wholemeal or regular pittas
115 g/4 oz spaghetti or tomato sauce
260 g/9 oz sliced vegetables (mushrooms, green peppers, tomatoes, onions)
115 g/4 oz grated mozzarella cheese
½ tsp dried oregano
2 tsp extra-virgin olive oil

Preheat the oven to 230°C/450°F/gas 8.

Split each pitta into 2 thin rounds. Place crust side down, on a large baking tray. Bake for 10 minutes, or just until crisp.

Remove from the oven and top each round evenly with sauce, vegetables, cheese, and oregano. Drizzle each with olive oil. Bake for 5–8 minutes, or until the cheese just melts.

Makes 4 servings

Per serving: *288 calories, 14 g protein, 37 g carbohydrates, 10 g fat, 610 mg sodium, 2 g fibre*

Diet Exchanges: *0 milk, 2 vegetable, 0 fruit, 1½ bread, ½ meat, 1 fat*

Tomato-Crab Bake
217 Calories

Majeda Casciano

"These crab cakes make an elegant lunch or starter. No one will guess that they're not high-fat. For brunch, top each with a poached egg."

70 g/2½ oz dried breadcrumbs

2 large tomatoes, cut into 1-cm/½-in. slices

225 g/8 oz fresh lump crabmeat, well-drained

115 g/4 oz grated low-fat mozzarella cheese

90 g/3 oz finely chopped black olives

35 g/1¼ oz finely chopped mushrooms

3 tbsp finely chopped parsley

1 garlic clove, finely chopped

½ tsp dried oregano

½ tsp dried basil

Preheat the oven to 190°C/350°F/gas 4. Coat a baking tray with non-stick spray.

Place the breadcrumbs on a plate. Coat both sides of the tomato slices with non-stick spray. Dip the tomato slices in the breadcrumbs to coat well. Place the tomato slices on the prepared baking tray.

In a large bowl, combine the crabmeat, cheese, olives, mushrooms, parsley, garlic, oregano, and basil. Spoon the crab mixture evenly onto the tomato slices.

Bake for 15 minutes, or until hot.

Makes 4 servings

Per serving: *217 calories, 17 g protein, 16 g carbohydrates, 9 g fat, 919 mg sodium, 1.5 g fibre*

Diet Exchanges: *0 milk, 1 vegetable, 0 fruit, 0 bread, 2 meat, 1 fat*

It Worked for Me!

Dinah Burnette

VITAL STATS

Weight lost: 45 kg/7 st 2 lb

Time kept it off: 2 years

Weight-loss strategies: Low-fat diet, drinks lots of water, walks and strength trains

Weight-maintenance strategies: Has a 2 kg/5 lb gain/loss window, drinks lots of water, avoids elastic waistbands

*D*inah Burnette dropped 45 kg, got out of her size 26 clothing, and slipped into a size 12. She continues to take control of her life.

'I was one of those people everybody hates because I could eat anything. Fast foods and chocolate chip cookies were my staples. I never thought about my weight because it never changed.

'Then, my doctor prescribed medication for anxiety, which caused me to gain weight. I admit that I used my medication to some extent as an excuse to let myself get out of shape. My afternoon snacks were two peanut butter sandwiches with chocolate milk. And I never exercised.

'Of course, the weight crept up. I didn't realize how serious my problem had become until I saw a photo of myself: 111 kg (17½ st) stuffed into a size 26 dress. It was then that I realized my medicine wasn't making me fat. I was.

'It was time to take control. When I finally admitted that I was responsible for my current weight, I also realized that I could change it. I drank 3.5 litres/6 pints of water every day. I also started walking – just under a kilometre (½ mile) at first. After a few weeks, I was walking twice as far. Then I joined the YMCA and started lifting weights. I added a daily 20-minute jog in the pool. I learned how breakfast kick-starts the metabolism, so I began each day with a slice of whole-grain bread, a box of raisins, and a glass of skimmed milk. I'd snack on fruit, low-fat yogurt, cereal, or raw veggies throughout the day.

'Within 6 months, I lost 23 kg (3½ st) and was down to a size 18. Even my shoes and rings were too big. And my double chin was disappearing. I loved the way I felt. I rediscovered energy that I hadn't had in years. Exactly one year later, I hit my goal.

'Today, good nutrition and exercise are central to my life. Every day, I run or walk 3 km (2 miles) and lift weights every other day.

Great nutrition isn't monotonous either, since I've learned to make my favourite recipes healthier.

'One trick I use to stay slim is that I refuse to wear any clothing with elastic waistbands. I'm also very careful about what I eat on weekdays, and I don't worry about the weekends. I don't want to be fat ever again. I want to stay healthy. I didn't like myself when I gained weight. I like myself so much more now.' ■

Dinah's
Shredded Chicken Spread

173 Calories

"This makes a great sandwich on pumpernickel bread. Or serve it on lettuce with your favourite raw vegetables and sliced fruit."

340 g/12 oz boneless, skinless chicken breast

225 g/8 oz fat-free or reduced-fat cream cheese, softened

1 small onion, finely chopped

1 celery stick, finely chopped

60 g/2 oz bottled pimientos, chopped

½ tsp salt

½ tsp cracked black pepper

Combine the chicken and enough water to cover in a very large saucepan over high heat. Heat to boiling. Reduce the heat to low and cook for 10 minutes, or until a thermometer inserted in the thickest breast

registers 70°C/160°F and the juices run clear. Transfer the chicken to a plate to cool. Using 2 forks, pull chicken into shreds.

In a large bowl, combine the chicken, cream cheese, onion, celery, pimientos, salt, and pepper. Cover and refrigerate for at least 2 hours to blend flavours.

Makes 4 servings

Per serving: *173 calories, 26 g protein, 3 g carbohydrates, 6 g fat, 304 mg sodium, 1 g fibre*

Diet Exchanges: *0 milk, 0 vegetable, 0 fruit, 1 bread, 1½ meat, 0 fat*

Roast Garlic Spread

Barb Pomaville

Garlic changes completely when you roast it. It takes on a sweet, almost buttery flavour and becomes soft and spreadable. I like this spread on melba toast. It's also good as a dip with cut-up vegetables.

1 whole garlic bulb

225 g/8 oz reduced-fat cream cheese, softened

85 g/3 oz fat-free mayonnaise

Preheat the oven to 190°C/350°F/gas 4.

Discard the papery skin from the garlic, but leave the bulb intact. Sprinkle the bulb with a little water and wrap it in foil. Place it on a baking tray and bake for 45 minutes.

Squeeze each clove of garlic from its skin into a medium bowl. Discard the skin. Add the cream cheese and mayonnaise to the bowl and mix well.

Makes 340 g/12 oz

Per 2 tablespoons: *72 calories, 3 g protein, 2 g carbohydrates, 1 g fat, 130 mg sodium, 0 g fibre*

Diet Exchanges: *0 milk, 0 vegetable, 0 fruit, ½ bread, 0 meat, ½ fat*

Herb Cheese Spread

76 Calories

Marjorie Mitchell

'Why give up cheese? There's no need when you have this easy spread recipe on hand. Serve with cream crackers or Belgian endive. I usually make this a day ahead to let the flavours develop.'

225 g/8 oz soured cream

115 g/4 oz grated reduced-fat Cheddar cheese

1 spring onion, finely chopped

2 tbsp chopped parsley

½ tsp dried thyme

½ tsp dried rosemary, crushed

½ tsp ground black pepper

In a medium bowl, combine the soured cream, cheese, spring onion, parsley, thyme, rosemary, and pepper. Cover and refrigerate up to 4 days.

Makes 340 g/12 oz

Per 1 heaped tablespoon: *76 calories, 4 g protein,1 g carbohydrates, 6 g fat, 86 mg sodium, 0 g fibre*

Diet Exchanges: *0 milk, 0 vegetable, 0 fruit, 0 bread, ½ meat, 0 fat*

Hot Bean Dip

81 Calories

Adriane Lockwood

Need a quick party dip or something easy to please the kids? This one's a hit every time. It's excellent with crisps or fresh vegetables. It's best hot, but good cold, too.

400 g/14 oz canned refried beans

200 g/7 oz reduced-fat soured cream

200 g/7 oz salsa

½ tsp salt

1 tsp ground black pepper

60 g/2 oz grated reduced-fat Cheddar cheese (optional)

Preheat the oven to 160°C/325°F/gas 3.

In a large bowl, combine the beans, soured cream, salsa, salt, and pepper. Spoon the mixture into a shallow 1-litre/ 2-pint ovenproof dish. Top with the cheese, if using. Bake for 10–15 minutes, or until heated through.

Makes 860 g/1¾ lb

Per 85 g/3 oz: *81 calories, 3 g protein, 8 g carbohydrates, 4 g fat, 240 mg sodium, 3 g fibre*

Diet Exchanges: *0 milk, 0 vegetable, 0 fruit, 1 bread, ½ meat, 0 fat*

Yogurt Fruit Smoothie

232 Calories

Michelle Keller

*"The refreshing creaminess of this drink comes from the yogurt.
But it's also good made with skimmed milk or low-fat soya milk. Use your
favourite frozen fruit or a combination of fruits."*

500 g/1 lb low-fat natural yogurt

1 ripe banana, cut into chunks

150 g/5 oz frozen unsweetened
   strawberries or peaches

2 tbsp honey

120 g/4 oz ice cubes

In a blender, combine the yogurt, banana, strawberries or peaches, honey, and ice. Blend until frothy.

Makes 2

Per smoothie: *232 calories, 14 g protein, 4 g carbohydrates, 2 g fat, 213 mg sodium, 2 g fibre*

Diet Exchanges: *1 milk, 0 vegetable, 2 fruit, 0 bread, 0 meat, 0 fat*

50 LOW-CALORIE SNACKS

The need to nibble can strike at any time. Below are snacks to satisfy your craving for any kind of sweet or salty nibble (even chocolate!). Each food listed contains about 50 calories. For a 150-calorie snack, choose three. Stash them in your car, handbag, desk drawer, or anywhere that will be handy when you might feel like having a little snack. There are plenty that don't need to be stored in a refrigerator.

150 g/5 oz strawberries
1 small orange
$\frac{1}{2}$ banana
1 thick or 3 thin slices of melon
20 g/$\frac{3}{4}$ oz raisins
120 g/4 oz cherries
150 g/5 oz blueberries
1 medium baked apple, no filling
2 prunes
140 ml/5 fl oz orange juice
2 sesame breadsticks
5 baked tortilla chips with 1
    tablespoon salsa
1 mini doughnut (2.5 cm/1 in. diameter)
2 cream crackers, dry
$\frac{1}{2}$ slice thick-cut, unbuttered
    wholemeal toast
2 mini pittas
1 stone-ground wheat biscuit
3 rye biscuits (such as Ryvita)
2 small Jaffa cakes
1 small wholemeal digestive biscuit
1 poppadum, microwaved
2 tablespoons low-fat muesli
1 tablespoon trail mix
1 handful plain air-popped popcorn

1 tablespoon toffee popcorn
1$\frac{1}{2}$ rice cakes
4 dried apricots (8 halves)
1 fig roll
2 fresh figs
225 ml/8 fl oz gazpacho
1 tablespoon chocolate chips
15 Smarties or M & Ms
20 g/$\frac{3}{4}$ oz reduced-fat Cheddar cheese
16 olives
75 g/2$\frac{1}{2}$ oz low-fat cottage cheese
150 ml/5 fl oz skimmed milk
1 small pot diet yogurt
1 small hard-boiled egg
85 g/3 oz refried beans
1$\frac{1}{2}$ peaches
2 teaspoons peanuts
1 teaspoon almonds
1 slice rye bread
2–3 plums
4 Ritz crackers
small handful of grapes
2 slices turkey breast
2 chocolates
2 kiwi fruit
5 liquorice allsorts

Peanut Butter and Banana Shake

329 Calories

Linda Quinonez

"Here's a smoothie with a new twist! Kids love it. Drink the whole thing for breakfast or lunch. I keep bananas in the freezer so they are ready to go. The peels darken, but the fruit is still fine."

225 g/8 oz fat-free natural yogurt
1 frozen banana
1 tbsp creamy peanut butter
1 tsp vanilla extract
1 tsp honey
½ tsp ground cinnamon

In a blender, combine the yogurt, banana, peanut butter, vanilla extract, honey, and cinnamon. Blend until smooth.

Makes 1

Per shake: *329 calories, 16 g protein, 46 g carbohydrates, 10 g fat, 241 mg sodium, 2 g fibre*

Diet Exchanges: *1½ milk, 0 vegetable, 2 fruit, 0 bread, 1 meat, 0 fat*

Purple Power Shake

347 Calories

Britt Isaac

"For an energy boost, my fiancé has one of these shakes before his tennis matches. I like it because it's a good source of calcium, fruit, vitamins, and soya protein. Even my most tofu-phobic friends love it. Use your favourite fruit and berries."

90 g/3 oz chopped fresh fruit (bananas, peaches, mangos)

75 g/2½ oz fresh or frozen berries (blueberries, strawberries, raspberries)

75 g/2½ oz frozen orange juice concentrate

115 g/4 oz silken tofu, drained

225 ml/8 fl oz skimmed milk or fat-free soya milk

In a blender, combine the fruit, berries, orange juice concentrate, tofu, and milk. Blend until smooth.

Makes 1

Per shake: *347 calories, 21 g protein, 57 g carbohydrates, 6 g fat, 141 mg sodium, 2 g fibre*

Diet Exchanges: *1 milk, 0 vegetable, 4 fruit, 0 bread, 0 meat, 0 fat*

TIP: Silken tofu has a creamier consistency than regular tofu.

Easy Evening Meals

Chicken and Rice Italiano

Erin Ruocco

"Here's my Italian twist on the Spanish arroz con pollo. For variety, serve the saucy chicken over cooked pasta instead of rice."

4 boneless, skinless chicken breasts

500g/1 lb pasta sauce with garlic and peppers

2 tbsp grated Parmesan cheese

1/2 tsp dried Italian seasoning

400 ml/14 fl oz fat-free chicken stock

140 g/5 oz Arborio or regular long-grain white rice

Preheat the oven to 230°C/450°F/gas 8.

Place the chicken in a shallow ovenproof dish. Spoon the sauce evenly over the top. Sprinkle with the cheese and Italian seasoning. Cover the dish with foil and bake for 18–22 minutes, or until a thermometer inserted in the thickest portion registers 70°C/160°F and the juices run clear.

Meanwhile, in a medium saucepan, heat the stock to boiling. Stir in the rice. Cover and reduce the heat to low. Simmer for 14 minutes, or until the rice is tender and the liquid is absorbed.

Divide the rice among 4 plates. Top with the chicken and sauce.

Makes 4 servings

Per serving: *344 calories, 37 g protein, 39 g carbohydrates, 6 g fat, 929 mg sodium, 1 g fibre*

Diet Exchanges: *0 milk, 0 vegetable, 0 fruit, 3 bread, 2 meat, 0 fat*

Chicken Fiesta

296 Calories

Betty Jimenez

"My family loves this simple chicken dish, especially when served with Spanish rice. When it's in season, I add corn on the cob to the menu."

4 boneless, skinless chicken breasts

2 tbsp ground cumin

2 tbsp garlic powder or finely chopped garlic

½ tsp salt

¼ tsp ground black pepper

225 g/8 oz salsa

85 g/3 oz grated reduced-fat extra-sharp Cheddar cheese

85 g/3 oz grated reduced-fat Red Leicester cheese

1 small avocado, stoned, peeled, and sliced (optional)

Preheat the oven to 180°C/350°F/gas 4.

Place the chicken in a medium non-stick ovenproof dish. Coat both sides of the chicken with non-stick spray. Sprinkle both sides evenly with the cumin, garlic powder or finely chopped garlic, salt, and pepper. Top with the salsa and bake for 20 minutes.

Remove the dish from the oven and sprinkle with the two cheeses. Bake for 10 minutes, or until the cheese is melted and a thermometer inserted in thickest portion registers 70°C/160°F and the juices run clear. Serve with the avocado, if using.

Makes 4 servings

Per serving: *296 calories, 42 g protein, 10 g carbohydrates, 14 g fat, 517 mg sodium, 2 g fibre*

Diet Exchanges: *0 milk, 0 vegetable, 0 fruit, 0 bread, 4 meat, 0 fat*

Crunchy Baked Chicken

408 Calories

Penny Lewiss

"I learned to cut out extraneous fat from my foods and replace the flavour with seasonings and spices. Now I have a toned and firmed body, atop which sits a head full of positive and happy wishes."

Preheat the oven to 190°C/375°F/gas 5.

In a small bowl, mix the garlic, lime juice, 1 tablespoon soy sauce, and ¼ teaspoon pepper. Rub into the chicken and refrigerate for 30 minutes.

In a shallow bowl, combine the yogurt, flour, garlic powder, milk, remaining soy sauce, and remaining pepper. Spread the breadcrumbs on greaseproof paper.

Dredge the chicken in the yogurt mixture, then press into the breadcrumbs on all sides. Place on a rack in a roasting tin and coat generously with non-stick spray.

Bake 45 minutes, or until a thermometer inserted in thickest portion registers 77°C/170°F and juices run clear.

Makes 4 servings

Per serving: *408 calories, 41 g protein, 57 g carbohydrates, 3 g fat, 954 mg sodium, 2 g fibre*

Diet Exchanges: *½ milk, 0 vegetable, 0 fruit, 2 bread, 2 meat, 0 fat*

(Asian Slaw recipe on page 230)

4 garlic cloves, crushed

1 tbsp lime juice

2 tbsp soy sauce

½ tsp ground black pepper

4 skinless bone-in chicken breasts or thighs

225 g/8 oz fat-free natural yogurt

60 g/2 oz plainflour

½ tsp garlic powder

2 tbsp skimmed milk

210 g/7½ oz dried breadcrumbs

Big-Flavour Chicken

302 Calories

Amy S. Hutchins

"We like to serve this dish with brown rice and a big green salad. It's a filling meal, yet easy enough to make on busy weeknights."

115 g/4 oz reduced-fat soured cream

1 packet Hollandaise sauce mix

75 ml/2½ fl oz dry white wine or alcohol-free wine

2 tbsp Worcestershire sauce

1 tbsp Dijon mustard

4 boneless, skinless chicken breasts

4 slices (20 g/¾ oz each) reduced-fat Cheddar cheese

60 g/2 oz dried bread stuffing mix

Preheat the oven to 180°C/350°F/gas 4. Coat a 23 × 23 cm/9 × 9 in. ovenproof dish with non-stick spray.

In a medium bowl, combine the soured cream, Hollandaise sauce mix, wine, Worcestershire sauce, and mustard. Spoon one-third of the mixture evenly into the prepared dish. Arrange the chicken in the dish and top each piece with a slice of cheese. Spoon the remaining soured-cream mixture over the chicken and top with the stuffing mix. Bake for 30–40 minutes, or until a thermometer inserted in the thickest portion registers 70°C/160°F and the juices run clear.

Makes 4 servings

Per serving: *302 calories, 32 g protein, 16 g carbohydrates, 11 g fat, 833 mg sodium, 1 g fibre*

Diet Exchanges: *0 milk, 0 vegetable, 0 fruit, ½ bread, 2½ meat, 0 fat*

Slimming Meal

1 serving Big-Flavour Chicken

60 g/2 oz steamed broccoli with lemon and garlic

2 tablespoons couscous with 1 teaspoon grated Parmesan cheese

⅛ honeydew melon

475 calories

Greek Island Chicken

359 Calories

Paige Morehouse

"I serve this high-flavour dinner over cooked rice to soak up the savoury sauce."

1 tbsp olive oil

4 boneless, skinless chicken breasts

1 onion, chopped

2 garlic cloves, finely chopped

85 g/3 oz mushrooms, sliced

225 ml/8 fl oz dry white wine or alcohol-
   free wine

225 g/8 oz bottled marinated artichoke
   hearts, drained

25 g/1 oz coarsely chopped dry-packed
   sun-dried tomatoes

45 g/1½ oz pitted Greek olives, halved

1 tsp lemon-pepper seasoning

1 tsp honey

¼ tsp salt

½ tsp dried oregano

½ tsp ground cinnamon

70 g/2½ oz crumbled feta cheese

4 lemon wedges or slices

Warm the oil in a large non-stick frying pan over medium-high heat. Add the chicken and cook for 5 minutes on each side, or until browned. Transfer to a plate.

Reduce the heat to medium and add the onion and garlic to the same frying pan. Cook for 5 minutes, or until the onion is tender. Stir in the mushrooms. Cook for 10 minutes, or until the mushrooms render their juices. Add the wine, artichokes, tomatoes, olives, lemon-pepper seasoning, honey, salt, oregano, cinnamon, and chicken. Reduce the heat to low, cover, and cook for 15 minutes.

Uncover and cook for 5 minutes, or until the sauce thickens slightly and a thermometer inserted in thickest portion registers 70°C/160°F and the juices run clear. Sprinkle with the cheese. Serve with the lemon for squeezing.

Makes 4 servings

Per serving: *359 calories, 41 g protein, 7 g carbohydrates, 15 g fat, 850 mg sodium, 1 g fibre*

Diet Exchanges: *0 milk, 1 vegetable, 0 fruit, 0 bread, 3 meat, 2 fat*

Mango Chicken

Pamela Valois

249 Calories

"Depending on what's in the house, I serve this over brown rice, couscous, or pasta. If you can't find fresh mango, look for bottled or substitute fresh papaya."

1 tsp vegetable oil

500 g/1 lb boneless, skinless chicken breasts, cubed

8 spring onions, chopped

2 tomatoes, deseeded and chopped

2 ripe mangos, peeled and chopped (see tip)

¾ tsp ground cumin

¾ tsp ground coriander

½ tsp salt

½ tsp ground black pepper

225 g/8 oz fat-free natural yogurt

225 ml/8 fl oz reduced-fat unsweetened coconut milk

20 g/¾ oz chopped fresh coriander leaves

Warm the oil in a non-stick frying pan or wok over medium-high heat. Add the chicken and spring onions. Cook for 5 minutes or until the chicken is browned. Add the tomatoes, mangos, cumin, coriander, salt, and pepper. Cook for 3 minutes. Add the yogurt and milk. Reduce the heat to low and cook for 10–15 minutes, or until the sauce thickens and the chicken is fork-tender and no longer pink. Sprinkle with the coriander leaves.

Makes 4 servings

Per serving: *249 calories, 34 g protein, 18 g carbohydrates, 5 g fat, 407 mg sodium, 3 g fibre*

Diet Exchanges: *0 milk, 1 vegetable, 1 fruit, 0 bread, 2½ meat, 0 fat*

TIP: To peel and chop a mango, stand it on end and slice off two 'fillets' from the flat sides of the fruit, cutting as close to the stone as possible. Cut crisscross diamond patterns into the flesh of the fillets, but don't cut through the peel. Use your thumbs to push the fruit from the peel side, turning the fillet inside out and exposing the cubes. Cut the cubes away from the peel. Discard the stone and peel.

Chicken Therese

237 Calories

Therese Meyer

"Fresh ingredients like mushrooms and flavour boosters like sherry and dry mustard really enhance the flavour of this chicken dish. You'd never guess that the sauce base is a canned soup. Serve over rice or noodles."

4 boneless, skinless chicken breasts

1 tsp garlic salt

¼ tsp ground black pepper

⅛ tsp ground red pepper

1 tbsp olive oil

10 mushrooms, sliced

1 onion, chopped

300 ml/10 fl oz canned cream of chicken soup

2 tbsp dry sherry

¾ tsp mustard powder

¼ tsp ground nutmeg

Rub each chicken breast with the garlic salt, black pepper, and red pepper.

Warm the oil in a large non-stick frying pan over medium-high heat. Add the chicken and cook until browned on both sides, turning once. Transfer the chicken to a plate and keep warm.

Add the mushrooms and onion to the same frying pan. Cook for 5 minutes, or until tender. Stir in the soup, sherry, mustard powder, and nutmeg. Heat to boiling and add the chicken. Reduce the heat to low, cover, and simmer for 20 minutes, or until a thermometer inserted in the thickest portion registers 70°C/160°F and the juices run clear.

Makes 4 servings

Per serving: *237 calories, 31 g protein, 7 g carbohydrates, 1 g fat, 376 mg sodium, 2 g fibre*

Diet Exchanges: *0 milk, 0 vegetable, 0 fruit, 1 bread, 1½ meat, 0 fat*

It Worked for Me!

Marlene Dropp

VITAL STATS

Weight lost: 27 kg/4 st 4 lb

Time kept it off: 12 years

Weight-loss strategies: Walking; weight training; low-fat diet; small, frequent meals

Weight-maintenance strategies: Has a 2–3 kg/5–7 lb gain/loss window, walks 8 km/5 miles a day, skis cross-country, uses clothing fit as a gauge

*D*aily *exercise and eating several small meals a day helped Marlene Dropp, mother of four, become lean, energized, and de-stressed.*

'After I had my first two children in my 20s, I was back in pre-pregnancy clothes in no time. But in my 30s, after my second two children, I gave in to munching on junk food. That left me at the 90 kg (14 st) mark. I tried dieting, but that didn't work. And between my family and my job, I had no time for exercise. It was a last priority.

'I was a blimp. To cheer me up and get me out of the house, my eldest daughter suggested we go for a walk. We walked only a short way, but, to my amazement, it felt great! Just the act of moving lifted my spirits and chased the blues away. I thought, "If it worked once, it'll work again." I walked the next day and the next. Each time, I came home full of energy and feeling good about myself. That's when I decided a morning walk would be a number one priority every day.

'My first goal was an 8-km (5-mile) walk. There are lots of 1-km (½-mile) circular roads in my neighbourhood, so every week I'd add another loop to the route. Afterward, I'd measure the distance with my car, then note my progress on the calendar. Within two months, I'd reached my goal.

'My next goal was to increase my speed and complete 1 km in 8 minutes. I didn't do as well with this goal. I thought that my diet might be the reason, so I cut out junk food and started eating four or five small, low-fat meals a day. After about a year of healthy eating habits and more walking, I finally did it. Best of all, just two years after my first short walk with my daughter, I had shed 27 kg.

'Walking every day has become a habit for me. It's what took the weight off and what keeps it off. I walk 8 km (5 miles) every day and still watch my fat and calorie intake. I also started cross-country skiing. When I work out, I feel better physically and emotionally.' ◼

Marlene's
Chicken and Vegetable Stir-Fry

505 Calories

"For this dish, I let the chicken marinate while I go for a walk.
When I return, it's ready to stir-fry."

3 tbsp soy sauce

2 tbsp cornflour

1 garlic clove, finely chopped

500 g/1 lb boneless, skinless chicken
  breast, cut into 2.5-cm/1-in. pieces

200 g/7 oz long-grain white rice

2 tbsp peanut or vegetable oil

500 g/1 lb frozen mixed
  vegetables, thawed

30 g/1 oz dry roasted peanuts (optional)

In a large bowl, combine the soy sauce, cornflour, and garlic. Add the chicken and toss to coat. Cover and refrigerate for 20 minutes or overnight.

Cook the rice according to the packet directions. Keep warm.

Warm 1 tablespoon of the oil in a large frying pan or wok over medium-high heat. Add the chicken, reserving the marinade. Cook for 5 minutes, or until browned, stirring frequently. Transfer the chicken to a plate. Add the remaining oil to the pan. Stir in the vegetables and cook for 5 minutes, or until the vegetables are tender.

Return the chicken to the pan. Add the reserved marinade and cook for 1 minute, or until the sauce is thickened and the chicken is no longer pink. Serve over the rice. Sprinkle with peanuts, if using.

Makes 4 servings

Per serving: 505 calories, 41 g protein, 60 g carbohydrates, 13 g fat, 804 mg sodium, 1 g fibre

Diet Exchanges: 0 milk, 2 vegetable, 0 fruit, 1½ bread, 3 meat, 0 fat

Splurge Meal

1 serving Marlene's Chicken and Vegetable Stir-Fry

1 portion cooked rice noodles sautéed with spring onions in ½ teaspoon sesame oil

10–12 ears of baby sweetcorn

1 coconut macaroon

1 scoop orange sorbet

811 calories

Orange-Almond Chicken

241 Calories

Lisa Pettit

"When I'm craving Chinese-style sweet-and-sour chicken but don't want the calories or fat, I turn to this recipe."

30 g/1 oz sliced almonds

1 tbsp peanut or vegetable oil

4 boneless, skinless chicken breasts

60 g/2 oz chopped shallots

85 g/3 oz mushrooms, sliced

100 g/3½ oz orange marmalade

3 tbsp soy sauce

¼ tsp ground black pepper

Orange slices (optional)

Place the almonds in a large non-stick frying pan. Toast over medium heat for 5 minutes or until fragrant, shaking the pan often. Transfer to a plate and set aside.

Warm the oil in the same frying pan over medium-high heat. Add the chicken and cook for 5 minutes, or until no longer pink, turning occasionally. Transfer to a plate.

Add the shallots to the pan and cook for 5 minutes, or until soft. Add the mushrooms and cook for 5 minutes, or until the mushrooms render their juices. Stir in the marmalade, soy sauce, and pepper. Return the chicken to the pan. Reduce the heat to low, cover, and simmer for 10 minutes, or until a thermometer inserted in the thickest portion registers 70°C/160°F and the juices run clear. Top with the almonds and the orange slices, if using.

Makes 4 servings

Per serving: *241 calories, 27 g protein, 20 g carbohydrates, 7 g fat, 723 mg sodium, 1 g fibre*

Diet Exchanges: *0 milk, 0 vegetable, 0 fruit, 1½ bread, 2 meat, 0 fat*

Chicken with Tomatoes

156 Calories

Caroline B. Hurley

"On days when you're tired but want both a tasty and a filling meal, this dish can't be beat. I serve it on aromatic jasmine rice, but any rice or pasta will do."

4 boneless, skinless chicken breasts

115 ml/4 fl oz fat-free Italian salad dressing

1 tbsp olive oil

410 g/14 oz canned tomatoes

½ tsp Italian seasoning

In a resealable plastic bag, combine the chicken and salad dressing. Set aside in the refrigerator for 20 minutes, then remove the chicken from the marinade, reserving the marinade.

Warm the oil in a medium frying pan over medium-high heat. Add the chicken and cook for 5 minutes, or until no longer pink, turning occasionally. Stir in the reserved marinade, tomatoes (with juice), and Italian seasoning. Heat to boiling. Reduce the heat to low, cover, and simmer for 15 minutes, or until a thermometer inserted in the thickest portion registers 70°C/160°F and the juices run clear.

Makes 4 servings

Per serving: *156 calories, 25 g protein, 3 g carbohydrates, 5 g fat, 100 mg sodium, 1 g fibre*

Diet Exchanges: *0 milk, 2 vegetable, 0 fruit, 0 bread, 1½ meat, 0 fat*

Slimming Meal

1 serving Chicken with Tomatoes

1 portion cooked egg noodles

2–3 tablespoons steamed baby carrots with dill

70 g/2½ oz blueberries with 115 g/4 oz low-fat lime yogurt

402 calories

Slow-Cooked Lemon Chicken

205 Calories

Leighanne C. Hersey

"This meal is perfect for workdays or any time you're busy in the evening. Just start the recipe in the morning (it takes only a a few minutes) and let it cook while you're at work or doing other things."

4 boneless, skinless chicken breasts
1 tbsp lemon-pepper seasoning
500 g/1 lb fresh soup vegetables, chopped
300 ml/10 fl oz canned cream of chicken soup
1 tsp dried rosemary, crushed

Coat the chicken with lemon-pepper seasoning. Coat a medium non-stick frying pan with non-stick spray and warm over medium-high heat. Add the chicken and cook for 5 minutes, or until browned on both sides, turning once.

Place the chicken in a slow cooker and add the vegetables.

In a medium bowl, combine the soup, half a soup can of water, and the rosemary. Pour this mixture over the vegetables and chicken. Cover and cook on low for 8 hours or on high for 4 hours.

Makes 4 servings

Per serving: *205 calories, 21 g protein, 18 g carbohydrates, 4 g fat, 940 mg sodium, 3 g fibre*

Diet Exchanges: *0 milk, 1 vegetable, 0 fruit, 1 bread, 1½ meat, 0 fat*

Slimming Meal

1 serving Slow-Cooked Lemon Chicken

3 tablespoons steamed green beans with slivered almonds

1 whole sliced tomato with 15 g/½ oz crumbled feta cheese

1 serving Black Cherry Baked Apples (page 272)

475 calories

SIX SIMPLE SAUCES FOR CHICKEN

On a busy night nothing's easier than grilled chicken breasts. And nothing more boring! Wake up your next chicken dinner with these super-quick, low-calorie sauces. Each recipe makes enough to accompany two boneless, skinless chicken breasts.

Caribbean Salsa

Combine 1 finely chopped mango or papaya, 75 g/2½ oz finely chopped pineapple, 2 tablespoons chopped fresh mint, 2 tablespoons chopped white onion, ¼ teaspoon salt, and ¼ teaspoon ground red pepper. Let rest for 1 hour to develop flavours.

Per serving: *54 calories, 1 g protein, 13 g carbohydrates, 0 g fat, 2,126 mg sodium, 3 g fibre*

Diet Exchanges: *0 milk, 0 vegetable, 1 fruit, 0 bread, 0 meat, 0 fat*

Lemon Goat's Cheese

Brown 15 g/½ oz butter in a small frying pan. Stir in 1 tablespoon flour. Cook for 1 minute. Whisk in 340 ml/12 fl oz chicken stock and cook until the sauce boils, stirring constantly. Blend in 115–170 g/

4–6 oz mild goat's cheese and ½ teaspoon grated lemon peel.

Per serving: *120 calories, 5 g protein, 5 g carbohydrates, 9 g fat, 1,374 mg sodium, 0 g fibre*

Diet Exchanges: *0 milk, 0 vegetable, 0 fruit, 0 bread, 1 meat, 1 fat*

Mushroom

Warm 1 teaspoon olive oil in a non-stick frying pan over medium heat. Add 130 g/ 4½ oz sliced mushrooms and 30 g/4 oz finely chopped onion and cook until the mushrooms are soft. Stir in 2 tablespoons soy sauce or balsamic vinegar and 1 tablespoon crushed fresh rosemary or thyme. Cover and cook for 2 minutes. Before serving, stir in ¼ teaspoon salt and a pinch of black pepper.

Per serving: *62 calories, 3 g protein, 6 g carbohydrates, 5 g fat, 1,060 mg sodium, 2 g fibre*

Diet Exchanges: *0 milk, 1 vegetable, 0 fruit, 0 bread, 0 meat, 0 fat*

Pepperonata

Warm 1 teaspoon olive oil in a medium non-stick frying pan over medium heat. Add

Chicken Fajitas

476 Calories

Kelly Stack

"When you start with boneless, skinless chicken breasts, dinner is only minutes away. This Mexican dish is a family favourite any night of the week."

225 g/8 oz boneless, skinless chicken breast, cut into strips

225 g/8 oz sliced red and green peppers

225 g/8 oz sliced onions

1 packet fajita seasoning mix

8 flour tortillas

115 g/4 oz low-fat soured cream

1 large tomato, finely chopped

100 g/3½ oz grated reduced-fat Cheddar cheese (optional)

Coat a large frying pan with non-stick spray. Add the chicken and cook, stirring occasionally, for 5–7 minutes, or until no longer pink. Add the vegetables and cook until heated through. Add the fajita mix and cook for 5 minutes more. Spoon some of the mixture into each tortilla and top with soured cream, tomato, and cheese, if using. Roll up each fajita like a cone.

Makes 4 servings

Per serving: *476 calories, 31 g protein, 73 g carbohydrates, 9 g fat, 521 mg sodium, 5 g fibre*

Diet Exchanges: *0 milk, 1 vegetable, 0 fruit, 4 bread, 1 meat, 0 fat*

Confetti Enchiladas

266 Calories

Sharon Swindle

"Traditionally, corn tortillas are fried before filling for enchiladas. I soften them in stock instead. It saves not only fat and calories but also time and mess. Sometimes, I make this in two dishes and freeze one."

340 g/12 oz cooked chicken, cubed

410 g/14½ oz canned chopped tomatoes, drained

125 g/4½ oz bottled or canned green chilli peppers, drained and chopped

225 g/8 oz fresh or frozen sweetcorn kernels

6 spring onions, chopped

4 tomatillos, chopped

80 g/3 oz chopped red pepper

115 g/4 oz low-fat natural yogurt

1 tsp salt

1 tsp chilli powder

½ tsp ground red pepper

170 g/6 oz grated reduced-fat Cheddar and Red Leicester cheese mixture

450 ml/16 fl oz chicken stock

16 corn tortillas

Preheat the oven to 180°C/350°F/gas 4. Spray a 33 × 23 cm/ 13 × 9 in. ovenproof dish (or two smaller ones) with non-stick spray.

In a large bowl, mix the chicken, tomatoes, chilli peppers, sweetcorn, spring onions, tomatillos, chopped red pepper, yogurt, salt, chilli powder, ground red pepper, and half the cheese.

Warm the stock in a large frying pan over low heat. Add the tortillas (in batches, if necessary) and cook for 2–3 minutes, or until softened.

Transfer the tortillas to kitchen paper. Spoon some filling along the middle of each tortilla. Roll up tightly and place, seam side down, in the prepared dish. Sprinkle with the remaining cheese. Cover with foil and bake for 25–30 minutes, or until hot and bubbly.

Makes 8 servings

Per serving: *266 calories, 23 g protein, 23 g carbohydrates, 9 g fat, 833 mg sodium, 1 g fibre*

Diet Exchanges: *0 milk, 2 vegetable, 0 fruit, 1 bread, 2 meat, 0 fat*

TIP: Tomatillos are a type of small green tomato with a papery husk.

Beef and Macaroni

329 Calories

Carole Plaza-O'Connell

"We updated this old family favourite to use less fat. Evaporated milk makes it creamy without having to use high-fat double cream. It's still a bit high in fat, so we save it for nights when we're celebrating."

115 g/4 oz macaroni

340 g/12 oz extra-lean ground steak

1 garlic clove, finely chopped

100 ml/3½ fl oz semi-skimmed evaporated milk

1½ packets chicken noodle soup mix

170 ml/6 fl oz water

¾ tsp ground black pepper

½ tsp dried Italian seasoning

115 g/4 oz grated reduced-fat extra-sharp Cheddar cheese

Cook the macaroni according to the packet directions. Drain.

In a large frying pan, cook the beef and garlic over medium-high heat for 10 minutes, or until the beef is no longer pink. Stir to break the beef into small pieces. Drain and discard the fat. Stir in the evaporated milk, soup mix, water, pepper, Italian seasoning, 2 tablespoons cheese, and the cooked macaroni. Top with the remaining cheese. Cover and cook over low heat for 10 minutes, or until hot and bubbly.

Makes 4 servings

Per serving: *329 calories, 33 g protein, 27 g carbohydrates, 11 g fat, 509 mg sodium, 1 g fibre*

Diet Exchanges: *0 milk, 0 vegetable, 0 fruit, 2 bread, 4 meat, 2 fat*

Splurge Meal

1 serving Beef and Macaroni

1 slice multigrain bread

170 g/6 oz chilled cooked green beans on shredded romaine lettuce with fat-free Italian dressing

1 scoop vanilla frozen yogurt with 1 tablespoon chocolate sauce and 1 teaspoon chopped peanuts

629 calories

Tomatoes and Courgettes with Meatballs

236 Calories

Kim Mustill

"I use this one-dish meal to sneak in a few extra servings of vegetables. Serve it in bowls with crusty Italian bread or spoon it over fettuccine."

225 g/8 oz extra-lean ground steak or turkey mince

35 g/1¼ dried seasoned dried breadcrumbs

1 egg

¾ tsp ground black pepper

40 g/1½ oz grated Parmesan cheese

1 tbsp olive oil

1 small onion, finely chopped

2 garlic cloves, finely chopped

2 small courgettes, halved lengthways and sliced

1 small yellow squash, halved lengthways and sliced

450 g/1 lb canned Italian-plum tomatoes, cut in half

450 g/1 lb canned chopped tomatoes

¼ tsp sugar

15 g/½ oz chopped fresh basil leaves

In a large bowl, combine the beef or turkey, breadcrumbs, egg, ½ teaspoon pepper, and 4 tablespoons Parmesan. Form into balls the size of walnuts.

Warm the oil in a large non-stick frying pan over medium-high heat. Add the meatballs, several at a time, and cook for 5 minutes, or until browned and no longer pink inside. Transfer to a bowl, leaving the drippings in the frying pan.

Add the onion and garlic to the warm drippings in the frying pan and cook over medium-high heat for 5 minutes, or until the onion is tender. Stir in the courgettes, yellow squash, cut tomatoes (with juice), chopped tomatoes, sugar, remaining Parmesan, remaining pepper, and meatballs. Heat to boiling, then reduce the heat to low, cover, and cook for 20 minutes. Stir in the basil.

Makes 4 servings

Per serving: *236 calories, 23 g protein, 16 g carbohydrates, 10 g fat, 290 mg sodium, 2 g fibre*

Diet Exchanges: *0 milk, 3 vegetable, 0 fruit, 0 bread, 2½ meat, 1 fat*

Taco Bake

Grace Schefter

"When I make this recipe in advance and store it covered in the refrigerator, the children cut squares and warm them in the microwave. Serve with baked tortilla chips and enjoy!"

225 g/8 oz extra-lean ground steak

225 g/8 oz turkey mince

425 g/15 oz red kidney beans, rinsed and drained

115 g/4 oz bottled or canned green chilli peppers, drained and chopped

1 packet taco seasoning mix

225 g/8 oz low-fat soured cream

115 g/4 oz grated reduced-fat Cheddar cheese

baked tortilla chips (optional)

Preheat the oven to 180°C/350°F/gas 4. Coat a 23 × 23 cm/9 × 9 in. ovenproof dish with non-stick spray.

Warm a large non-stick frying pan over medium-high heat. Add the beef and turkey, stirring to break the meat into pieces. Cook for 10 minutes, or until no longer pink. Stir in the beans, peppers, and taco seasoning mix. Spoon into the prepared dish, spread the soured cream evenly over the top and sprinkle with the cheese. Bake 30 minutes, or until heated through and the cheese is bubbly. Serve with tortilla chips, if using.

Makes 4 servings

Per serving (without tortilla chips):
359 calories, 41 g protein, 15 g carbohydrates, 15 g fat, 563 mg sodium, 5 g fibre

Diet Exchanges: *0 milk, 0 vegetable, 0 fruit, 2 bread, 4 meat, 0 fat*

Red Chilli Steak Burritos

551 Calories

Marie Yakes

"These burritos are the real deal – steak, chillis, and tomatoes cooked up right and served in flour tortillas. If you like, add reduced-fat Cheddar cheese and low-fat soured cream."

2 tsp olive oil

1 onion, finely chopped

3 garlic cloves, finely chopped

500 g/1 lb lean steak, finely chopped

1 tbsp plain flour

260 g/9 oz bottled or canned green chilli peppers, drained and chopped

800 g/1¾ lb canned tomatoes

1 tsp ground black pepper

8 large flour tortillas

Warm the oil in a large saucepan over medium heat. Add onion and garlic and cook for 10 minutes, or until tender. Toss the beef with the flour. Add the beef to the saucepan and cook for 5 minutes, or until no longer pink. Stir in the chilli peppers, tomatoes (with juice), and black pepper. Heat to boiling over high heat. Reduce the heat to low, cover, and simmer for 45 minutes, or until the meat is very tender, breaking up the tomatoes with the back of a spoon.

Using a slotted spoon, place about 3 tablespoons of meat on a tortilla. Roll the tortilla like an envelope to make an enclosed packet. Repeat with the remaining meat and tortillas. Top with the sauce left in the pan.

Makes 4 servings

Per serving: *551 calories, 38 g protein, 79 g carbohydrates, 12 g fat, 443 mg sodium, 5 g fibre*

Diet Exchanges: *0 milk, 1 vegetable, 0 fruit, 3 bread, 3 meat, 1 fat*

Splurge Meal

1 serving Red Chilli Steak Burritos

1 ear corn on the cob with 2 tablespoons Roast Garlic Spread (page 106)

½ sliced mango with
1 scoop frozen chocolate yogurt sprinkled with chilli powder

722 calories

Slow-Cooked Pork Stew

C. Barber

"The pork and vegetables in this dish taste best when cooked slowly. The meat becomes so tender you can tear it with a fork. I usually make it in a slow cooker, but you can bake it in a covered casserole, too. Follow the recipe using a large casserole instead of a slow cooker. Cover tightly and bake at 135°C/275°F/gas 1 for 5 hours without disturbing."

900 g/2 lb lean pork loin, cut into 2.5-cm/1-in. cubes

225 g/8 oz baby carrots

3 large potatoes, cut into 2.5-cm/1-in. cubes

2 parsnips, cut into 2.5-cm/1-in. cubes

2 onions, cut into wedges

3 garlic cloves, finely chopped

2 tsp ground black pepper

1 tsp dried thyme

1 tsp salt

570 ml/1 pint canned vegetable juice

2 tbsp brown sugar

1 tbsp mustard

4 tsp tapioca

Place the pork in a slow cooker. Add the carrots, potatoes, parsnips, onions, garlic, pepper, thyme, and salt.

In a medium bowl, combine the vegetable juice, brown sugar, mustard, and tapioca. Pour it over the meat and vegetables.

Cover and cook on low for 6 hours or on high for 4 hours.

Makes 6 servings

Per serving: *315 calories, 36 g protein, 30 g carbohydrates, 6 g fat, 350 mg sodium, 4 g fibre*

Diet Exchanges: *0 milk, 1 vegetable, 0 fruit, 3 bread, 3½ meat, 0 fat*

Fettuccine with Chicken Sauce

Lisa Smith

"For a healthy twist to meat sauce, I use skinless chicken pieces instead of fatty minced beef."

521 Calories

1 tbsp olive oil

500 g/1 lb boneless, skinless chicken breast, cubed

1 green pepper, chopped

800 g/1¾ oz canned tomatoes packed in purée, or chopped tomatoes

1 small onion, quartered

4 garlic cloves

2 tsp sugar

2 tsp dried basil

½ tsp ground black pepper

115 g/4 oz pitted, sliced black olives, drained (optional)

225 g/8 oz dried fettuccine

Warm the oil in large saucepan over medium-high heat. Add the chicken and green pepper and cook for 5 minutes, or until the chicken is no longer pink.

In a blender, combine the tomatoes (with juice), onion, garlic, sugar, basil, and black pepper. Blend until smooth. Add to the chicken, reduce the heat to medium-low and simmer for 25 minutes, or until slightly thickened. Stir in the olives, if using.

Meanwhile, cook the fettuccine according to packet directions. Drain.

Serve the fettuccine topped with the chicken sauce.

Makes 4 servings

Per serving: *521 calories, 47 g protein, 54 g carbohydrates, 14 g fat, 817 mg sodium, 6 g fibre*

Diet Exchanges: *0 milk, 1 vegetable, 0 fruit, 3 bread, 2 meat, 0 fat*

FROM THE PROS

Canyon Ranch Health Resorts

Canyon Ranch Health Resorts have the good fortune of having menu consultant and low-fat cooking guru Jeanne Jones on the staff. She created this herb-infused spa favourite.

LAMB CHOPS WITH APRICOT AND HERB SAUCE

237 Calories

4 boneless lamb steaks (115 g/4 oz each), trimmed of all visible fat and skewered

½ tsp garlic salt

½ tsp ground black pepper

115 g/4 oz dried apricot halves

400 ml/14 fl oz chicken stock

½ tsp balsamic vinegar

½ tsp dried oregano

½ tsp dried thyme

¼ tsp dried rosemary, crushed

¼ tsp salt

⅛ tsp ground nutmeg

Sprinkle both sides of the lamb evenly with the garlic salt and pepper. Warm a large non-stick frying pan over medium heat until hot. Add the lamb and brown well on both sides.

In a medium saucepan, combine the apricots and stock. Heat to boiling over high heat. Reduce the heat to low and simmer for 5 minutes, or until the apricots are very soft. Transfer half of the apricots and all of the liquid to a blender or food processor. Add the vinegar, oregano, thyme, rosemary, salt, and nutmeg. Purée. Pour over the lamb. Sprinkle the meat with the remaining cooked apricots. Reduce the heat to low, cover, and simmer for 10 minutes, or until a thermometer inserted in centre of a lamb steak registers 70°C/160°F and the juices run clear.

Makes 4 servings

Per serving: *237 calories, 25 g protein, 13 g carbohydrates, 10 g fat, 695 mg sodium, 2 g fibre*

Diet Exchanges: *0 milk, 0 vegetable, 0 fruit, 1 bread, 2 meat, 0 fat*

Spicy Spaghetti

578 Calories

Bonnie Voight

"This very simple sauce can be doubled to serve later over tortellini or ravioli. Refrigerate the sauce for up to a week or freeze it for up to 6 months. For a spicier sauce, add more red-pepper flakes."

500 g/1 lb spaghetti

2 tbsp olive oil

1 small onion, chopped

3 garlic cloves, finely chopped

225 ml/8 fl oz red wine or alcohol-free wine

800 g/1¾ lb canned plum tomatoes, chopped

2 tsp dried basil

½ tsp red-pepper flakes

Cook the spaghetti according to packet directions. Drain.

Meanwhile, warm the oil in a large saucepan over medium heat. Add the onion and cook for 5 minutes. Stir in the garlic and cook for 1 minute. Stir in the wine and cook for 2 minutes. Add the tomatoes (with juice), basil, and red-pepper flakes, and cook, uncovered, for 20 minutes, or until reduced by one-third. Serve with the spaghetti.

Makes 4 servings

Per serving: *578 calories, 18 g protein, 101 g carbohydrates, 10 g fat, 87 mg sodium, 6 g fibre*

Diet Exchanges: *0 milk, 2 vegetable, 0 fruit, 5 bread, 0 meat, 2 fat*

Splurge Meal

1 serving Spicy Spaghetti

60 g/2 oz frisée lettuce with croutons and 1 chopped hard-boiled egg

1 slice whole-wheat Italian bread rubbed with garlic and ½ teaspoon olive oil

1 serving Roast Fruit Wraps with Dipping Sauce (page 278)

1,144 calories

Easy Rigatoni

Lori Varney

"This is a good make-in-advance-and-freeze recipe. I often make a double batch. It's reassuring to know that I have it in the freezer to rescue me on busy nights! It's very filling, but not fattening."

2 tbsp olive oil

1 onion, chopped

3 garlic cloves, crushed

170 g/6 oz tomato purée

800 g/1¾ lb canned chopped tomatoes

1 tsp sugar

1½ tsp dried oregano

1½ tsp dried basil

1 tsp salt

½ tsp ground black pepper

225 g/8 oz rigatoni

2 tbsp grated Parmesan cheese

Warm the oil in a medium frying pan over medium heat. Add the onion and garlic and cook for 10 minutes, or until tender. Add the tomato purée and cook for 3 minutes. Stir in the tomatoes, sugar, oregano, basil, salt, and pepper. Heat to boiling. Reduce the heat to medium-low, cover, and cook for 30 minutes, stirring occasionally.

Meanwhile, cook the rigatoni according to packet directions. Drain. Toss the pasta with the sauce and serve with the cheese.

Makes 4 servings

Per serving: *364 calories, 13 g protein, 58 g carbohydrates, 11 g fat, 728 mg sodium, 5 g fibre*

Diet Exchanges: *0 milk, 4 vegetable, 0 fruit, 3 bread, 0 meat, 2 fat*

The Spa at Doral

Guests of the Spa at Doral enjoy great-tasting food. The secret
to intensifying the flavour of tomatoes is to remove some of the water. Add a
pinch of crushed red-pepper flakes for a little extra kick.

LINGUINE MONTECATINI

263
Calories

8 plum tomatoes, cut in half
2 tsp olive oil
8 garlic cloves, peeled and thinly sliced
115 g/4 oz fresh spinach
225 g/8 oz linguine

Preheat the oven to 110°C/200°F/gas
¼. Place the tomatoes, cut side up, on a
rack in a large ovenproof dish and bake
for 20 minutes, or until slightly dry.
Chop coarsely.

Warm the oil in a large non-stick frying
pan over medium heat. Add the garlic,
spinach and tomatoes, and cook until the
spinach is wilted.

Cook the linguine according to packet
directions. Drain, add to the frying pan,
and toss well.

Makes 4 servings

Per serving: *263 calories, 7 g protein,
51 g carbohydrates, 4 g fat, 60 mg sodium,
3 g fibre*

Diet Exchanges: *0 milk, 2 vegetable, 0 fruit,
3 bread, 0 meat, ½ fat*

Mushroom and Tofu Fettuccine

372 Calories

George Toro

*"Evaporated milk adds richness without fat in this creamy pasta dish.
The tofu adds protein without the cholesterol of meat and eggs."*

225 g/8 oz dried fettuccine or 170 g/
  6 oz fresh

1 tbsp olive oil

115 g/4 oz low-fat firm tofu, drained
  and cut into small cubes

85 g/3 oz shiitake or button
  mushrooms, chopped

2 garlic cloves, finely chopped

200 ml/7 fl oz semi-skimmed
  evaporated milk

3 tbsp chopped fresh parsley

2 tbsp finely chopped pitted black olives

2 tbsp finely chopped fresh chives

¾ tsp salt

½ tsp ground black pepper

40 g/1½ oz grated Parmesan cheese

Cook the fettuccine according to packet directions. Drain.

Warm the oil in a large frying pan over medium-high heat. Add the tofu and cook for 5 minutes, or until lightly browned. Add the mushrooms and cook for 5 minutes, or until golden. Add the garlic and cook for 1 minute. Reduce the heat to low and add the evaporated milk, parsley, olives, chives, salt, and pepper. Cook for 5 minutes, stirring occasionally. Add the pasta and toss to mix. Cook for 2 minutes, or until heated through. Serve with the cheese.

Makes 4 servings

Per serving: *372 calories, 18 g protein,
51 g carbohydrates, 12 g fat, 599 mg sodium,
2 g fibre*

Diet Exchanges: *0 milk, 0 vegetable, 0 fruit,
3 bread, 2 meat, 0 fat*

Mediterranean Pasta

Tina Groves

"Bring home the flavours of the sun-drenched islands with this easy dish."

40 g/1½ oz dry-packed sun-dried tomatoes

225 g/8 oz angel hair pasta or
thin spaghetti

1 tbsp olive oil

2 onions, chopped

1 tsp dried oregano

300 g/10 oz fresh spinach, chopped, or
frozen chopped spinach, thawed and
squeezed dry

2 tbsp chopped pitted kalamata olives or
black olives

140 g/5 oz crumbled feta cheese

Soak the tomatoes in hot water for 10 minutes, or until soft. Drain and chop.

Cook the pasta according to packet directions, and drain.

Meanwhile, warm the oil in a large non-stick frying pan over medium heat. Add the onions and oregano, and cook for 10 minutes, or until the onions are tender. Add the spinach, cover, and cook for 5 minutes, or until the spinach is wilted. Add the olives, tomatoes, and pasta, and toss to mix. Sprinkle with the cheese.

Makes 4 servings

Per serving: *404 calories, 15 g protein, 48 g carbohydrates, 18 g fat, 813 mg sodium, 4 g fibre*

Diet Exchanges: *0 milk, 2 vegetable, 0 fruit, 3 bread, 1 meat, 3 fat*

EYES ON THE SIZE

Knowing and doing are two different things. You may know that you want to eat 1 serving of pasta with your pork, beef or chicken dinner, but dishing out 1 serving is another matter entirely. That doesn't mean you have to pull out the scales. Use a few visual cues instead. Picture the following objects when serving your favourite foods. (To find out what counts as a serving and how many servings to eat, see pages 9, 14, 15, and 18.)

• Closed fist = 2 servings pasta, potatoes, cereal or starchy vegetables
• Tennis ball = 1 serving canned fruit or ice cream
• Ping-Pong ball = 2 tablespoons
• Deck of cards = 85 g/3 oz (of cooked meat, fish, or chicken, for instance)
• Top of thumb (from tip to middle joint) = 1 teaspoon
• Top of thumb (from tip to middle joint) = 30 g/1 oz (of cheese, for instance)

Angel Hair Pasta with Clam Pesto

427 Calories

Tracy Viselli

"Classic pesto recipes are made with lots of olive oil, and that means lots of calories. Adding breadcrumbs cuts the fat and calories way back without losing body. The herbal taste is still intense and fresh. I sometimes add finely chopped tomatoes for more flavour."

225 g/8 oz angel hair pasta

500 g/1 lb finely chopped canned clams

1 slice white bread, crust removed

30 g/1 oz loosely packed fresh basil

3 tbsp pine nuts

2 garlic cloves

½ tsp salt

2 tbsp olive oil

85 g/3 oz finely chopped tomatoes (optional)

2 tbsp grated Parmesan cheese

Cook the pasta according to packet directions. Drain and place in a large bowl.

Meanwhile, drain the clams, reserving 60 ml/2 fl oz liquid.

Tear the bread into large pieces and place it in a food processor or blender. Process or blend to fine crumbs. Add the basil, pine nuts, garlic, salt, oil, and clam liquid. Process to a smooth paste.

Add the clams, basil mixture, and tomatoes (if using) to the hot pasta, and toss to mix. Serve with the cheese.

Makes 4 servings

Per serving: *427 calories, 30 g protein, 49 g carbohydrates, 14 g fat, 1,892 mg sodium, 2 g fibre*

Diet Exchanges: *0 milk, 0 vegetable, 0 fruit, 4 bread, 2½ meat, 0 fat*

Slimming Meal

1 serving Angel Hair Pasta with Clam Pesto

3 tablespoons chilled steamed green beans

1 scoop vanilla frozen yogurt splashed with warm espresso

493 calories

FROM THE PROS

Carolina Wellness Retreat

To make lifestyle changes that last, food should be easy to make and delicious. That's the approach of Colleen Wracker, RD, a nutritionist at the Carolina Wellness Retreat. This simple recipe is like a breath of fresh air.

COD DIJON

139 Calories

4 large carrots, cut into matchsticks
2 tbsp chopped parsley
1 tsp olive oil
⅛ tsp salt
⅛ tsp ground black pepper
4 cod fillets (120 g/4 oz each)
2 tsp stone-ground Dijon mustard
1 tsp honey

In a 28 × 18 cm/11 × 7 in. microwave dish, combine the carrots, parsley, oil, salt, and pepper. Cover with greaseproof paper. Microwave on high power for 5 minutes, stirring once. Fold any thin fillets to make each an even thickness. Place on top of the carrots in the corners of the dish with the thickest parts towards the outside.

In a small bowl, combine the mustard and honey. Spread over the fish and cover with greaseproof paper. Microwave on high for 2 minutes. Rotate the fillets, placing the cooked parts towards the centre, and cook for 1–3 minutes more, or until the fish flakes easily. Let stand, covered, for 2 minutes.

Makes 4 servings

Per serving: *139 calories, 21 g protein, 8 g carbohydrates, 3 g fat, 204 mg sodium, 2 g fibre*

Diet Exchanges: *0 milk, 1 vegetable, 0 fruit, 0 bread, 2 meat, 0 fat*

Slimming Meal

1 serving Cod Dijon

85 g/3 oz boiled potatoes tossed with Dijon mustard and chopped chives

60 g/2 oz peas with chopped mint

1 chocolate wafer biscuit

1 orange

| 407 calories |

Crab Cakes

Kathy Fruendt

"When I make these crab cakes, I use cream crackers, but table water biscuits work, too. Serve with low-fat coleslaw."

75 g/2½ oz creamcrackers, crushed
   (about 13 crackers)

2 egg whites

1 tbsp Worcestershire sauce

2 tsp crab-boil seasoning (see tip)

¼ tsp crushed red-pepper flakes

6 tbsp reduced-fat mayonnaise

500 g/1 lb crabmeat

1 tsp finely chopped sweet gherkins

1 tsp finely chopped onion

4 lemon wedges

Per serving: *382 calories, 28 g protein, 17 g carbohydrates, 23 g fat, 1,335 mg sodium, 0 g fibre*

Diet Exchanges: *0 milk, 0 vegetable, 0 fruit, 1 bread, 2 meat, 0 fat*

TIP: To make crab-boil seasoning, mix ½ teaspoon each of the following dried herbs and spices in a jar: mustard seed, coriander seed, dill seed, whole allspice, ground cloves, and crumbled bay leaf. Cover the jar tightly and shake

In a large bowl, combine the crackers, egg whites, Worcestershire sauce, crab-boil seasoning, red-pepper flakes, and 2 tablespoons mayonnaise. Gently fold in the crabmeat. Form into 4 patties.

Coat a large frying pan with non-stick spray and warm over medium heat. Add the crab cakes and cook for 20 minutes or until crispy, turning once.

In a small bowl, combine the gherkins, onion, and remaining mayonnaise. Serve the crab cakes with the sauce and lemon wedges.

Makes 4 servings

Splurge Meal

1 serving Crab Cakes

1 serving Asian Slaw (page 230)

1 wholemeal roll

½ grilled peach with 2 tablespoons low-fat vanilla yogurt

645 calories

Salmon with Lemon-Caper Cream Sauce

Michael Ostrowsky

A sinfully rich tasting lemony sauce makes salmon a real treat. I sometimes serve this with almond green beans and roast potatoes.

2 tsp olive oil

1 garlic clove, finely chopped

60 ml/2 fl oz lemon juice

2 tbsp capers

1 tsp lemon-pepper seasoning

115 g/4oz) low-fat soured cream

4 salmon steaks (170 g/6 oz each)

Coat a grill pan with non-stick spray. Preheat the grill.

In a small saucepan, warm the oil over medium heat. Add the garlic and cook for 1 minute. Reduce the heat to low. Stir in the lemon juice, capers, and lemon-pepper seasoning, and cook for 5 minutes. Add the soured cream and cook for 5 minutes more, or until heated through.

Meanwhile, place the salmon on the prepared grill pan. Grill 10 cm/4 in. from the heat for 5 minutes. Turn and grill for 5 minutes more, or until the fish is just opaque. Serve with the sauce.

Makes 4 servings

Per serving: *389 calories, 35 g protein, 27 g carbohydrates, 14 g fat, 88 mg sodium, 0 g fibre*

Diet Exchanges: *0 milk, 0 vegetable, 0 fruit, 0 bread, 4 meat, 0 fat*

Prawns Creole

Sara D. Gullett

"I think the best way to serve prawns is á la Creole. Here's a lower-fat and quicker way to enjoy the traditional dish. Serve over hot cooked rice."

2 rashers streaky bacon

1 onion, chopped

½ green pepper, chopped

1 celery stick, chopped

1 garlic clove, finely chopped

450 g/1 ln canned chopped tomatoes

1 bay leaf

½ tsp salt

¼ tsp ground black pepper

¼ tsp Worcestershire sauce

¼ tsp hot-pepper sauce

500 g/1 lb fresh or thawed frozen medium prawns, peeled and deveined

Cook the bacon in a large frying pan over medium heat until crisp. Transfer to kitchen paper to drain, then crumble when cool. Remove and discard all but 1 tablespoon of fat from the frying pan.

Cook the onion, pepper, and celery in the hot fat over medium heat for 5 minutes, or until tender. Stir in the garlic and cook for 1 minute. Add the tomatoes (with juice), bay leaf, salt, black pepper, Worcestershire sauce, and hot-pepper sauce. Heat to boiling. Reduce the heat to low and simmer for 20 minutes. Add the prawns and bacon, and cook for 10 minutes, or until the prawns are opaque. Remove the bay leaf before serving.

Makes 4 servings

Per serving: *162 calories, 26 g protein, 6 g carbohydrates, 4 g fat, 1,377 mg sodium, 2 g fibre*

Diet Exchanges: *0 milk, 3 vegetable, 0 fruit, 0 bread, 1 meat, 0 fat*

Slimming Meal

1 serving Prawns Creole

4 tablespoons cooked brown rice

30 g/1 oz frisée lettuce with 1 rasher shredded bacon and 1 tablespoon low-fat vinaigrette

1 slice watermelon

363 calories

Brown Rice Vegetable Stir-Fry

248 Calories

Conrad and Tricia Holsomback

"This is a great dish for using leftover rice. Add bits of cooked meat, prawns, and/or tofu for more protein. Water chestnuts, green beans, and sprouts also make great additions to the sautéed vegetables."

200 g/7 oz brown rice

570 ml/1 pint chicken stock

1 tbsp sesame or peanut oil

2 large leeks, white part only, sliced

2 celery sticks, thinly sliced

2 carrots, thinly sliced

2 garlic cloves, finely chopped

2 tbsp soy sauce

1 tbsp rice vinegar or cider vinegar

1 tbsp oyster sauce

Cook and stir the rice in a large, dry saucepan over medium heat for 5 minutes, or until fragrant and toasted. Add the stock. Reduce the heat to low, cover, and simmer for 40–45 minutes, or until the rice is tender and the liquid is absorbed.

Meanwhile, warm the oil in a large frying pan over medium-high heat. Add the leeks, celery, carrots, and garlic. Cook 5 minutes, stirring frequently, or until the vegetables are crisp-tender. Stir in the rice, soy sauce, vinegar, and oyster sauce.

Makes 4 servings

Per serving: *248 calories, 5 g protein, 47 g carbohydrates, 6 g fat, 749 mg sodium, 3 g fibre*

Diet Exchanges: *0 milk, 3 vegetable, 0 fruit, 2 bread, 0 meat, 1 fat*

Quick Black Bean Enchiladas

722 Calories

Wendie Clark

"Fifteen-minute meals are a godsend in my house. This one tastes like you spent more time on it. Make it as spicy or mild as you like by using more or less of the chilli peppers and hot or mild salsa."

340 g/12 oz low-fat cottage cheese

800 g/1¾ lb cooked black beans, rinsed and drained

1–2 jalapeño chilli peppers, deseeded and chopped (wear rubber gloves when handling)

225 g/8 oz grated reduced-fat Cheddar cheese

8 flour tortillas

500 g/1 lb salsa

Preheat the oven to 180°C/350°F/gas 4. Coat a 33 × 23 cm/13 × 9 in. ovenproof dish with non-stick spray.

In a large bowl, mix the cottage cheese, beans, peppers, and half the cheese. Spoon a quarter of the mixture on each tortilla. Roll them up Swiss-roll style, place them seam side down in the prepared dish, and pour the salsa evenly over them.

Sprinkle with the remaining cheese, cover with foil, and bake for 20 minutes. Remove the foil and bake for 10 minutes, or until hot and bubbly.

Makes 4 servings

Per serving: *722 calories, 51 g protein, 104 g carbohydrates, 14 g fat, 1,762 mg sodium, 6 g fibre*

Diet Exchanges: *0 milk, 0 vegetable, 0 fruit, 5 bread, 3 meat, 0 fat*

Splurge Meal

1 serving Quick Black Bean Enchiladas

2 tablespoons salsa

½ sliced avocado with orange sections and low-fat vinaigrette with fresh oregano

1 serving Quick Rice Pudding (page 259)

1,172 calories

Black Bean and Corn Burritos

322 Calories

Lissa Hill

"These are very messy to eat yet very satisfying. (Use a fork if necessary.) With so many tastes and textures, there's no need for lots of cheese here."

1 tsp vegetable oil

40 g/1½ oz chopped red pepper

115 g/4 oz bottled or canned green chilli peppers, drained and chopped

115 g/4 oz frozen sweetcorn, thawed

½ tsp chilli powder

¼ tsp ground black pepper

500 g/1 lb cooked black beans, rinsed and drained

4 tortillas (whole-wheat, if available), warmed

115 g/4 oz low-fat soured cream

115 g/4 oz salsa

115 g/4 oz chopped red onion or spring onions

½–2 jalapeño chilli peppers, deseeded and chopped (wear rubber gloves when handling)

2 tbsp lime juice

3 tbsp chopped fresh coriander leaves

Warm the oil in a medium non-stick frying pan over medium heat. Add the red pepper and cook for 5 minutes, or until soft.

Add the green chilli peppers, sweetcorn, chilli powder, and black pepper. Cook for 1 minute. Add the beans, mashing them with the back of a wooden spoon until slightly creamy, and cook for 8 minutes.

Spread the bean mixture on the tortillas and top each with soured cream, salsa, red onion or spring onions, jalapeño chile peppers, lime juice, and coriander. Roll up like an envelope to make an enclosed packet.

Makes 4

Per burrito: *322 calories, 17 g protein, 60 g carbohydrates, 3 g fat, 682 mg sodium, 10 g fibre*

Diet Exchanges: *0 milk, 1 vegetable, 0 fruit, 2 bread, 0 meat, 0 fat*

Slimming Meal

1 serving Black Bean and Corn Burritos

1 whole sliced tomato with red onions

1 scoop lemon sorbet

1 Chocolate Chunk Cookie (page 264)

404 calories

Mexican Salad

Stephanie Goddard

"This is a great salad of contrasts – warm and cold, soft and crunchy."

Cook the bulgur according to packet directions.

Warm the oil in a large frying pan over medium heat. Add the onion and cook 5 minutes. Add the garlic and cook 2 minutes, or until the onion is tender. Reduce the heat to low. Stir in the beans, cumin, salt, and cooked bulgur. Cook 5 minutes, or until hot.

For each serving, arrange a layer of one-quarter of the tortilla chips on a plate. Add layers of lettuce, bulgur mixture, tomatoes, cucumber, pepper, olives, and cheese. Finish with 1 tablespoon soured cream.

Makes 4 big servings

Per serving: *589 calories, 25 g protein, 70 g carbohydrates, 24 g fat, 1,439 mg sodium, 12 g fibre*

Diet Exchanges: *0 milk, 1 vegetable, 0 fruit, 4 bread, 1 meat, 2 fat*

150 g/5¼ oz bulgur

2 tbsp olive oil

1 small onion, chopped

2 garlic cloves, finely chopped

450 g/1 lb canned refried beans

1 tsp ground cumin

¼ tsp salt

100 g/2½ oz crumbled baked tortilla chips

200 g/7 oz shredded lettuce

2 tomatoes, finely chopped

1 cucumber, peeled, deseeded, and finely chopped

1 green pepper, finely chopped

85 g/3 oz olives, chopped

115 g/4 oz grated low-fat Cheddar cheese

60 g/2 oz soured cream

Splurge Meal

225 ml/8 fl oz gazpacho

1 corn muffin

1 serving Mexican Salad

½ sliced mango with cinnamon sugar

902 calories

Delightful Weekend Dinners

Chicken Fettuccine

480 Calories

Cheryl Tomasz

"I save this dish for those busy weekends when I don't feel like cooking. It comes together quickly, yet still has an elegant flavour."

1 large onion, sliced

2 garlic cloves, finely chopped

225 ml/8fl oz dry white wine or alcohol-free white wine

500 g/1 lb boneless, skinless chicken breasts, cut into thin strips

225 g/8 oz black olives, sliced

1 large tomato, chopped

225 g/8 oz tomato sauce

½ tsp ground thyme

¼ tsp ground black pepper

225 g/8 oz dried fettuccine or 170 g/6 oz fresh

1 bunch chives or 2 spring onions, chopped

Coat a large non-stick frying pan with non-stick spray and warm over medium heat. Add the onion and garlic. Cook for 4 minutes, or until soft. Add the wine and heat to boiling over high heat. Reduce the heat to medium and simmer for 5 minutes.

Add the chicken and simmer for 10 minutes, or until no longer pink. Add the olives, tomato, tomato sauce, thyme, and pepper. Heat through.

Meanwhile, cook the fettuccine according to packet directions. Drain.

Serve the pasta topped with the chicken and sauce. Sprinkle with the chives or spring onions.

Makes 4 servings

Per serving: *480 calories, 39 g protein, 50 g carbohydrates, 12 g fat, 1,380 mg sodium, 5 g fibre*

Diet Exchanges: *0 milk, 3 vegetable, 0 fruit, 3 bread, 2 meat, 0 fat*

FROM THE PROS

Canyon Ranch Health Resorts

Guests at Canyon Ranch Health Resorts have come to expect good food that tastes great. Menu consultant Jeanne Jones keeps them happy and healthy with this simple Asian-flavoured chicken.

CHINESE CHICKEN IN A BAG
229 Calories

1 whole chicken (1.5–2 kg/3–4 lb)
1 tsp ground ginger
½ tsp Chinese five-spice powder
1½ tsp salt
3 spring onions, cut into 7.5-cm/3-in. pieces
1 tbsp plain flour
3 tbsp hoisin sauce
3 tbsp honey
2 tbsp dry sherry or apple juice
½ tsp coarsely ground black pepper

Rinse the chicken inside and out with cold water and pat dry with kitchen paper. In a cup, mix the ginger, five-spice powder, and ½ teaspoon salt. Rub all over the inside of the chicken. Place the spring onions in the cavity.

Put the flour in a large oven-safe cooking bag and shake to coat the inside of the bag.

In a small bowl, mix the hoisin sauce, honey, sherry or apple juice, pepper, and remaining salt. Rub all over the outside of the chicken. Place the chicken in the bag with any remaining sauce. Seal the bag and put it in the refrigerator for at least 4 hours.

Preheat the oven to 180°C/350°F/gas 4. Cut six 1.5-cm/½-in. slits in the top of the bag and place it in an ovenproof dish in the oven, making sure that the bag does not overhang the dish. Bake for 1 hour, or until a thermometer inserted in a breast registers 82°C/180°F and juices run clear.

Remove the chicken from the oven and allow to stand for 10 minutes. Carefully cut open the bag, remove the chicken and pour the juices into a bowl. Place the bowl in the freezer for a few minutes so that fat can congeal for easy removal. Cut the chicken into serving pieces and serve with the degreased juices.

Makes 8 servings

Per serving: *229 calories, 36 g protein, 3 g carbohydrates, 8 g fat, 378 mg sodium, 0 g fibre*

Diet Exchanges: *0 milk, 0 vegetable, 0 fruit, 1½ bread, 1½ meat, 0 fat*

Lemon Red Snapper with Jalapeño Peppers

165 Calories

"This is an elegant but easy dish. It's cooked in foil so that the fish stays moist and flavourful without added fat. And there are no pans to clean up!"

Marlene Agnely

4 firm-flesh fish fillets (about 170 g/6 oz each), such as snapper, cod, or halibut

60 ml. 2 fl oz low-fat Italian salad dressing

2 spring onions, cut into matchsticks

2 tsp lemon-pepper seasoning

1 jalapeño chilli pepper, deseeded and chopped (wear rubber gloves when handling)

¼ tsp salt

Preheat the oven to 190°C/375°F/gas 5.

Cut 8 pieces of foil, each about 25-cm/ 10-in. long, depending on the size of the fish. Place each fillet on a piece of foil. Top each one with 1 tablespoon salad dressing, one-quarter of the spring onions, ½ teaspoon lemon-pepper seasoning, one-quarter of the chilli pepper, and a pinch of salt. Cover with another piece of foil and crimp the edges to seal. Place on a baking tray. Bake for 10 minutes, or until the fish flakes easily.

Makes 4 servings

Per serving: *165 calories, 34 g protein, 1 g carbohydrates, 3 g fat, 404 mg sodium, 0 g fibre*

Diet Exchanges: *0 milk, 0 vegetable, 0 fruit, 0 bread, 2 meat, 0 fat*

Slimming Meal

1 serving Lemon Red Snapper with Jalapeño Peppers

85 g/3 oz roast sliced potatoes with mint

85 g/3 oz steamed sugar snap peas with roast red peppers and basil

½ grilled peach with 1 scoop vanilla frozen yogurt sprinkled with nutmeg

394 calories

White Chicken Chilli

295 Calories

Debbie Wilson

"I serve this slow-cooked chilli with a small amount of soured cream or fat-free yogurt. If you don't have a slow-cooker, cook it in a covered casserole in the oven set at 120°C/250°F/gas ½."

1 tbsp olive oil

340 g/12 oz boneless, skinless chicken breast, cubed

1 large onion, chopped

2 garlic cloves, finely chopped

225 ml/8 fl oz dry white wine or chicken stock

700 g/1½ lb canned cannellini beans, rinsed and drained

1 tsp mustard powder

1 tsp ground cumin

½ tsp salt

⅛ tsp ground black pepper

115 g/4 oz baked tortilla chips

60 g/2 oz grated reduced-fat extra-sharp Cheddar cheese

Warm the oil in a large frying pan over medium-high heat. Add the chicken and cook for 10 minutes, or until the chicken is no longer pink, stirring frequently. Remove and set aside. Add the onion and garlic to the pan and cook for 5 minutes, or until tender.

Spoon the chicken, onion, and garlic into a slow cooker. Add the wine or stock, beans, mustard powder, cumin, salt, and pepper. Simmer on low for 5–6 hours. Serve over the tortilla chips and sprinkle with the cheese.

Makes 6 servings

Per serving: *295 calories, 25 g protein, 28 g carbohydrates, 10 g fat, 756 mg sodium, 7 g fibre*

Diet Exchanges: *0 milk, 0 vegetable, 0 fruit, 2½ bread, 2 meat, 0 fat*

Chilli Loco

219 Calories

Kelly Gracey

*"This is a crazy kind of chilli. (In Spanish, loco means crazy.)
I modified my beef chilli recipe to make this tasty variation. If you like your chilli spicy,
don't remove the seeds from the jalapeño pepper."*

1 onion, chopped

2 tsp olive oil

500 g/1 lb minced turkey breast

2 garlic cloves, finely chopped

1 jalapeño chilli pepper, deseeded and chopped (wear rubber gloves when handling)

1 tbsp ground cumin

800 g/1¾ lb canned tomatoes with herbs

800 g/1¾ lb canned tomato sauce

115 g/4 oz canned mushrooms, drained

450 g/1 lb canned cannellini beans, rinsed and drained

450 g/1 lb canned borlotti beans, rinsed and drained

60 g/2 oz grated reduced-fat Cheddar cheese

Sauté the onion in the oil in a large saucepan over medium heat until soft. Add the turkey and cook for 5 minutes, or until no longer pink. Add the garlic, pepper, and cumin. Cook for 5 minutes longer. Add the tomatoes (with juice), tomato sauce, and mushrooms. Heat to boiling. Reduce the heat to low, cover, and simmer over medium-low heat for 30 minutes, stirring frequently. Add the beans and continue cooking for another 15 minutes. Serve in a bowl and top with the cheese.

Makes 8 servings

Per serving: *219 calories, 25 g protein, 20 g carbohydrates, 5 g fat, 152 mg sodium, 6 g fibre*

Diet Exchanges: *0 milk, 3 vegetable, 0 fruit, 1 bread, 1 meat, 0 fat*

Roast Sirloin Steak

276 Calories

Scott Mingus

"Whenever I really want beef, I turn to this ultra-simple recipe."

700 g/1½ lb sirloin steak (5 cm/2 in. thick), trimmed of visible fat
225 ml/8 fl oz low-fat Italian dressing
½ tsp ground black pepper

Per serving: *276 calories, 42 g protein, 5 g carbohydrates, 10 g fat, 419 mg sodium, 0 g fibre*

Diet Exchanges: *0 milk, 0 vegetable, 0 fruit, 0 bread, 3 meat, 0 fat*

Place the steak in a large roasting tin and coat it completely with the dressing. Cover and marinate in the refrigerator for 2–8 hours, turning occasionally. Drain and discard the marinade.

Preheat the oven to 200°C/400°F/gas 6.

Uncover the tin and roast the steak in the oven for 35–40 minutes, or until a thermometer inserted in centre registers 65°C/145°F for medium-rare. Remove the meat from the oven and sprinkle it with black pepper. Let stand 10 minutes before slicing.

Makes 4 servings

TIP: This dish tastes great with vegetables added to the roasting tin. While the steak is roasting, place another 60 ml/2 fl oz Italian dressing in a medium bowl. Add 300 g/10 oz chopped vegetables, such as halved and sliced courgettes, red onion wedges, and halved cherry tomatoes. Toss to coat. Let sit for 5 minutes. Remove the steak from the oven after 20 minutes of cooking time and place the vegetables in the tin around it. Roast for 15–20 minutes, or until the vegetables are soft.

(Twice-Baked Potatoes recipe on page 209)

It Worked for Me!

Joan Lunden

VITAL STATS

Weight lost: 23 kg/3½ st

Time kept it off: 10 years

Weight-loss strategies: Kept food diary, low-fat foods, daily exercise

Weight-maintenance strategies: Healthy eating, exercise, stress reduction through meditation and visualization

Choosing a goal to motivate her has enabled Joan to find inspiration and maintain balance and health in her life.

'I chose to make a life change at age 39. I was very overweight, unhappy with my life, and downright frightened about my health. One thing I knew for sure was that, if I got healthy, I would get happy. So I changed the way I ate, and I changed the way I thought about and perceived food and exercise.'

Joan tried every diet out there, but she soon realized that dieting is a false state of living that she could not maintain. Joan is a great example of the principle that changes come slowly if they are going to be permanent. 'There's no magic bullet. It takes time, effort, desire, and the right information and strategy to make the change,' she explains. 'Once you've learned the ground rules, they will become second nature. And eating healthfully can become an integral and painless part of your lifestyle.' She has the same approach to her exercise commitment.

Joan admits that the idea of going to the gym to get into shape was a bore at first. Then, her friend and trainer suggested that she look at working out the way an athlete does: as training for a particular goal. Once Joan figured out what sport she was training for (mountain climbing) and set a date for her event (6 months later), she had a goal to work towards. Going to the gym became exciting and fun. 'Exercise isn't about suffering,' she says. 'Exercise is about finding something you enjoy doing that also happens to protect your health, lift your mood, and give your energy level a boost.'

Joan realized that being physically fit and eating healthy were only part of the equation: lasting health also meant taking care of her mind and spirit. She learned about the mind–body connection and used this concept to improve her overall well-being. 'I have been on the most fantastic journey, seeking out great adventures for my mind, body, and spirit,' she smiles. 'I'm constantly reaching for a happier, healthier life.' ∎

Joan's
Jewel of the Nile Chicken Kebabs

196 Calories

'These kebabs are always a hit with the family. The colourful vegetables are like jewels on a skewer and the marinade gives them a Middle Eastern flavour. They make great party food, too.'

3 tbsp chopped parsley

60 g/2 oz fat-free natural yogurt

60 ml/2 fl oz lemon juice

2 tbsp olive oil

1 tbsp chopped fresh coriander leaves

1 tbsp paprika

1 tbsp curry powder

2 tsp ground cumin

2 small garlic cloves, finely chopped

½ tsp salt

½ tsp ground black pepper

500 g/1 lb boneless, skinless chicken breasts, cubed

1 small yellow or orange pepper, cut into 2.5-cm/1-in. pieces

1 yellow summer squash, sliced 6 mm/¼ in. thick

8 cherry tomatoes

1 onion, cut into 2-cm/½-in. wedges

In a large bowl, combine the parsley, yogurt, lemon juice, oil, coriander, paprika, curry powder, cumin, garlic, salt, and black pepper. Add the chicken and toss to coat. Cover and refrigerate for at least 20 minutes or up to 2 hours.

Heat a large saucepan of lightly salted water to boiling. Drop in the chopped pepper and cook for 2 minutes. Remove with a slotted spoon and drain. Drop in the squash and cook for 1 minute. Remove with a slotted spoon and drain. Thread a cherry tomato on each of 4 skewers, then alternately thread on marinated chicken, pepper, squash, and onion, ending with a cherry tomato.

Preheat the grill and coat the grill rack with non-stick spray. Grill the kebabs 10–15 cm/4–6 in. from the heat for 3–4 minutes per side, or until the chicken is no longer pink and the juices run clear.

Makes 4 servings

Per serving: *196 calories, 32 g protein, 8 g carbohydrates, 4 g fat, 286 mg sodium, 2 g fibre*

Diet Exchanges: *0 milk, 2 vegetable, 0 fruit, 0 bread, 2½ meat, 0 fat*

Confetti Meat Loaf

215 Calories

Helaine Ferebee

"To reduce the fat and calories in my ordinary meat loaf, I use brown rice to extend the beef. The rice also keeps the meat loaf moist and lends a nutty flavour. I keep cooked rice in the freezer for fast and easy preparation. This makes a nice meal with roast potatoes and steamed broccoli."

90 g/3 oz brown rice

1 tbsp olive oil or vegetable oil

1 small onion, chopped

170 g/6 oz chopped red and green peppers

500 g/1lb extra-lean ground steak and/or minced turkey breast

225 g/8 oz chunky salsa

1 egg

¾ tsp salt

½ tsp ground black pepper

¼ tsp celery seeds

Cook the rice according to packet directions.

Preheat the oven to 180°C/350°F/gas 4.

Warm the oil in a small frying pan over medium heat. Add the onion and peppers. Cook for 5 minutes, or until tender.

In a large bowl, combine the meat, salsa, egg, salt, black pepper, and celery seeds. Stir in the vegetables and rice. Place the mixture in an oblong ovenproof dish or loaf tin. Bake for 45–50 minutes, or until thermometer inserted in centre registers 70°C/160°F and the meat is no longer pink.

Makes 6 servings

Per serving: *215 calories, 22 g protein, 14 g carbohydrates, 8 g fat, 271 mg sodium, 1 g fibre*

Diet Exchanges: *0 milk, 1 vegetable, 0 fruit, 1 bread, 2 meat, 0 fat*

El Dorado Casserole

298 Calories

Kelly Tinsle

"This healthier version of a popular Mexican-style casserole is hearty and satisfying. It's easy to make in advance, too. It's still a bit high in fat, so I like to save it for times when I want to splurge."

500 g/1 lb extra-lean ground steak or minced turkey breast

1 onion, chopped

225 g/8 oz ricotta cheese

225 g/8 oz reduced-fat cream cheese

225 g/8 oz bottled or canned green chilli peppers, chopped

115 g/4 oz black olives, drained and chopped

115 g/4 oz coarsely broken baked tortilla chips

85 g/3 oz grated reduced-fat Red Leicester cheese

85 g/3 oz grated reduced-fat Cheddar cheese

Salsa (optional)

Preheat the oven to 190°C/375°F/gas 5. Coat a 33 × 23 cm/13 × 9 in. ovenproof dish with non-stick spray.

In a large non-stick frying pan over medium-high heat, cook the beef or turkey and onion, stirring occasionally, 10 minutes, or until the meat is no longer pink and the onion is tender. Drain off any fat.

In a large bowl, combine the ricotta, cream cheese, chilli peppers (with liquid), and olives.

Spoon half of the meat into the prepared dish. Top with half of the ricotta mixture, and then half of the tortilla chips. Sprinkle with half of the Red Leicester and half of the Cheddar. Repeat the layers with the remaining meat mixture, ricotta mixture, chips, and grated cheeses.

Cover and bake for 20 minutes. Uncover and bake for 10 minutes, or until hot and bubbly. Serve with the salsa, if using.

Makes 8 servings

Per serving: 298 calories, 28 g protein, 11 g carbohydrates, 16 g fat, 646 mg sodium, 2 g fibre

Diet Exchanges: 0 milk, 0 vegetable, 0 fruit, 1 bread, 2 meat, 2 fat

Grilled Pork Chops

95 Calories

Lori Carillo

"To cook pork chops evenly without them becoming too browned and tough on the outside, I turn them often. Grill vegetables and a few chunks of pineapple to round out the meal."

Preheat the grill and coat the grill rack with non-stick spray. Cook the chops 10 cm/4 in. from the heat, turning once halfway through the cooking time of 10–12 minutes, or until a thermometer inserted in the centre of a chop registers 70°C/160°F and the juices run clear.

Makes 4 servings

Per serving: *95 calories, 17 g protein, 1 g carbohydrates, 3 g fat, 297 mg sodium, 0 g fibre*

Diet Exchanges: *0 milk, 0 vegetable, 0 fruit, 0 bread, 2½ meat, 0 fat*

4 boneless centre-cut pork loin chops, trimmed of visible fat (each about 85 g/ 3 oz and 4 cm/1½ in. thick)

1 tbsp Worcestershire sauce

2 garlic cloves, finely chopped

½ tsp salt

½ tsp paprika

⅛ tsp ground black pepper

Sprinkle the pork chops all over with the Worcestershire sauce, garlic, salt, paprika, and pepper. Cover and refrigerate for at least 20 minutes or up to 2 hours.

Slimming Meal

1 serving Grilled Pork Chops

1 skewer grilled sliced aubergine, courgettes, and potatoes

2 rings grilled pineapple drizzled with 1 teaspoon honey

214 calories

(Herb Rice recipe on page 216)

Chickpea and Sausage Soup

290 Calories

Janet Fry

"Here's my favourite soup – satisfying yet calorie-wise. The sausage is drained, so you get the spice but not much fat. Sometimes I vary the vegetables to get different flavours."

500 g/1 lb dried chickpeas

120 g/4 oz chorizo, thinly sliced

3 leeks, white part only, chopped

2 celery sticks, chopped

2 shallots, finely chopped

2 garlic cloves, finely chopped

170 g/6 oz tomato purée

1.5 litres/2½ pints chicken stock

2 tsp dried Italian seasoning

425 g/15 oz canned sweetcorn, drained

400 g/14 oz canned or cooked sliced carrots, drained

Wash the chickpeas and discard any stones or shrivelled peas. Place the chickpeas in a large saucepan with enough water to cover and let soak for 12 hours or overnight. Drain. (Alternatively, use the quick-soak method: heat the chickpeas and water to boiling, boil for 2 minutes, then remove the pan from the heat, cover, and let stand for 1 hour. Drain.)

In a large saucepan over medium-high heat, cook the sausage until no longer pink. Transfer to a bowl with a slotted spoon. Drain and discard all but 1 tablespoon of the fat from the pan. Stir in the leeks, celery, and shallots. Cook for 5 minutes. Stir in the garlic and cook for 1 minute. Stir in the tomato purée, stock, Italian seasoning, and chickpeas. Heat to boiling, then reduce the heat to low and simmer for 2 hours, or until the chickpeas are tender. Add the sweetcorn and carrots and cook for 5 minutes.

Makes 8 servings

Per serving: *290 calories, 19 g protein, 38 g carbohydrates, 8 g fat, 832 mg sodium, 9 g fibre*

Diet Exchanges: *0 milk, 2 vegetable, 0 fruit, 3 bread, 1 meat, 0 fat*

Spicy Pork and Bean Stew

449 Calories

Valorie Rogers

"I love to cook, and I indulge in this hobby every chance I get. At work, I always find that my co-workers are willing taste-testers. They absolutely loved this stew. Serve it over rice or noodles, or have it with cornbread on the side."

1 tbsp olive oil

340 g/12 oz lean pork tenderloin, cut into 2.5-cm/1-in. cubes

1 green pepper, chopped

1 large onion, chopped

6 garlic cloves, finely chopped

2 jalapeño chilli peppers, deseeded and finely chopped (wear rubber gloves when handling)

3 tsp chilli powder

1 tsp ground cumin

½ tsp ground black pepper

¼ tsp ground red pepper

425 g/15 oz canned chopped tomatoes

425 g/15 oz canned chopped tomatoes with chilli peppers

900 g/2 lb canned red kidney beans, rinsed and drained

500 g/ 1 lb cooked black beans or canned borlotti beans, rinsed and drained

Warm the oil in a large non-stick saucepan over medium heat. Add the pork and cook until no longer pink. Stir in the green pepper, onion, garlic, chilli peppers, chilli powder, cumin, black pepper, and ground red pepper. Cook for 8 minutes, or until the vegetables are tender. Stir in the chopped tomatoes (with juice), chopped tomatoes with chilli peppers (with juice), kidney beans, and black or borlotti beans. Cook for 10–15 minutes, or until the flavours are blended.

Makes 4 servings

Per serving: *449 calories, 41 g protein, 56 g carbohydrates, 9 g fat, 847 mg sodium, 16 g fibre*

Diet Exchanges: *0 milk, 2 vegetable, 0 fruit, 3 bread, 3½ meat, 0 fat*

Seafood Chowder

Tammy L. DePriest.

350 Calories

"I love my chowder milky and rich. I didn't want to give it up, so I found a way to make it low in fat and calories."

30 g/1 oz butter or margarine

1 small onion, chopped

1 celery stick, chopped

425 ml/15 fl oz chicken stock

85 g/3 oz small shell pasta

1 bay leaf

¼ tsp dried thyme

⅛ tsp ground nutmeg

⅛–¼ tsp ground red pepper

370 ml/13 fl oz semi-skimmed evaporated milk

225 g/8 oz fresh or thawed frozen peeled and deveined prawns and/or scallops

450 g/1 lb canned clams or oysters

225 g/8 oz fresh, or frozen and thawed, fish fillets, cut into 2.5-cm/1-in. cubes

2 tbsp chopped pimiento

2 tbsp chopped parsley

Warm the butter or margarine in a large saucepan over medium heat. Add the onion and celery and cook for 5 minutes, or until tender. Add the stock, pasta, bay leaf, thyme, nutmeg, and ground red pepper.

Heat to boiling. Reduce the heat to low and cook for 15 minutes, or until the pasta is tender. Stir in the evaporated milk, prawns and/or scallops, clams or oysters (with liquid), fish, pimiento, and parsley. Heat gently for 10 minutes, or until the fish flakes easily. Remove and discard the bay leaf before serving.

Makes 4 servings

Per serving: *350 calories, 43 g protein, 24 g carbohydrates, 10 g fat, 2,072 mg sodium, 1 g fibre*

Diet Exchanges: *1 milk, 0 vegetable, 0 fruit, 1 bread, 1½ meat, 0 fat*

EAT MORE FOOD AND FEWER CALORIES

The next time you visit a salad bar or self-service food counter, notice what's at the front of the line: iceberg lettuce, rice, pasta, and other salads. It's no accident. Restaurateurs know that when you pile your plate with fluffy (and inexpensive) foods like lettuce, you'll have less room down the line for more expensive items like prawns.

Fortunately for you, giving more space to bulky foods like grains, beans, lettuce, and pasta is calorie-wise, too. Consider the numbers: fatty foods like prime rib of beef have more calories per gram than carbohydrate-rich or protein-rich foods like pasta or beans (9 calories per gram for fats versus 4 calories per gram for carbohydrates and proteins). The easiest way to cut calories but not volume from your meals is to cut back on the amount of fats that you eat and increase the amount of carbohydrate and protein foods.

Here are a few calorie equations that make the point. Every one of these portions has the same number of calories. Sure, some examples are extreme – broccoli is no substitute for ice cream – but they paint a clear picture. Notice that the higher the fibre and the lower the fat in a food, the more you can eat for the same number of calories.

Food	Calories	Fibre (g)	Fat (g)
1 scoop premium ice cream	230	0	17
160 g/5 oz cooked brown rice	230	4	2
100 g/3½ oz cooked pasta	230	2	2
3 scoops fat-free frozen yogurt	230	0	0
200 g/7 oz cooked couscous	230	3	0
2⅛ bananas	230	8	2
2⅝ apples	230	11	3
3⅓ slices wholemeal bread	230	6	4
700 g/1½ lb steamed broccoli	230	17	6
700 g/1½ lb carrots	230	17	1
50 g/1¾ oz plain air-popped popcorn	230	9	3
7 cream crackers	230	3	9
800 g/1¾ lb lettuce	230	30	0
29 baked tortilla chips	230	4	2
3 choclate digestive biscuits	230	1	11

Prawn Risotto

267 Calories

Michael Woodward

"The secret to creamy – but not fattening – risotto is to use short-grain Arborio rice and to stir it constantly while it cooks."

700 ml/1¼ pints chicken stock

225 ml/8 fl oz water

1 tbsp extra-virgin olive oil

1 small onion, chopped

1 garlic clove, finely chopped

2 tbsp tomato purée

400 g/14 oz Arborio rice

340 g/12 oz medium fresh or frozen and thawed prawns, peeled and deveined

125 ml/4 fl oz white wine (optional)

30 g/1 oz grated Parmesan cheese

In a medium saucepan, combine the stock and water. Heat to simmering. Reduce the heat to low and keep warm.

Warm the oil in a large shallow saucepan over medium heat. Add the onion and garlic, and cook for 10 minutes, or until the onion is tender. Stir in the tomato purée and cook for 10 minutes. Stir in the rice. Reduce the heat to medium-low. Add about a ladleful of warm stock and cook, stirring constantly, until almost completely absorbed. Continue adding stock, a ladle at a time, stirring constantly, until the rice is barely tender. Stir in the prawns and wine, if using. Cook for 5 minutes, or until the rice is tender yet firm and the prawns are opaque. Serve with the cheese.

Makes 8 servings

Per serving: *267 calories, 14 g protein, 42 g carbohydrates, 4 g fat, 528 mg sodium, 1 g fibre*

Diet Exchanges: *0 milk, 0 vegetable, 0 fruit, 3 bread, 1 meat, 0 fat*

Prawns in Tomato Sauce over Pasta

385 Calories

Frances Lobiondo

"My husband and I try to keep calories down for almost all of our home-cooked meals. Since cooking is my passion, I'm constantly creating low-fat recipes. Here's one we come back to again and again."

1 tbsp olive oil

1 small bunch spring onions, chopped

2 garlic cloves, finely chopped

800 g/1¾ lb canned chopped tomatoes

170 ml/6 fl oz dry white wine or alcohol-free white wine

1 tbsp sugar

30 g/1 oz chopped flat-leaf parsley or basil

12 fresh or frozen and thawed jumbo prawns, peeled and deveined

225 g/8 oz spaghetti

30 g/1 oz grated Parmesan cheese

Warm the oil in a medium saucepan over medium heat. Add the spring onions and garlic. Cook for 10 minutes, or just until the spring onions begin to turn golden.

Add the tomatoes, wine, sugar, and two-thirds of the parsley or basil. Heat to boiling, then reduce the heat to low, cover, and simmer 20–25 minutes, or until the sauce is slightly thickened.

Add the prawns and return to a simmer. Cook for 4–5 minutes, or until the prawns are opaque.

Meanwhile, cook the spaghetti according to packet directions. Drain and transfer to a large bowl. Add the sauce and toss to mix.

Sprinkle with the Parmesan and the remaining parsley or basil.

Makes 4 servings

Per serving: *385 calories, 25 g protein, 50 g carbohydrates, 8 g fat, 748 mg sodium, 3 g fibre*

Diet Exchanges: *0 milk, 2 vegetable, 0 fruit, 3 bread, 1 meat, 1 fat*

Asian Veggie Wraps

289 Calories

Micara Morency

"I've lost 23 kg (3½ st) by increasing the amount of vegetables in my diet. And I'm still losing! These wraps are one of my favourite ways to eat vegetables."

2 tbsp vegetable oil

225 g/8 oz shredded bok choy or green cabbage

2 carrots, cut into matchsticks

1 small courgette, cut into matchsticks

115 g/4 oz mushrooms, sliced

5 spring onions, cut into matchsticks

60 g/2 oz broccoli florets

3 tbsp soy sauce

1 tbsp sesame oil

4 flour tortillas

Preheat the oven to 200°C/400°F/gas 6. Coat a baking tray with non-stick spray.

Warm the vegetable oil in a large frying pan over medium heat. Add the bok choy or cabbage, carrots, courgette, mushrooms, spring onions, and broccoli. Cook, stirring frequently, for 5 minutes, or until the carrots and broccoli are crisp-tender. Stir in the soy sauce and sesame oil.

Spoon a quarter of the mixture along the centre of a tortilla and fold it like an envelope. Place, folded edges down, on the prepared baking tray. Repeat with the remaining ingredients. Bake for 10 minutes, or until golden brown.

Makes 4

Per wrap: *289 calories, 7 g protein, 39 g carbohydrates, 12 g fat, 811 mg sodium, 4 g fibre*

Diet Exchanges: *0 milk, 3 vegetable, 0 fruit, 1 bread, 0 meat, 2½ fat*

Very Vegetable Soup

113 Calories

Debra Davies

*"It's easy to get your 5 servings of vegetables a day
when this stewlike soup is part of your menu."*

2 tbsp olive oil

1 large onion, chopped

2 green and/or red peppers, chopped

4 garlic cloves, finely chopped

½ tsp ground cumin

½ small green cabbage, sliced

2 large carrots, sliced

1 courgette, chopped

1 yellow squash, chopped

410 g/14½ oz canned tomatoes

1.25 litres/2¼ pints canned or bottled
vegetable juice

½ tsp ground black pepper

¼ tsp crushed red-pepper flakes

Warm the oil in a large saucepan over
medium heat.

Add the onion and chopped peppers, and
cook for 5 minutes, or until tender. Add the
garlic and cumin, and cook for 1 minute.
Add the cabbage, carrots, courgette, squash,
tomatoes (with juice), vegetable juice, black
pepper, and red-pepper flakes. Heat to
boiling. Reduce the heat to low, cover, and
simmer for 1 hour.

Makes 6 servings

Per serving: *113 calories, 3 g protein,
13 g carbohydrates, 6 g fat, 38 mg sodium,
5 g fibre*

Diet Exchanges: *0 milk, 5 vegetable, 0 fruit,
0 bread, 0 meat, 1 fat*

Slimming Meal

1 serving Very Vegetable Soup

1 serving Warm Pepper and Pork
    Salad (page 242)

1 slice wholemeal bread

1 pear

378 calories

Vegetable Lasagne

Anna Riester

279 Calories

"Sure, this dish can be enjoyed right away, but like many casseroles, it tastes even better the next day!"

1 tsp olive oil

1 courgette, chopped

450 g/1 lb ricotta cheese

1 egg

1 tsp dried basil

¼ tsp salt

⅛ tsp ground black pepper

500 g/1 lb prepared pasta sauce

225 g/8 oz no-cook lasagne (about 9 sheets)

300 g/10 oz frozen broccoli, thawed

800 g/1¾ lb canned chopped tomatoes

30 g/1 oz grated Parmesan cheese

30 g/1 oz reduced-fat mozzarella cheese, grated

Preheat the oven to 180°C/350°F/gas 4. Coat a 33 × 23 cm/13 × 9 in. ovenproof dish with non-stick spray.

Warm the oil in a medium frying pan over medium heat. Add the courgette and cook 5 minutes, or until crisp-tender. Remove from the heat and set aside.

In a medium bowl, mix the ricotta, egg, basil, salt, and pepper. Reserve a quarter of the pasta sauce.

Place 3 sheets of lasagne in the prepared dish. Evenly spoon half of the remaining pasta sauce over the lasagne. Top with half of the ricotta mixture, half the broccoli, half the courgette, half the tomatoes (with juice), and half the Parmesan. Repeat layering with 3 more sheets of lasagne and the remaining ingredients. End with the remaining sheets of lasagne. Spoon the reserved pasta sauce over the top and sprinkle with the mozzarella.

Cover with foil and bake for 25 minutes. Uncover and bake for 20 minutes, or until hot and bubbly. Let stand for 10 minutes before serving.

Makes 8 servings

Per serving: *279 calories, 16 g protein, 30 g carbohydrates, 11 g fat, 552 mg sodium, 3 g fibre*

Diet Exchanges: *0 milk, 2 vegetable, 0 fruit, 1 bread, 1 meat, 0 fat*

Spinach Lasagne

Carrie Wright

300 Calories

"For a less fussy lasagne, I use a no-cook sauce and no-boil lasagne. If you prefer the taste and texture, use fresh sheets and cook according to packet directions before assembling the lasagne."

800 g/1¾ lb canned or bottled
tomato sauce

800 g/1¾ lb canned tomatoes, drained

2 tsp dried oregano

2 tsp dried basil

1 tsp dried thyme

¼ tsp ground black pepper

300 g/10 oz fresh spinach, chopped, or
frozen chopped spinach, thawed and
squeezed dry

225 g/8 oz no-cook lasagne (about
9 sheets)

425 g/15 oz ricotta cheese

225 g/8 oz reduced-fat mozzarella
cheese, grated

Preheat the oven to 190°C/375°F/gas 5.

In a large bowl, combine the tomato sauce, tomatoes, oregano, basil, thyme, and pepper. Break up whole tomatoes with the back of a spoon. Set aside.

Coat a medium non-stick frying pan with non-stick spray. Add the spinach and cook for 4 minutes, or until wilted.

Spread 120 g/4 oz of the tomato mixture into a 33 × 23 cm/13 × 9 in. ovenproof dish. Place 3 sheets of lasagne on top (they will not completely cover the bottom of the dish). Spread half of the ricotta over the lasagne. Layer with half the spinach. Top with a third of the remaining sauce and sprinkle with a third of the mozzarella. Cover with 3 more sheets, the remaining ricotta, and then the remaining spinach. Spoon on about a third of the remaining sauce and about a third of the remaining mozzarella. Cover with 3 more sheets and top with remaining sauce and mozzarella.

Cover and bake for 30 minutes. Uncover and bake for 15 minutes, or until hot and bubbly. Let stand for 10 minutes before serving.

Makes 8 servings

Per serving: *300 calories, 17 g protein, 33 g carbohydrates, 12 g fat, 1,221 mg sodium, 14 g fibre*

Diet Exchanges: *0 milk, 1 vegetable, 0 fruit, 2 bread, 1 meat, 0 fat*

Beef and Bean Stew

414 Calories

Holly Smail

"Call it a casserole or call it Mexican lasagne. Either way, it'll be a favourite."

1 tsp olive oil

1 green pepper, deseeded and chopped

1 onion, chopped

225 g/8 oz mince substitute

1 sachet taco seasoning mix

800 g/1¾ lb canned tomatoes, tomatoes

4 large flour tortillas

450 g/1 lb canned red kidney beans, rinsed and drained

450 g/1 lb canned white cannellini beans, rinsed and drained

115 g/4 oz grated reduced-fat Cheddar cheese

Warm the oil in a large non-stick frying pan over medium heat. Add the pepper and onion. Cook for 10 minutes, or until tender. Stir in the mince substitute, taco seasoning mix (also add water if directed on the label), and tomatoes (with juice). Heat to boiling. Reduce the heat to low, cover, and simmer for 15–20 minutes.

Preheat the oven to 180°C/350°F/gas 4.

Lightly coat a 23 × 23 cm/9 × 9 in. ovenproof dish with non-stick spray. Cut the tortillas into 5 cm/2 in. wide strips. Arrange a single layer in the bottom of the prepared dish and top with half the taco filling, half the kidney beans, half the cannellini beans, and one-third of the cheese. Arrange another layer of tortilla strips and top with the remaining taco filling, beans, and a third of the cheese. Top with the remaining tortilla strips and sprinkle with the remaining cheese.

Cover with foil and bake for 20 minutes. Uncover and bake for 10 minutes, or until hot and bubbly.

Makes 4 servings

Per serving: *414 calories, 16 g protein, 36 g carbohydrates, 24 g fat, 611 mg sodium, 7 g fibre*

Diet Exchanges: *0 milk, 3 vegetable, 0 fruit, 4 bread, 2 meat, 0 fat*

Splurge Meal

1 serving Beef and Bean Stew

1 corn muffin with 1 serving Herb Cheese Spread (page 107)

4 tablespoons brown rice

½ papaya with 115 g/4 oz lemon yogurt

880 calories

It Worked for Me!

Jodie Wissmiller

VITAL STATS

Weight lost: 20 kg/3 st 3 lb

Time kept it off: 2 years

Weight-loss strategies:
Studying nutrition and exercise, low-fat diet, strength training, aerobics

Weight-maintenance strategies:
Eating low-calorie and low-fat, daily workouts

Life for a 15-year-old weighing 82 kg/12 st 9 lb was not fun. When Jodie Wissmiller realized that her weight was messing up her life, she finally did something about it. Now she's a role model for her family.

'As if adolescence weren't difficult enough, my weight added to the struggle in my teens. It seemed as though all I did was eat, sleep, cry, and complain. I was constantly being teased about my weight, which made me shy and self-conscious. At the same time, I admired my thin, outgoing friends. I wanted to look up to myself, too.

'During half-term in spring one year I realized I had to do something about my weight. I read everything I could find on weight loss and exercise. I clipped and copied articles and arranged them by subject in a ring binder.

'I learned that muscle burns more calories than fat, and that if I developed my muscles, it would be easier to lose weight. I began with 45 minutes of stretching and strength training twice a day. I gave up evening TV for crunches, leg lifts, and free weights.

'I read about nutrition and learned that the easiest way to cut calories was to cut down on the fat I ate. That meant giving up fatty school lunches like burgers and chips. I took my own lunch, which was usually a turkey sandwich, a piece of fruit, and juice. I changed my breakfast to cereal, fruit, and plain toast. While the rest of my family was eating take-aways, I cooked my own meals. At first, I made steamed vegetables and poached chicken breast. Then I started collecting recipes. Within a few weeks my weight started dropping. Eventually my mum started to change the way she cooked, and she started exercising with me. She has lost 6 kg (1 st) so far and has helped me convince Dad to start walking and riding his bike.

'I no longer want to hide my body. I'm happy and confident. I can't tell you how good that feels.' ■

Jodie's Pineapple Pizza

470 Calories

"This is my favourite food in the whole world! The crust is so nice and thick, I'm fully satisfied after two slices."

375–435 g/13–15 oz plain flour

1 sachet fast-action dried yeast

¾ tsp salt

225 ml/8 fl oz very warm water (50°C/120°F)

2 tbsp vegetable oil

225 g/8 oz prepared pizza topping

115 g/4 oz low-fat mozzarella cheese, grated

570 g/1¼ lb canned pineapple chunks, drained

¼ tsp garlic powder

Preheat the oven to 200°C/400°F/gas 6. Coat a 30 cm/12 in. pizza pan with non-stick spray.

In a large bowl, combine 250 g/9 oz flour, the yeast, and salt. Stir in the water and oil. Add 125 g/4 oz flour, or enough to make a soft dough.

Turn the dough out on to a floured surface and knead for 10 minutes, or until smooth and elastic, adding more flour, if necessary. Let the dough rest for 10 minutes.

With a floured rolling pin, roll the dough into a 33 cm/13 in. circle. Place it in the prepared pizza pan and pinch up the edges to form a rim. Spread the topping on the dough, sprinkle evenly with the cheese, and spoon the pineapple evenly on top. Sprinkle with the garlic powder. Bake for 20–30 minutes, or until the crust is golden brown.

Makes 8 slices

Per 2 slices: *470 calories, 16 g protein, 92 g carbohydrates, 6 g fat, 746 mg sodium, 4 g fibre*

Diet Exchanges: *0 milk, 0 vegetable, 1 fruit, 4 bread, 2 meat, 0 fat*

Splurge Meal

2 slices Jodie's Pineapple Pizza

85 g/3 oz spinach salad with low-fat ranch dressing

2 scoops low-fat frozen yogurt

596 calories

Veggie Cassoulet 285 Calories

Wanda Lea O'Keefe

"At 30 years old, Pat, my husband, had sky-high cholesterol. That's when I learned to cut the fat out of our diet. Now, Pat's cholesterol is at acceptable levels and our sons are pictures of health."

115 g/4 oz dried white haricot beans

1 litre/1¾ pints water

2 large onions, chopped

3 garlic cloves, finely chopped

2 leeks, white part only, thinly sliced

4 vegetarian sausages, sliced

200 g/7 oz bottled or canned roast red peppers, drained and chopped

2 large carrots, thinly sliced

1 tsp salt

½ tsp ground black pepper

40 g/1½ oz dry-packed sun-dried tomatoes

½ tsp dried rosemary, crushed

30 g/1 oz fresh wholemeal breadcrumbs

Rinse the beans and discard any stones or shrivelled beans.

In a medium saucepan, combine the beans and 700 ml/1¼ pints water. Soak the beans overnight. Drain and return the beans to the pan. Add the onions, garlic, and remaining water. Heat to boiling over high heat, then reduce the heat to low, cover, and simmer for 1 hour. Remove from the heat and stir in the leeks, sausages, roast peppers, carrots, salt, and black pepper.

While the beans are cooking, soak the tomatoes in hot water for 10 minutes, or until soft. Drain, reserving the soaking liquid. Chop the tomatoes.

Preheat the oven to 160°C/325°F/ gas 3. Coat a large ovenproof dish with non-stick spray.

Stir the tomatoes and soaking liquid into the bean mixture. Spoon into the prepared dish, sprinkle with the rosemary, and top with the breadcrumbs. Bake for 1 hour, or until the carrots are tender and the breadcrumbs are golden brown.

Makes 4 servings

Per serving: *285 calories, 17 g protein, 35 g carbohydrates, 10 g fat, 855 mg sodium, 10 g fibre*

Diet Exchanges: *0 milk, 2 vegetable, 0 fruit, 2½ bread, 1 meat, 0 fat*

Black-Eyed Bean Stew

538 Calories

Kim Swearington

"This aromatic dish is packed with flavour, and it's a great source of fibre. Cooking with dried beans is really simple. Just put the beans to soak before you go to bed the night before. Alternatively, use the quick-soak method: Place rinsed beans in a large saucepan with enough water to cover and heat to boiling. Cook for 2 minutes; remove from the heat, cover, and let stand for 1 hour."

500 g/1 lb dried black-eyed beans

2 tbsp olive oil

2 onions, cut into 1-cm/½-in. pieces

1 green pepper, cut into 1-cm/½-in. pieces

8 garlic cloves, finely chopped

2 large potatoes, peeled and cut into
   1-cm/½-in. cubes

800 g/1¾ lb canned tomatoes

1 tbsp dried oregano

1 tbsp dried thyme

3 bay leaves

¼ tsp crushed red-pepper flakes

125 ml/4 fl oz chicken stock (optional)

Wash the beans and discard any stones or shrivelled beans. Place the beans in a large saucepan with enough water to cover. Cover and soak for 12 hours or overnight. Drain.

In a large saucepan, combine the beans and fresh water to cover. Heat to boiling over high heat. Reduce the heat to low and simmer for 25–30 minutes, or until tender. Set aside.

Warm the oil in a large saucepan over medium heat. Add the onions and pepper. Cook for 5 minutes, or until tender. Add the garlic and cook for 1 minute. Stir in the potatoes, tomatoes (with juice), oregano, thyme, bay leaves, red-pepper flakes, and beans with about a quarter of the cooking liquid. Heat to boiling. Reduce the heat to low and simmer for 1¼ hours. If the mixture becomes dry, add stock. Remove and discard the bay leaves before serving.

Makes 4 servings

Per serving: *538 calories, 34 g protein, 94 g carbohydrates, 5 g fat, 127 mg sodium, 14 g fibre*

Diet Exchanges: *0 milk, 3 vegetable, 0 fruit, 2 bread, 0 meat, 1½ fat*

Braised Tofu

Rowena Low

"Tofu is a high-quality, low-fat, inexpensive protein source. And it's heart-healthy. In this dish, I use spices and seasonings to intensify tofu's mild flavour. To complement its soft texture, I serve the tofu over brown rice, which has a nutty chewiness."

2 whole star anise

3 whole cloves

2 cardamom pods

2 cinnamon sticks

1 tbsp toasted sesame oil

5 slices fresh ginger

2 tbsp oyster sauce

3 tbsp low-sodium tamari or soy sauce

500 g/1 lb extra-firm tofu, drained and cubed

170 ml/6 fl oz water

2 tbsp rice vinegar

50 g/³⁄₄ oz packed brown sugar

⅛ tsp crushed red-pepper flakes

2 tbsp chopped fresh coriander leaves

2 tbsp chopped peanuts or sesame seeds (optional)

Heat a large frying pan over medium heat until hot. Add the anise, cloves, cardamom, and cinnamon. Cook for 1 minute, or until fragrant, shaking the pan often. Add the oil, ginger, oyster sauce, tamari or soy sauce, and tofu. Cook for 2 minutes. Add the water, vinegar, brown sugar, and red-pepper flakes. Heat to boiling.

Reduce the heat to low, cover, and simmer, for 30 minutes, or until sauce is thickened turning the tofu occasionally. Carefully lift out the tofu.

With a slotted spoon, remove and discard the anise, cloves, cardamom, and cinnamon. Stir in 1 tablespoon of the chopped coriander. Spoon the sauce over the tofu. Sprinkle with the remaining coriander and the peanuts or sesame seeds, if using.

Makes 4 servings

Per serving: *290 calories, 29 g protein, 22 g carbohydrates, 12 g fat, 316 mg sodium, 0 g fibre*

Diet Exchanges: *0 milk, 0 vegetable, 0 fruit, 1 bread, 1½ meat, 0 fat*

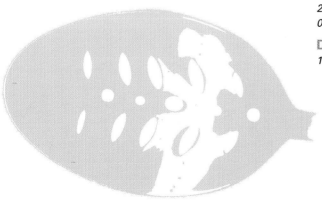

Green Mountain at Fox Run

At Green Mountain at Fox Run weight loss is a matter
of balance. 'Eating healthfully doesn't have to be restrictive,' says nutrition
director Marsha Hudnall. 'People can eat high-fat, high-calorie foods within a
balanced diet and still achieve and maintain healthy weights.' Another principle
at Green Mountain is simplicity. How can only three ingredients
add up to a delicious meal? Try it and find out.

AUBERGINE PARMESAN

205 Calories

1 aubergine, peeled and sliced 3 mm/
$\frac{1}{8}$ in. thick
340 ml/12 fl oz tomato sauce
185 g/6$\frac{1}{2}$ oz mozzarella cheese, grated

Per serving: *205 calories, 14 g protein,
14 g carbohydrates, 6 g fat, 325 mg sodium,
2 g fibre*

Diet Exchanges: *0 milk, 3 vegetable, 0 fruit,
0 bread, 1 meat, 0 fat*

Preheat the grill.
   Place the aubergine on a baking tray
and grill for 5 minutes on each side to
remove moisture. Remove from the grill.
   Preheat the oven to 150°C/300°F/gas 2.
   Spoon some tomato sauce into a 23 ×
23 cm/9 × 9 in. ovenproof dish. Top with
a layer of aubergine, some cheese, and
more sauce. Repeat until all the
ingredients are used, ending with cheese.
Cover with foil and bake for 2 hours, or
until the aubergine is tender. Let stand for
10 minutes before serving.

Makes 4 servings

Slimming Meal

1 serving Aubergine Parmesan
40 g/1$\frac{1}{2}$ oz small pasta with
   $\frac{1}{2}$ teaspoon olive oil and
   1 tablespoon grated
   Parmesan cheese
Small bowl tossed greens with
   jarred marinated artichokes
1 poached pear

389 calories

Unstuffed Cabbage

Tahmina Muradova

"All the lovely flavours of stuffed cabbage, but without the difficult and time-consuming steps."

1 tablespoon olive oil

1 onion, chopped

1 carrot, chopped

1 green bell pepper, cut into 2.5-cm/
   1-in. pieces

4 garlic cloves, finely chopped

1 small Chinese cabbage, cut into
   2.5-cm/1-in. pieces

1 tomato, cut into 2.5-cm/1-in. pieces

1 potato, chopped

125 ml/4 fl oz spicy canned
   vegetable juice

1 bay leaf

1 teaspoon salt

1 cup rice

3 tbsp chopped parsley

Warm oil in a large saucepan over medium heat. Add onion, carrot, pepper, and garlic. Cook 10 minutes, or until vegetables are tender. Add cabbage, tomato, potato, vegetable juice, bay leaf, and salt. Heat to boiling. Reduce heat to low and simmer 20 minutes, or until cabbage is tender and liquid is reduced. Remove and discard bay leaf before serving.

Meanwhile, cook rice according to packet directions. Serve rice topped with cabbage. Sprinkle with parsley.

Makes 4 servings

Per serving: *184 calories, 4 g protein, 32 g carbohydrates, 4 g fat, 526 mg sodium, 2 g fibre*

Diet Exchanges: *0 milk, 2 vegetable, 0 fruit, 2 bread, 0 meat, 1 fat*

Mediterranean Stuffed Aubergine

271 Calories

Janie Clark

"Incorporating whole grains, nuts, and seeds into my diet is increasingly important to me."

150 g/5¼ oz brown rice

285 ml/½ pint vegetable or chicken stock

2 small aubergines, halved lengthways

20 g/¾ oz dry-packed sun-dried tomatoes

2 tsp olive oil

1 onion, chopped

1 garlic clove, finely chopped

40 g/1½ oz sliced black olives

20 g/¾ oz chopped spring onions

4 tbsp chopped fresh oregano or
   2 tbsp dried

70 g/2½ oz crumbled feta cheese

3 tbsp lemon juice

½ tsp salt

⅛ tsp ground black pepper

In a medium saucepan, combine the rice and stock. Heat to boiling over high heat. Reduce the heat to low, cover, and simmer for 40–45 minutes, or until the rice is tender.

Preheat the oven to 180°C/350°F/gas 4. Lightly coat a baking tray with non-stick spray.

Cut out the aubergine flesh, cube it, salt it, and place it in a colander to drain for 15 minutes. Rinse and place in a large bowl.

Place the aubergine shells, cut side down, on the baking tray, sprinkle with 1 tablespoon water, and bake for 10 minutes. Cool.

Soak the tomatoes in hot water for 10 minutes. Drain, chop, and add to the cubes.

Warm the oil in a large frying pan over medium heat. Add the onion and garlic, and cook for 10 minutes. Add to the aubergine cubes with the olives, spring onions, oregano, rice, half the cheese, lemon juice, salt, and pepper. Mix well. Use to stuff each aubergine shell. Top with the remaining cheese.

Place the stuffed shells on the baking tray. Bake for 25–30 minutes, or until hot and the cheese is lightly browned.

Makes 4 servings

Per serving: *271 calories, 8 g protein, 37 g carbohydrates, 12 g fat, 1,014 mg sodium, 4 g fibre*

Diet Exchanges: *0 milk, 1 vegetable, 0 fruit, 2 bread, 0 meat, 1 fat*

Slimming Meal

1 serving Mediterranean Stuffed Aubergine

40 g/1½ oz orecchiette pasta with ½ teaspoon olive oil and chopped fresh basil

6 chilled asparagus spears with grated orange peel and tarragon

1 Chocolate Chunk Cookie (page 264)

421 calories

Simply Sides

Mediterranean Courgettes

129 Calories

Marie J. Brubaker

"The microwave oven makes this side dish in minutes. Perfect for pasta or rice."

1 courgette, cut into 1-cm/½-in. pieces
900 g/2 lb canned Italian plum tomatoes
450 g/1 lb canned red kidney beans, rinsed and drained
½ tsp ground black pepper

In a large microwavable bowl, combine the courgette, tomatoes (with juice), beans, and pepper. Microwave on high power 5–7 minutes, stirring once, or until the courgette is crisp-tender.

Makes 4 servings

Per serving: *129 calories, 9 g protein, 23 g carbohydrates, 1 g fat, 429 mg sodium, 8 g fibre*

Diet Exchanges: *0 milk, 3 vegetable, 0 fruit, 1 bread, 0 meat, 0 fat*

Mushroom Sauce

10 Calories

Dixie Lunderville

"This gravy doesn't start with fat, drippings, or butter. Instead, I used sautéed mushrooms and beef stock for flavour. Pour it on lean grilled beef or pork, or serve over a baked potato. For onion gravy, omit the mushrooms."

40 g/1½ oz mushrooms, finely chopped
60 g/2 oz finely chopped onion
2 tbsp cornflour
410 ml/14½ fl oz beef or chicken stock
2 tbsp chopped parsley
1 tbsp dry sherry (optional)

Coat a medium saucepan with non-stick spray and warm over medium heat. Add the mushrooms and onion. Cook for 10 minutes, or until tender, stirring often.

In a small bowl, combine the cornflour and 60 ml/2 fl oz stock. Stir until smooth. Add to the mushrooms with the parsley, sherry (if using), and remaining stock. Heat to boiling, stirring constantly. Reduce the heat to low and cook for 1 minute, stirring.

Makes 450 ml/16 fl oz

Per 2 tablespoons: *10 calories, 1 g protein, 2 g carbohydrates, 0 g fat, 0 mg cholesterol, 8 mg sodium, 0 g fibre*

Diet Exchanges: *0 milk, ½ vegetable, 0 fruit, 0 bread, 0 meat, 0 fat*

FROM THE PROS

Green Mountain at Fox Run

Food can be very personal. For many people, it signals a particular memory or the comforts of better times. The people at the Green Mountain weight-management community at Fox Run understand this principle. That's why they feature calming comfort foods like these super spuds.

TWICE-BAKED POTATOES

294 Calories

4 small baking potatoes, scrubbed and patted dry

3 tbsp skimmed milk

115 g/4 oz low-fat cottage cheese

1½ tsp finely chopped onion

1½ tsp chopped chives

¼ tsp paprika

¼ tsp garlic powder

60 g/2 oz grated Jarlsberg cheese

Preheat the oven to 180°C/350°F/gas 4.
Prick the potatoes with a fork and bake on an oven rack for 45 minutes, or until tender. Let cool. Cut off the top lengthways and scoop out the filling, leaving a 6 mm/¼ in. shell. Place the filling in a medium bowl or in a food processor. Add the milk, cottage cheese, onion, chives, paprika, and garlic powder. Mash with a fork or pulse until combined. Spoon back into the potato skins. Sprinkle each with 2 tablespoons cheese. Bake for 20 minutes, or until heated through and the cheese melts.

Makes 4

Per potato: *294 calories, 15 g protein, 49 g carbohydrates, 6 g fat, 201 mg sodium, 4 g fibre*

Diet Exchanges: *0 milk, 0 vegetable, 0 fruit, 3 bread, 1 meat, 0 fat*

(Photograph on page 173)

Orange Sweet Potatoes

204 Calories

Cheryl Olson

*"These make a great alternative to plain sweet potatoes.
When topped with fresh coriander, they pair well with grilled fish."*

15 g/1½ oz butter
3 large sweet potatoes or yams
225 ml/8 fl oz orange juice
1 tsp grated orange peel
¾ tsp salt
½ tsp grated nutmeg
¼ tsp ground black pepper
50 g/¾ oz brown sugar

Preheat the oven to 190°C/375°F/gas 5. Coat a 23 × 23 cm/9 × 9 in. ovenproof dish with non-stick spray.

Brown the butter in a small frying pan over medium heat, swirling the pan, until the butter turns a nutty colour. Remove from the heat and set aside.

Peel the sweet potatoes or yams, cut in half lengthways, and then into 1-cm/½-in. thick slices. Place in the prepared dish. Pour the orange juice over the sweet potatoes or yams. Sprinkle with the orange peel, salt, nutmeg, and pepper. Top with the brown sugar and browned butter. Cover and bake for 40–45 minutes, or until the sweet potatoes or yams are crisp-tender. Uncover and cook for 12–15 minutes, or until the juices are almost absorbed.

Makes 4 servings

Per serving: *204 calories, 2 g protein, 45 g carbohydrates, 3 g fat, 334 mg sodium, 2 g fibre*

Diet Exchanges: *0 milk, 0 vegetable, ½ fruit, 1½ bread, 0 meat, ½ fat*

FROM THE PROS

The Spa at Doral

You'll see sweet potatoes on the menu at many health spas. It's not that nutritionists think white potatoes are unhealthy, but sweet potatoes offer so much more flavour and nutrients per bite. The guests at the Spa at Doral love this creamy alternative to traditional mashed potatoes.

SWEET POTATO MASH

276 Calories

1 kg/2½ lb sweet potatoes
2 tbsp honey
10 g/⅓ oz butter or margarine
60 ml/2 fl oz semi-skimmed evaporated milk
½ tsp salt

Preheat the oven to 180°C/350°F/gas 4. Prick the sweet potatoes with a fork and bake on an oven rack for 1 hour, or until tender. Remove from the oven and set aside for 15 minutes, or until cool enough to handle. Cut the potatoes in half and scoop the flesh into a large bowl. Stir in the honey, butter or margarine, milk, and salt, mashing the potatoes as you stir.

Makes 4 servings

Per serving: *276 calories, 4 g protein, 61 g carbohydrates, 4 g fat, 147 mg sodium, 6 g fibre*

Diet Exchanges: *0 milk, 0 vegetable, 0 fruit, 4 bread, 0 meat, 1 fat*

Sherried Squash Bake

Daria Zawistowski

This comforting casserole makes a satisfying accompaniment to roast poultry. Any hard-skinned winter squash can be used, such as butternut, acorn, or kabacha.

1 kg/2 lb butternut squash, peeled, deseeded, and cut into cubes

115 ml/4 fl oz skimmed milk

2 tbsp plain flour

1 egg

2 tbsp cream sherry or apple juice

65 g/2¼ oz brown sugar

½ tsp salt

¼ tsp ground white or black pepper

⅛ tsp ground cinnamon

In a covered saucepan, heat 2.5 cm/1 in. of lightly salted water to boiling. Place the squash in a steamer basket and insert into the saucepan. Cover and simmer for 7 minutes, or until very tender.

Preheat the oven to 160°C/325°F/gas 3. Coat a 23 × 23 cm/9 × 9 in. ovenproof dish with non-stick spray.

In a large bowl with a mixer at medium speed, beat the squash, milk, flour, egg, sherry or apple juice, brown sugar, salt, and pepper. Spoon the mixture into the prepared dish. Sprinkle with the cinnamon. Bake for 30 minutes, or until a wooden cocktail stick inserted in the centre comes out clean.

Makes 8 servings

Per serving: 105 calories, 3 g protein, 23 g carbohydrates, 1 g fat, 127 mg sodium, 2 g fibre

Diet Exchanges: *0 milk, 0 vegetable, 0 fruit, 1 bread, 0 meat, 0 fat*

It Worked for Me!

Mark Ballard

VITAL STATS

Weight lost: 57 kg/8 st 13 lb

Time kept it off: 3½ years

Weight-loss strategies: Walking, vegetarian diet, keeping a food and exercise log

Weight-maintenance strategies: Has a 2-kg/4½-lb gain/loss window, weighs in twice a month, uses clothing fit as a guide, exercises daily

From 136 kg/ 21 st 6 lb and housebound to 79 kg/12½ st and an active life, Mark Ballard knows that losing weight and keeping it off takes a daily commitment.

'My first diet was in secondary school, but it wasn't until I turned 30 that I made a commitment to lose the weight and keep it off. By then, my weight wasn't the only thing that was unhealthfully high. My blood pressure began to soar as well. Ever since I could remember, my parents took blood pressure medication. I had friends whose families had never taken these drugs, and I wanted to be like them.

'My track record with diets wasn't very good, so this time I turned to exercise. I decided to start a walking programme. On my first day out, I made it only a short distance. I was so hot and tired, I wanted to give up then and there. But instead, I kept

going. Every day, I'd set little goals: "Tomorrow, I'll see if I can make it to that brown house and back." Within 6 months, I was walking for an hour and a half without stopping. Eventually, I picked up the pace and after a year and a half, I even ran a 10-km (6-mile) race just to prove to myself that I could do it.

'Once I started exercising, I started losing weight, which spurred me to change my eating habits, too. I didn't think I could give up sweets entirely, but I could do without fried foods and fatty meats. I didn't give up everything. If I wanted a piece of cake, I'd have it. But I kept tabs on myself. Everything I ate I recorded on a calendar. That kept me honest about just how many pieces of cake I'd had lately. The weight kept coming off.

'Now, I take part in life like I never have. I go out with my chilren to the gym or to parks. I go to parties. I have so much more energy. My career as an artist and designer is booming – I'm getting more clients – and that's a lot more fun than hanging around the kitchen sneaking biscuits.

'I've found that the motivation has to come from inside you. When you're losing weight, people comment and reinforce the loss. It gives you a little kick each time you drop a few kilos. But when you're just maintaining your weight, the comments stop. To stay motivated, I think back on what it took to get me to where I am today. I know by now that it's easier to keep the weight off than to have to go through taking it all off again.' ■

Mark's
Potatoes and Tomatoes Vinaigrette

213 Calories

"This makes a great side dish for grilled fish. Sometimes I have it as a light supper or lunch by itself. It keeps in the fridge for 3 to 4 days."

3 potatoes, cut into 2.5-cm/1-in. cubes

3 tbsp olive oil

60 ml/2 fl oz white wine vinegar

1 tbsp chopped fresh basil or 1 tsp dried

1 tbsp chopped fresh oregano or
   1 tsp dried

1 tsp garlic powder

2 tomatoes, finely chopped

1 green pepper, cut into 1-cm/½-in. strips

1 red pepper, cut into 1-cm/½-in. strips

1 small sweet onion, sliced

Place the potatoes in a large saucepan. Cover with water and heat to boiling over high heat. Reduce the heat to low, cover, and simmer for 10 minutes, or until the potatoes are tender. Drain and cool.

In a large bowl, combine the oil, vinegar, basil, oregano, and garlic powder. Add the tomatoes, peppers, onion, and potatoes. Toss to coat. Cover and marinate for 2 hours at room temperature.

Makes 4 servings

Per serving: *213 calories, 4 g protein, 24 g carbohydrates, 12 g fat, 15 mg sodium, 4 g fibre*

Diet Exchanges: *0 milk, 1 vegetable, 0 fruit, 2 bread, 0 meat, 1 fat*

Herb Rice

221 Calories

Scott Mingus

"I don't like to cook complicated dishes. This one is easy and tasty, and it goes with just about anything."

1 tsp olive oil
1 small onion, finely chopped
1 small garlic clove, finely chopped
200 g/7 oz long-grain white rice
1 tsp dried Italian seasoning
¼ tsp ground black pepper
1 bay leaf
450 ml/¾ pint vegetable stock
a knob of butter

Warm the oil in a medium saucepan over medium heat. Add the onion and garlic. Cook for 5 minutes, or until soft. Add the rice. Cook for 1 minute to coat with oil. Add the Italian seasoning, pepper, bay leaf, and stock. Heat to boiling. Reduce the heat to low, cover, and simmer for 20 minutes, or until the rice is tender and the liquid is absorbed. Remove and discard the bay leaf. Stir in the butter until distributed. Fluff with a fork before serving.

Makes 4 servings

Per serving: *221 calories, 4 g protein, 42 g carbohydrates, 4 g fat, 313 mg sodium, 1 g fibre*

Diet Exchanges: *0 milk, 0 vegetable, 0 fruit, 1¼ bread, 0 meat, 0 fat*

(Photograph on page 180)

Portobello Brown Rice

Ellen Burr,

"Meaty, earthy portobello mushrooms are a great complement to the nutty flavour of brown rice."

117 Calories

100 g/3½ oz brown rice
1 tbsp vegetable oil
170 g/6 oz portobello mushrooms, sliced
1 small onion, chopped
2 garlic cloves, finely chopped
½ tsp lemon-pepper seasoning
¼ tsp ground turmeric
¼ tsp dried thyme
30 g/1 oz dried cranberries
30 g/1 oz shelled pistachios, chopped
3 tbsp chopped parsley

Cook the rice according to packet directions.

Meanwhile, warm the oil in a large non-stick frying pan over medium-high heat. Add the mushrooms, onion, garlic, lemon-pepper seasoning, and turmeric. Cook for 5 minutes, or until the onion is tender. Stir in the thyme, cranberries, pistachios, parsley, and rice. Reduce the heat to low and cook for 5 minutes, or until heated through.

Makes 4 servings

Per serving: *117 calories, 3 g protein, 23 g carbohydrates, 2 g fat, 5 mg sodium, 4 g fibre*

Diet Exchanges: *0 milk, 1 vegetable, 0 fruit, 2 bread, 0 meat, 1 fat*

Black Beans and Rice

369 Calories

Connie Gregg

"Some nights, my daughter and I make a big green salad and make a dinner out of this dish. It also complements Mexican-style main dishes like burritos and enchiladas."

200 g/7 oz white rice

500 g/1 lb cooked black beans, rinsed and drained

115 g/4 oz bottled or canned green chilli peppers, drained and chopped

225 g/8 oz salsa

60 g/2 oz grated reduced-fat Cheddar cheese (optional)

Cook the rice according to packet directions.

Preheat the oven to 180°C/350°F/gas 4.

Add the beans, peppers, and salsa to the cooked rice. Place over low heat and cook, stirring frequently, for 5 minutes, or until heated through. Spoon into a serving dish. Sprinkle with the cheese, if using.

Bake for 10 minutes, or until the cheese melts.

Makes 4 servings

Per serving: *369 calories, 20 g protein,65 g carbohydrates, 4 g fat, 309 mg sodium, 4 g fibre*

Diet Exchanges: *0 milk, 0 vegetable, 0 fruit, 2 bread, 0 meat, 0 fat*

FROM THE PROS

Green Mountain at Fox Run

Marsha Hudnall, the owner and resident dietitian at this health resort, is a firm believer that healthy weight comes from a healthy relationship with food. At Green Mountain, that means serving great-tasting meals that fill your body and soul.

ALMOND-MUSHROOM RICE CASSEROLE

458 Calories

350 g/12 oz sliced mushrooms

2 tbsp chopped onion

75 g/2¾ oz slivered almonds

1 tsp dried basil

½ tsp dried oregano

1¼ tsp dried thyme

450 g/1 lb cooked brown rice

225 g/8 oz low-fat cottage cheese

125 ml/4 fl oz vegetable or chicken stock

1 tsp reduced-sodium soy sauce

115 g/4 oz grated Jarlsberg cheese

Preheat the oven to 180°C/350°F/gas 4.

Coat a large non-stick frying pan with non-stick spray and warm over medium heat. Add the mushrooms, onion, almonds, basil, oregano, and thyme. Cook 8 minutes, or until mushrooms release their liquid. Remove from the heat and spoon into a large bowl. Stir in the rice, cottage cheese, stock, and soy sauce. Spoon into a 23 × 23 cm/9 × 9 in. ovenproof dish and top with the cheese.

Cover and bake for 10 minutes, or until the cheese is melted.

Makes 4 servings

Per serving: *458 calories, 25 g protein, 40 g carbohydrates, 23 g fat, 717 mg sodium, 4 g fibre*

Diet Exchanges: *0 milk, 0 vegetable, 0 fruit, 3 bread, 1¼ meat, 0 fat*

Broccoli-Cheese Spoon Bread

259 Calories

Julie DeMatteo

"I believe that healthful eating habits should be taught to our children at an early age. One way is to serve vegetables in a child-friendly style. My two sons love this low-fat dish."

200 ml/7fl oz semi-skimmed evaporated milk

75 g/2¾ oz yellow cornmeal

½ tsp sugar

¼ tsp ground white or black pepper

60 g/2 oz grated reduced-fat extra-sharp Cheddar cheese

2 large eggs

2 large egg whites

340 g/12 oz frozen chopped broccoli, thawed and drained

60 g/2 oz chopped roasted red peppers

¼ tsp salt

Preheat the oven to 190°C/375°F/gas 5. Coat a 1-litre/2-pint ovenproof dish with non-stick spray.

In a medium saucepan over medium heat, gently stir the evaporated milk. Gradually add the cornmeal and cook, stirring constantly, for 2–3 minutes, or until thickened. Remove from the heat and stir in the sugar, white or black pepper, and 6 tablespoons of cheese. Stir until cheese melts.

Place the eggs in a small bowl. Add 4 tablespoons of the milk mixture, stirring constantly. Stir the egg mixture back into the milk mixture.

In a medium bowl, beat the egg whites until stiff. Fold into the milk mixture. Fold in the broccoli, roasted peppers, and salt. Pour into the prepared dish. Bake for 45–50 minutes, or until set. Sprinkle with the remaining cheese.

Makes 4 servings

Per serving: *259 calories, 21 g protein, 24 g carbohydrates, 9 g fat, 376 mg sodium, 3 g fibre*

Diet Exchanges: *½ milk, 2 vegetable, 0 fruit, 0 bread, 1 meat, 0 fat*

Chicken Stuffing Casserole

Pamela Wheeler

76 Calories

"Cooking a turkey or chicken stuffing in an ovenproof dish speeds up the time needed to roast the bird. And it's healthier from a food-safety point of view because leftovers are stored separately."

225 g/8 oz poultry-flavoured stuffing

30 g/1 oz dried mushrooms (shiitake or porcini)

20 g/¾ oz dry-packed sun-dried tomatoes

1 tbsp olive oil

1 small onion, chopped

1 celery stick, chopped

370 ml/13 fl oz hot vegetable or chicken stock

40 g/1½ oz raisins

2 tbsp chopped parsley

½ tsp dried rosemary, crumbled

¼ tsp ground black pepper

Place stuffing in a 2-litre/3½-pint ovenproof dish.

Soak the mushrooms and tomatoes in hot water for 12 minutes, or until soft. Drain and chop. Stir into the stuffing.

Preheat the oven to 230°C/450°F/gas 8.

Warm the oil in a medium frying pan over medium heat. Add the onion and celery, and cook for 5 minutes, or until soft. Add to the stuffing with the stock, raisins, parsley, rosemary, and pepper. Mix well. Cover and bake for 30 minutes, or until heated through.

Makes 8 servings

Per serving: *76 calories, 1 g protein, 10 g carbohydrates, 4 g fat, 291 mg sodium, 1 g fibre*

Diet Exchanges: *0 milk, 1 vegetable, 0 fruit, 1½ bread, 0 meat, ½ fat*

Diet Exchanges: *0 milk, 0 vegetable, 0 fruit, 1 bread, 0 meat, 0 fat*

EASY WAYS TO EAT MORE VEGETABLES AND FRUIT

You've heard the recommendation about eating more fruit and vegetables. The trick is adding them when they're not the main attraction. That way, you'll focus on the main dish but still get the benefits of eating these good-for-you foods. Another benefit is that you'll be full before you overeat. The fibre in vegetables and fruit is very filling and helps keep digestion moving smoothly.

Five servings a day is considered the absolute minimum. It's not as difficult as you think. First, most servings are just a couple of tablespoons. So, if you normally start your day with a small glass of orange juice, you've knocked off two servings right there. A sandwich made with lots of tomatoes and lettuce is another. A mid-afternoon fruit snack and a serving of vegetables at dinner, and you've nailed it. Not so bad. Here are some more ideas.

- Toss broccoli florets, red or green pepper strips, grated carrots, shredded spinach, peas, or sun-dried tomatoes into the cooking water before draining your pasta. These veggies will cook in minutes and add flavour, texture, and colour (not to mention nutrients) to your meal.

- Keep a bag of fresh baby carrots in your handbag, briefcase, or desk drawer. Munch on those whenever you feel the need to nibble.

- Add spinach, broccoli, or red or green peppers to your pizza, and tomatoes or sprouts to your sandwiches.

- Start your next restaurant meal with a salad. (See page 245 for the Best Salad Add-Ins.)

- End your next meal with sorbet, fruit crumble, marinated fruit, or another fruit-based dessert.

- Use the last of the warm coals from your barbecue to grill fruits for dessert. When grilled, the natural sugars in fruit caramelize, creating a rich flavour. Try sliced pineapple, bananas (in their skins), apple chunks skewered with pears, and whole peaches. They're delicious served with low-fat vanilla frozen yogurt and sprinkled with grated nutmeg or ground cinnamon.

- Choose fruit juice or vegetable juice instead of carbonated soft drinks. (With that choice, you'll also save about 125 calories, on average.)

- Eat the orange wedges that are served at the end of a meal in a Chinese restaurant, or eat the fruit or vegetable garnishes that come with just about any restaurant meal.

Slimming Salads and Dressings

Sweet and Creamy Spinach Salad

93 Calories

Helen Gelb

"This soured cream-based dressing is good on any greens, but I especially like it on fresh spinach with crumbled bacon. The children love it, too, so it's a good way to get them to eat their greens without a fuss."

115 g/4 oz soured cream

1 tbsp milk

2 tbsp sugar

1 tbsp red wine vinegar

½ tsp salt

¼ tsp ground black pepper

300 g/10 oz fresh spinach, torn

1 head romaine lettuce, torn

2 celery sticks, thinly sliced

1 small red onion, thinly sliced

4 rashers streaky bacon, cooked
   and crumbled

In a small bowl, mix the soured cream, milk, sugar, vinegar, salt, and pepper.

In a large bowl, combine the spinach, lettuce, celery, onion, and bacon. Add the dressing and toss to coat.

Makes 8 servings

Per serving: *93 calories, 4 g protein, 6 g carbohydrates, 6 g fat, 308 mg sodium, 1 g fibre*

Diet Exchanges: *0 milk, 2 vegetable, 0 fruit, 0 bread, 0 meat, ½ fat*

Hail Caesar Salad

104 Calories

Susan Nichols

"My husband and I both like to cook and eat. We try to come up with recipes that are low-fat and healthy. Here's one of our successes. We added and subtracted ingredients until it met our standards for taste and health."

2 tbsp extra-virgin olive oil

2 tbsp chicken stock

1 tbsp fat-free natural yogurt

½ tsp lemon juice

½ tsp Worcestershire sauce

½–1 tsp anchovy paste

1 garlic clove, finely chopped

¼ tsp ground black pepper

⅛ tsp hot-pepper sauce

1 head romaine lettuce, torn

3 tbsp grated Parmesan cheese

30 g/1 oz plain croutons

In a large bowl, mix the oil, stock, yogurt, lemon juice, Worcestershire sauce, anchovy paste, garlic, black pepper, and hot-pepper sauce. Add the lettuce, cheese, and croutons. Toss to coat.

Makes 4 servings

Per serving: *104 calories, 4 g protein, 5 g carbohydrates, 8 g fat, 164 mg sodium, 1 g fibre*

Diet Exchanges: *0 milk, 2 vegetable, 0 fruit, 3 bread, 0 meat, 1½ fat*

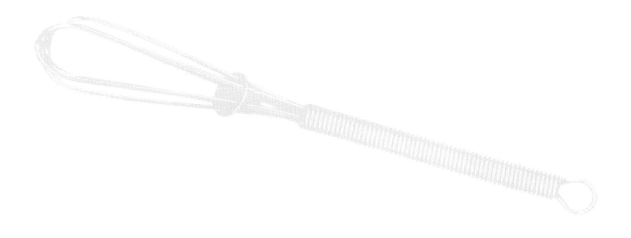

Deirdra Price, PhD

Author and weight-loss expert Deirdra Price, PhD, has a simple eating philosophy: weight control is a matter of enjoying, not being afraid of, food. We couldn't agree more. Here's a satisfying salad that's not fattening or frightening.

PERSIAN CUCUMBER SALAD

49 Calories

1 cucumber, peeled and cubed

2 plum tomatoes, deseeded and finely chopped

30 g/1 oz chopped red onion

3 tbsp chopped parsley

2 tbsp lemon juice

1 tbsp extra-virgin olive oil

⅛ tsp salt

⅛ tsp ground black pepper

In a medium bowl, combine the cucumber, tomatoes, onion, and parsley.

In a small bowl, mix the lemon juice, oil, salt, and pepper. Pour over the salad and toss to mix. Let marinate for 30 minutes to allow the flavours to develop.

Makes 4 servings

Per serving: *49 calories, 1 g protein, 3 g carbohydrates, 4 g fat, 104 mg sodium, 1 g fibre*

Diet Exchanges: *0 milk, 2 vegetable, 0 fruit, 0 bread, 0 meat, ½ fat*

Teriyaki Turkey Salad

298 Calories

Paul Serkin.

"Depending on the weather, I grill or barbecue the turkey for this versatile dish. It can be served warm or cold over salad greens or pasta."

50 g/1¾ oz brown sugar

50 ml/1¾ fl oz reduced-sodium soy sauce

2 tbsp lemon juice

1 tbsp vegetable oil

1 tbsp sesame oil

1 garlic clove, finely chopped

¼ tsp ground ginger

500 g/1 lb boneless, skinless turkey breast, cut into 2.5-cm/1-in. cubes

75 g/2½ oz mixed salad greens (red leaf, round, rocket, watercress)

4 tbsp toasted cashews

In a large resealable plastic bag, combine the brown sugar, soy sauce, lemon juice, vegetable oil, sesame oil, garlic, and ginger. Add the turkey. Seal and refrigerate for at least 20 minutes or up to 3 hours, stirring occasionally.

Coat the grill rack with non-stick spray and preheat the grill. Thread the meat on to 4 metal skewers. Barbecue over medium-hot coals or grill 10 cm/4 in. from the heat for 15 minutes, or until the centre of the meat is no longer pink and the juices run clear, turning occasionally.

Divide the salad greens between 4 plates. Top each with a skewer and garnish with the cashews.

Makes 4 servings

Per serving: *298 calories, 33 g protein, 15 g carbohydrates, 12 g fat, 783 mg sodium, 1 g fibre*

Diet Exchanges: *0 milk, 0 vegetable, 0 fruit, 1 bread, 3 meat, 0 fat*

Asian Slaw

Paige Morehouse

*"When I feel like grilling fish or burgers, I serve this on the side.
In the cooler months, I add 300 g/10 oz of cooked rice and 225 g/8 oz of shredded
cooked chicken to make a complete meal."*

85 g/3 oz grated broccoli stems

85 g/3 oz grated carrots

60 g/2 oz chopped celery

40 g/1½ oz mushrooms, sliced

30 g/1 oz sliced red pepper

60 ml/2 fl oz seasoned rice vinegar

1 tbsp vegetable oil

1 tsp sesame oil

2–3 drops hot-pepper sauce

1 tbsp chopped dry roasted peanuts

1 tbsp chopped fresh coriander leaves

In a large bowl, combine the broccoli stems, carrots, celery, mushrooms, and pepper.

In a small bowl, mix the vinegar, vegetable oil, sesame oil, and hot-pepper sauce. Pour over the salad. Garnish with the peanuts and coriander leaves.

Makes 4 servings

Per serving: *55 calories, 2 g protein, 3 g carbohydrates, 5 g fat, 56 mg sodium, 2 g fibre*

Diet Exchanges: *0 milk, 2 vegetable, 0 fruit, 0 bread, 0 meat, ½ fat*

(Photograph on page 118)

Grilled Summer Salad

Darlene Fairfax

"This very low-fat salad can be made in advance and served at room temperature. Remember it when you're grilling chicken or fish or even to dress up burgers."

DRESSING

115 g/4 oz apricot jam

75 ml/3 fl oz balsamic vinegar

1 garlic clove, finely chopped

1 tsp chopped fresh rosemary or
    ½ tsp dried

¼ tsp salt

SALAD

1 small aubergine, quartered lengthways

1 large sweet onion, sliced 1-cm/
    ½-in. thick

1 large courgette, sliced 1-cm/½-in. thick

1 large red, yellow, or orange pepper, cut
    into strips

140 g/5 oz assorted salad greens (red leaf,
    round, rocket, watercress)

To make the dressing:

In a small saucepan, combine the jam, vinegar, garlic, rosemary, and salt. Heat to boiling over medium heat, stirring frequently. Remove from the heat.

To make the salad:

Preheat the barbecue or grill. Coat the grill rack with non-stick spray.

Barbecue the aubergine, onion, courgette, and pepper over medium-hot coals or grill 10 cm/4 in. from the heat for 8–10 minutes, or until tender. Turn the vegetables occasionally and brush with the dressing.

Arrange the salad greens on a serving platter and top with the grilled vegetables. Pour any remaining dressing over the vegetables.

Makes 4 servings

Per serving: *69 calories, 2 g protein, 14 g carbohydrates, 1 g fat, 209 mg sodium, 3 g fibre*

Diet Exchanges: *0 milk, 4 vegetable, 0 fruit, ½ bread, 0 meat, 0 fat*

DRESSINGS TO LIVE BY

A plate of greens is a good thing. Just be smart about what goes on top. A major source of fat in an otherwise healthy diet is salad dressing.

Here are some satisfying, but not sabotaging, salad dressings. If you have a small jar with a tight-fitting lid, you can shake up these dressings and store them in the fridge for a few days.

Each recipe makes enough to coat about 4 servings.

TAHINI DRESSING

2 tbsp extra-virgin olive oil

1 tbsp tahini (sesame paste)

1 tbsp umeboshi plum vinegar
(see tip)

1 tbsp cider vinegar

1 tsp Dijon mustard

$\frac{1}{4}$ tsp salt

$\frac{1}{8}$ tsp ground black pepper

In a jar or small bowl, mix the oil, tahini, plum vinegar, cider vinegar, mustard, salt, and pepper.

Per serving: *89 calories, 1 g protein, 1 g carbohydrates, 10 g fat, 99 mg sodium, 0 g fibre*

Diet Exchanges: *0 milk, 0 vegetable, 0 fruit, 0 bread, 0 meat, 2 fat*

TIP: *Umeboshi plum vinegar is a tart, salty Japanese vinegar available in Oriental food stores and health food stores.*

RANCHO LA PUERTA BASIL YOGURT DRESSING

60 g/2 oz fat-free natural yogurt

1 shallot, finely chopped

1 spring onion, chopped

1 garlic clove, finely chopped

2 tbsp red wine vinegar

2 tbsp balsamic vinegar

2 tbsp water

1 tbsp chopped fresh basil

$\frac{1}{2}$ tsp ground black pepper

$\frac{1}{2}$ tsp chopped fresh thyme

$\frac{1}{4}$ tsp chopped fresh coriander leaves

In a jar or small bowl, mix the yogurt, shallot, spring onion, garlic, red wine vinegar, balsamic vinegar, water, basil, pepper, thyme, and coriander leaves.

Per serving: *12 calories, 1 g protein, 2 g carbohydrates, 0 g fat, 12 mg sodium, 0 g fibre*

Diet Exchanges: *0 milk, $\frac{1}{2}$ vegetable, 0 fruit, 0 bread, 0 meat, 0 fat*

CREAMY RANCH DRESSING

2 tbsp low-fat cottage cheese
2 tsp grated Parmesan cheese
1½ tsp low-fat natural yogurt
1 tsp lemon juice
1 tsp water
1 shallot, finely chopped
1 garlic clove, finely chopped
½ tsp chopped fresh basil
½ tsp chopped fresh oregano
Pinch of ground black pepper

In a jar or small bowl, mix the cottage cheese, Parmesan, yogurt, lemon juice, water, shallot, garlic, basil, oregano, and pepper.

Per serving: *26 calories, 2 g protein, 1 g carbohydrates, 1 g fat, , 57 mg sodium, 0 g fibre*

Diet Exchanges: *0 milk, 0 vegetable, 0 fruit, 0 bread, 0 meat, ½ fat*

BLUE CHEESE DRESSING

30 g/1 oz crumbled blue cheese
2 tbsp extra-virgin olive oil
2 tbsp brewed strong black tea
1 tbsp red wine vinegar
1 shallot, finely chopped
1 tsp Dijon mustard
¼ tsp Worcestershire sauce
¼ tsp salt
Pinch of ground black pepper

In a jar or small bowl, mix the blue cheese, oil, tea, vinegar, shallot, mustard, Worcestershire sauce, salt, and pepper.

Per serving: *99 calories, 2 g protein, 1 g carbohydrates, 10 g fat, 199 mg sodium, 0 g fibre*

Diet Exchanges: *0 milk, 0 vegetable, 0 fruit, 0 bread, 0 meat, 2 fat*

ROAST GARLIC LEMON DRESSING

1 whole bulb garlic
3 tbsp lemon juice
1 tbsp oil
1 tbsp water
⅛ tsp salt
2 tbsp chopped parsley

Preheat the oven to 200°C/400°F/ gas 6. Wrap the garlic in foil and bake on an oven rack for 45 minutes, or until soft. Cool slightly. Squeeze the garlic from its skins into a blender or food processor. Add the lemon juice, oil, water, and salt. Blend or process until smooth. Stir in the parsley.

Per serving: *45 calories, 1 g protein, 2 g carbohydrates, 4 g fat, 100 mg sodium, 1 g fibre*

Diet Exchanges: *0 milk, 0 vegetable, 0 fruit, 0 bread, 0 meat, 1 fat*

Romaine Salad with Sherry Vinaigrette

M. Baldwin

"The nutty flavour of sherry vinegar pairs well with walnuts and blue cheese."

108 Calories

2 tbsp extra-virgin olive oil

3 tbsp sherry vinegar

1 tbsp low-fat mayonnaise

1 tbsp lemon juice

1 tsp sugar

¼ tsp salt

¼ tsp ground white or black pepper

1 head romaine lettuce, torn

1 red pepper, chopped

60 g/2 oz toasted walnuts, chopped

30 g/1 oz crumbled blue cheese

In a small bowl, mix the oil, vinegar, mayonnaise, lemon juice, sugar, salt, and white or black pepper.

In a large bowl, combine the lettuce, red pepper, walnuts, and cheese. Add the dressing and toss to coat.

Makes 8 servings

Per serving: *108 calories, 2 g protein, 2 g carbohydrates, 10 g fat, 104 mg sodium, 2 g fibre*

Diet Exchanges: *0 milk, 1 vegetable, 0 fruit, 0 bread, 0 meat, 2 fat*

Wonderful Tuna Salad

Doretha Coval

"This salad makes a fantastic toasted sandwich with crusty bread. When the weather's cool, I fry the sandwich in a frying pan with a little non-stick spray. Don't let the pineapple put you off – it's delicious."

340 g/12 oz canned tuna in water, drained

85 g/3 oz fat-free natural yogurt

120 g/4 oz canned crushed pineapple, drained

1 celery stick, finely chopped

3 tbsp finely chopped sweet pickles or gherkins

20 g/³⁄₄ oz pecans, chopped

1 tsp yellow mustard

¹⁄₈ tsp ground cinnamon

In a medium bowl, mix the tuna, yogurt, pineapple, celery, sweet pickles or gherkins, pecans, mustard, and cinnamon.

Makes 4 servings

Per serving: *139 calories, 20 g protein, 6 g carbohydrates, 4 g fat, 306 mg sodium, 1 g fibre*

Diet Exchanges: *¹⁄₂ milk, 0 vegetable, 1 fruit, 0 bread, 1 meat, 0 fat*

139 Calories

Crab Salad

254 Calories

Suzanne Exler

"I especially enjoy this in the summer with a fresh baguette and some greens."

300 g/10 oz low-fat natural yogurt

60 g/2 oz low-fat mayonnaise

4 tbsp chopped fresh dill

1 tbsp chopped fresh tarragon or
   1 tsp dried

2 tsp Dijon mustard

¼ tsp salt

500 g/1 lb crabmeat, chopped

2 cucumbers, deseeded and chopped

4 spring onions, chopped

In a large bowl, mix the yogurt, mayonnaise, dill, tarragon, mustard, and salt. Stir in the crabmeat, cucumbers, and spring onions. Cover and refrigerate for at least 3 hours to blend the flavours.

Makes 4 servings

Per serving: *254 calories, 26 g protein, 10 g carbohydrates, 12 g fat, 689 mg sodium, 1 g fibre*

Diet Exchanges: *1 milk, 0 vegetable, 0 fruit, 0 bread, 2 meat, 0 fat*

Tuscan Tuna Salad

137 Calories

Kristen O'Brien

"This isn't your ordinary tuna salad. A light and flavourful vinaigrette and white beans turn the old sandwich filling into a satisfying meal. If there's no bread in the house, I serve it on a bed of salad greens."

2 tbsp lemon juice

2 tbsp whole-grain mustard

1 tbsp olive oil

1 tbsp balsamic or red wine vinegar

1 garlic clove, finely chopped

¼ tsp salt

¼ tsp ground black pepper

450 g/1 lb canned cannellini beans, rinsed and drained

170 g/6 oz canned tuna in water, drained

3 tbsp chopped fresh basil

tomato wedges (optional)

In a large bowl, mix the lemon juice, mustard, oil, vinegar, garlic, salt, and pepper. Add the beans, tuna, and basil. Toss to mix. Serve with the tomato wedges, if using.

Makes 4 servings

Per serving: *137 calories, 8 g protein, 17 g carbohydrates, 5 g fat, 103 mg sodium, 3 g fibre*

Diet Exchanges: *0 milk, 0 vegetable, 0 fruit, 1½ bread, 1 meat, 0 fat*

Sesame Chicken Salad

344 Calories

Cherie Groves

"You don't have to bread and deep-fry chicken to make it crunchy and crisp. This recipe uses sesame seeds for crunch and oven heat for cooking. Teriyaki sauce keeps the chicken moist and flavourful."

500 g/1 lb boneless, skinless chicken breasts, cut into thin strips

3 tbsp teriyaki sauce

30 g/1 oz sesame seeds

500 g/1 lb coleslaw mix

140 g/5 oz Oriental fried noodles

115 g/4 oz low-fat honey Dijon salad dressing

Place the chicken in a shallow bowl, toss with the teriyaki sauce, and let sit for 10 minutes.

Preheat the oven to 180°C/350°F/gas 4.

Place the sesame seeds on greaseproof paper. Roll the chicken in sesame seeds to coat. Arrange on a baking tray and bake for 10–12 minutes, or until chicken is no longer pink, turning once.

Divide the coleslaw between 4 plates. Top each with chicken and noodles, and drizzle with the dressing.

Makes 4 servings

Per serving: *344 calories, 41 g protein, 11 g carbohydrates, 15 g fat, 310 mg sodium, 3 g fibre*

Diet Exchanges: *0 milk, 1 vegetable, 0 fruit, 1 bread, 2 meat, 0 fat*

Warm Pepper and Pork Salad

117 Calories

Karen Gazaway

"When I'm in a real hurry, I use leftover pork or chicken and bottled roast peppers instead of starting with fresh. I just warm them in the microwave. A sprinkle of sunflower seeds on top is nice, too."

3 red, green, and/or yellow peppers, deseeded and quartered

225 g/8 oz lean pork tenderloin

2 tsp olive oil

½ onion, thinly sliced

¼ red cabbage, thinly sliced

2 celery sticks, thinly sliced

½ tsp salt

⅛ tsp ground black pepper

60 ml/2 fl oz balsamic vinaigrette dressing

30 g/1 oz mozzarella cheese, grated

Preheat the grill. Place the peppers on a grill pan and cook 10 cm/4 in. from the heat, turning occasionally, until the skins are bubbly and brown all over. Transfer to a paper bag, seal, and set aside for 5 minutes, or until cool enough to handle. Remove and discard skin, ribs, and seeds. Cut the peppers into strips.

Place the pork on the grill pan and cook for 12–15 minutes, turning once, or until a thermometer inserted in the centre reaches 68°C/155°F and the juices run clear. Let stand for 10 minutes, then cut into thin slices.

Warm the oil in a medium frying pan over medium heat. Add the onion, cabbage, celery, salt, and black pepper. Cook for 10 minutes, or until tender, stirring frequently.

Divide the cabbage mixture between 4 plates. Arrange the peppers and pork on top. Drizzle each with the dressing and sprinkle with 1 tablespoon cheese.

Makes 4 servings

Per serving: *117 calories, 15 g protein, 6 g carbohydrates, 4 g fat, 469 mg sodium, 2 g fibre*

Diet Exchanges: *0 milk, 3 vegetable, 0 fruit, 0 bread, 1½ meat, 0 fat*

Pork Salad with Black-Eyed Bean Dressing

187 Calories

Nancy Rossi Brownell

"A little freshly ground black pepper and some hot crusty bread, and this meal is complete. Use a mix of greens like round, frisée, radicchio, mâche, and romaine for more texture, flavour, and colour."

410 ml/14½ fl oz chicken stock

60 ml/2 fl oz dry sherry or apple juice

1 tbsp chopped fresh tarragon or
  1 tsp dried

2 garlic cloves, finely chopped

½ tsp paprika

¼ tsp ground sage

¼ tsp ground cumin

1 large sweet onion, thinly sliced

2 boneless centre-cut pork loin chops,
  trimmed of visible fat (about 60–85 g/
  2–3 oz each)

500 g/1 lb cooked black-eyed beans,
  rinsed and drained

1 tbsp Dijon mustard

300 g/10 oz mixed salad greens (red leaf,
  round, rocket, watercress)

In a medium frying pan over medium-high heat, combine 115 ml/4 fl oz stock, the sherry or apple juice, tarragon, garlic, paprika, sage, cumin, and onion. Heat to boiling and add the pork. Reduce the heat to low, cover, and simmer, turning the meat once, for 5 minutes, or until a thermometer inserted in centre of the pork registers 68°C/155°F and the juices run clear. Transfer the pork to a plate and set aside. Stir in the remaining stock, black-eyed beans, and mustard. Increase the heat to medium-high and heat to boiling. Cook, uncovered, for 10 minutes, or until the mixture is reduced by half.

Thinly slice the pork on the diagonal. Divide the salad greens between 4 large plates. Arrange the pork on top and drizzle with the dressing.

Makes 4 servings

Per serving: *187 calories, 16 g protein, 28 g carbohydrates, 2 g fat, 306 mg sodium, 5 g fibre*

Diet Exchanges: *0 milk, 2 vegetable, 0 fruit, 1 bread, 1 meat, 0 fat*

BEST SALAD ADD-INS

Salad bars have become the food equivalent of the Internet: too many choices! Here's a hint for navigating your way down the line: the shinier the item, the more fattening it is. How can we be so sure? Because shiny equals oil, as in salad dressings. A thick coating of oil also ensures that ingredients, which have to withstand long hours of display, don't dry out. So go easy on the glossy choices.

Here are the healthiest items on display, plus a few crunchy treats that won't boost calories too much. They're listed from highest to lowest according to calories.

Food	Calories	Food	Calories
2 tablespoons sesame seeds	110	3 tablespoons red onions	15
2 tablespoons chickpeas	91	3 tablespoons grated carrots	12
2 pickled beetroot	65	3 tablespoons chopped peppers	10
2 tablespoons raisins	54	2 tablespoons radicchio	9
2 tablespoons bacon bits	48	2 tablespoons romaine lettuce	8
5 pieces baby corn	43	3 tablespoons mung bean sprouts	8
2 tablespoons chopped hard-boiled eggs	40	3 tablespoons alfalfa sprouts	7
2 tablespoons chow mein noodles	30	2 tablespoons endive	7
2 tablespoons red kidney beans	28	2 tablespoons iceberg lettuce	7
2 tablespoons sliced fennel	27	2 tablespoons spinach	7
5 olives	25	3 tablespoons sliced mushrooms	6
2 tablespoons croutons	23	2 tablespoons rocket	5
5 baby carrots	19	2 tablespoons chopped spring onions	4
5 cherry tomatoes	18	2 tablespoons watercress	4
2 tablespoons grated cabbage	17	5 cucumber slices	3
		2 tablespoons chopped celery	2

Kidney Bean and Corn Salad

263 Calories

Robin Kenwood

"If you like high-flavour food, try this salad. It serves 4 as a main-dish salad or 6 as a side dish. It keeps in the refrigerator for a couple of days."

425 g/15 oz canned kidney beans, rinsed and drained

500 g/1 lb sweetcorn, fresh or frozen and defrosted

2 jalapeño chilli peppers, deseeded and finely chopped (wear rubber gloves when handling)

2 plum tomatoes, deseeded and chopped

60 g/2 oz finely chopped red onion

2 garlic cloves, finely chopped

3 tbsp chopped fresh coriander leaves

2 tbsp lime juice

1 tbsp olive oil

2 tsp taco or fajita seasoning mix

¼ tsp salt

In a large bowl, combine the beans, sweetcorn corn, peppers, tomatoes, onion, garlic, and coriander leaves.

In a small bowl, mix the lime juice, oil, seasoning mix, and salt. Pour over the salad. Cover and refrigerate for 1 hour to allow the flavours to develop.

Makes 4 servings

Per serving: *263 calories, 12 g protein, 41 g carbohydrates, 7 g fat, 690 mg sodium, 9 g fibre*

Diet Exchanges: *0 milk, 1 vegetable, 0 fruit, 2 bread, 0 meat, ½ fat*

Lentil–Rice Salad

374 Calories

Frances Taylor

"I like the fennel in this salad, but another flavour can be used, such as ground coriander or cumin. Sometimes I serve it without the onion and dressing for a nutritious hot rice dish."

100 g/3½ oz dry brown lentils

1 tbsp curry powder

300 g/10 oz cooked basmati rice

60 g/2 oz finely chopped Spanish onion

70 g/2½ oz pine nuts

85 g/3 oz raisins or currants

1 tsp fennel seeds, crushed (see tip)

2 tbsp extra-virgin olive oil

1 tbsp white wine vinegar

½ tsp mustard powder

½ tsp salt

Place the lentils in a large saucepan. Cover with water and add the curry powder. Heat to boiling over high heat. Reduce the heat to low, cover, and simmer for 20 minutes. Drain and set aside to cool. Add the rice, onion, nuts, raisins or currants, and fennel seeds.

In a small bowl, mix the oil, vinegar, mustard powder, and salt. Pour over the salad and toss to mix.

Makes 4 servings

Per serving: *374 calories, 20 g protein, 43 g carbohydrates, 20 g fat, 212 mg sodium, 2 g fibre*

Diet Exchanges: *0 milk, 0 vegetable, 0 fruit, 3 bread, 0 meat, 4 fat*

TIP: To crush fennel seeds, use a pestle and mortar. Alternatively, place the seeds between sheets of greaseproof paper and crush with a rolling pin or the bottom of a small, heavy saucepan.

Beans, Beans, Beans Salad

135 Calories

Navarre Bautista

"I took a classic three-bean salad and updated it. It's still a winner. Use your favourite bean combination, like kidney beans, green beans, chickpeas, or cannellini beans."

1.25 kg/3 lb cooked or canned beans (such as kidney, green, cannellini), rinsed and drained

1 green pepper, cut into thin strips

1 small red onion, thinly sliced

200 g/7 oz bottled roasted red peppers, drained and cut into strips

75 ml/2½ fl oz balsamic vinegar

60 ml/2 fl oz olive oil

1 tsp salt

1 tsp dried Italian seasoning

½ tsp mustard powder

¼ tsp ground black pepper

In a large bowl, combine the beans, greenpepper, onion, roasted peppers, vinegar, oil, salt, Italian seasoning, mustard powder, and black pepper. Toss to mix. Cover and refrigerate for 2 hours or overnight.

Makes 8 servings

Per serving: *135 calories, 5 g protein, 11 g carbohydrates, 8 g fat, 525 mg sodium, 4 g fibre*

Diet Exchanges: *0 milk, 0 vegetable, 0 fruit, 2 bread, 0 meat, 1 fat*

Dean Ornish, MD

In his research at the Preventive Medicine Research Institute in Sausalito, California, Dr Dean Ornish demonstrated that heart disease can be reversed without drugs or surgery. One of the best 'side effects' of his plan is weight loss. Dr Ornish's approach includes exercise, stress control, and a mostly vegetarian diet. But that doesn't mean eating bizarre food. This delicious salad is about as mainstream, yet lean, as you can get.

OLD-FASHIONED POTATO SALAD

190 Calories

3 eggs

1.25 kg/3 lb potatoes

3 celery sticks, finely chopped

1 small red onion, finely chopped

170 g/6 oz low-fat mayonnaise

60 ml/2 fl oz cider vinegar

3 tbsp finely chopped sweet pickles or gherkins

1 tbsp chopped parsley

1½ tsp salt

¼ tsp ground black pepper

Place the eggs in a small saucepan. Cover with hot water and heat to boiling over high heat. Reduce the heat to low, cover, and simmer for 12 minutes. Drain and cool in cold water. Remove and discard the egg shells. Cut the eggs in half. Remove and discard the yolks. Chop the whites.

Heat 5 cm/2 in. water to boiling in a large saucepan. Put potatoes in a steamer basket and place in the saucepan. Cover and steam for 30–35 minutes, or until fork-tender. Remove from the heat and set aside to cool. When cool enough to handle, peel and cut into small cubes.

In a large bowl, combine the celery, onion, mayonnaise, vinegar, sweet pickles or gherkins, parsley, salt, pepper, potatoes, and egg whites.

Makes 8 servings

Per serving: *190 calories, 5 g protein, 30 g carbohydrates, 6 g fat, 359 mg sodium, 3 g fibre*

Diet Exchanges: *0 milk, 0 vegetable, 0 fruit, 2 bread, ½ meat, 0 fat*

Tabbouleh Salad

111 Calories

Katia Nessif

*"I serve this traditional Lebanese salad on lettuce or grape leaves,
stuffed inside pitta bread, or as a dip with pitta chips for scooping."*

40 g/1½ oz chopped parsley

15 g/½ oz chopped fresh mint

60 g/2 oz chopped spring onions

115 ml/4 fl oz lemon juice

3 tbsp extra-virgin olive oil

½ tsp salt

¼ tsp allspice

100 g/3½ oz bulgur wheat

2 tomatoes, deseeded and chopped

In a large bowl, combine the parsley, mint, spring onions, lemon juice, oil, salt, and allspice.

Place the bulgur in another large bowl. Cover with boiling water. Cover the bowl and let stand for 4 minutes, or until the bulgur is just tender. Drain.

Stir the bulgur into the parsley mixture. Cover and refrigerate for 2 hours or overnight. Stir in the tomatoes just before serving.

Makes 8 servings

Per serving: *111 calories, 3 g protein, 12 g carbohydrates, 6 g fat, 111 mg sodium, 2 g fibre*

Diet Exchanges: *0 milk, 0 vegetable, 0 fruit, 1 bread, 0 meat, 1 fat*

Sweet Treats

Peanut Butter Cake with Chocolate Icing

131 Calories

Don Mauer

"When my friend Peter had a birthday, I created a peanut-butter cake using reduced-fat peanut butter. I iced it with a rich, smooth chocolate icing. It had only 3 grams of fat per serving, and Peter said it was his best birthday cake ever."

CAKE

150 g/5¼ oz unsweetened apple sauce

250 g/9 oz sifted self-raising flour

3 tsp baking powder

130 g/4½ oz peanut butter

200 g/7 oz brown sugar

1 tsp vanilla extract

2 large eggs

1 large egg white

170 ml/6 fl oz skimmed milk

ICING

265 g/9¼ oz sifted icing sugar

85 g/3 oz low-fat margarine or butter

50 g/1¾ oz cocoa powder

1 tsp vanilla extract

3 tsp skimmed milk

To make the cake:

Place a sieve lined with muslin over a deep bowl. Spoon in the apple sauce and let drain for 15 minutes (makes about 75 g/2½ oz drained apple sauce). Discard the liquid.

Preheat the oven to 180°C/350°F/gas 4. Coat a 33 × 23 cm/13 × 9 in. cake tin with non-stick spray.

In a medium bowl, combine the flour and baking powder.

In a large bowl, beat the peanut butter with an electric mixer for 2 minutes. Add the drained apple sauce and beat for 2 minutes. Beat in the brown sugar for 3 minutes, or until creamy. Beat in the vanilla extract and then the eggs, one at a time. Beat in the egg white, and then the milk. Add the flour mixture and mix on low until moistened.

Pour the batter into the cake tin and bake for 20–25 minutes, or until the centre of the cake springs back when pressed. Cool completely in the tin on a rack.

To make the icing:

In a food processor or large bowl, combine half of the icing sugar, the margarine or butter, cocoa, and vanilla extract. Process or beat until the icing sugar dissolves. Add the remaining icing sugar and 2 teaspoons milk. Process or beat just until smooth. If the icing is too thick, add the remaining milk.

Spread the icing on the cooled cake.

Makes 24 servings

Per serving: *131 calories, 3 g protein, 31 g carbohydrates, 3 g fat, 174 mg sodium, 1 g fibre*

Diet Exchanges: *0 milk, 0 vegetable, 0 fruit, 1½ bread, 0 meat, 1 fat*

Chocolate-Raspberry Avalanche Cake

Lisa Keys

"This cake is easier than it looks (and sounds!). It's all done in a square cake tin and ends up like a chocolate brownie cake served with chocolate sauce and raspberry cream. Yum!"

197 Calories

220 g/7½ oz plain flour
225 g/8 oz sugar
50 g/1¾ oz unsweetened cocoa powder
1 tsp baking powder
½ tsp bicarbonate of soda
¼ tsp salt
340 g/12 oz low-fat natural yogurt
2 tbsp sunflower oil
1 tsp vanilla extract
3 egg whites
200 g/7 oz fresh raspberries
2 tbsp honey
2 tbsp hot water
85 g/3 oz raspberry jam

Preheat the oven to 180°C/350°F/gas 4. Coat a 23 × 23 cm/9 × 9 in. cake tin with non-stick spray.

In a large bowl, combine the flour, half the sugar, half the cocoa, the baking powder, bicarbonate of soda, and salt.

In a medium bowl, combine 225 g/8 oz yogurt, the oil, and vanilla extract.

In a small bowl, beat the egg whites until soft peaks form. Gradually beat in the remaining sugar until stiff peaks form. Stir the yogurt mixture into the flour mixture just until moistened. Fold in the egg whites.

Pour into the cake tin. Sprinkle evenly with 150 g/5 oz raspberries. Bake for 40 minutes, or until a wooden cocktail stick inserted in centre comes out clean. Cool in the tin on a rack for 10 minutes. Remove from the tin and cool completely. Cut into 12 squares.

In another small bowl, mix the honey, water, and remaining cocoa.

In a medium bowl, mix the remaining yogurt and the jam. Serve each square with a dollop of raspberry cream and a drizzle of chocolate sauce.

Makes 12 servings

Per serving: *197 calories, 5 g protein, 40 g carbohydrates, 3 g fat, 199 mg sodium, 1 g fibre*

Diet Exchanges: *0 milk, 0 vegetable, ½ fruit, 2 bread, 0 meat, ½ fat*

FROM THE PROS

Dean Ornish, MD

Despite it's healthy sounding name, carrot cake is one of the most fattening dessert choices you can make. It's typically prepared with loads of oil. Luckily, in the hands of healthy heart guru Dean Ornish this cake becomes as good for you as it is tasty. Look for carrot purée in the baby food section of your supermarket.

CARROT CAKE WITH CREAM CHEESE ICING

 200 Calories

- 340 g/12 oz grated carrots (about 2 large)
- 170 g/6 oz sugar
- 115 g/4 oz canned crushed pineapple
- 115 g/4 oz carrot purée
- 4 egg whites
- 2 tsp vanilla extract
- ½ tsp salt
- 150 g/5¼ oz plain flour
- 150 g/5¼ oz oat bran
- 2 tsp bicarbonate of soda
- 1½ tsp ground cinnamon
- 225 g/8 oz low-fat cream cheese, softened

Preheat the oven to 220°C/425°F/gas 7. Coat a 23 cm/9 in. round cake tin with non-stick spray.

In a large bowl, mix the carrots, 115 g/4 oz sugar, the pineapple (with juice), carrot purée, egg whites, vanilla extract, and salt.

In another large bowl, combine the flour, oat bran, bicarbonate of soda, and cinnamon. Fold in the carrot mixture just until combined.

Pour into the tin and bake for 30 minutes, or until lightly browned and firm to the touch. Cool in the tin on a rack for 10 minutes. Remove from the tin.

In a medium bowl, beat the cream cheese and remaining sugar with an electric mixer. Spread evenly over the cake.

Makes 12 servings

Per serving: *200 calories, 6 g protein, 38 g carbohydrates, 4 g fat, 281 mg sodium, 2 g fibre*

Diet Exchanges: *0 milk, 1 vegetable, 1 fruit, 1 bread, 0 meat, 0 fat*

Quick Rice Pudding

215 Calories

Laura Janese.

"When you're craving something creamy and homey-tasting, here's a fat-free alternative to high-fat splurges."

900 ml/1¾ pints skimmed milk

200 g/6 oz quick-cooking long-grain white rice

45 g/1½ oz raisins

130 g/1 oz sachet vanilla-flavoured blancmange

2 egg whites

¼ tsp ground cinnamon

⅛ tsp ground nutmeg

In a medium saucepan, combine the milk, rice, raisins, blancmange mix, and egg whites. Heat to boiling over medium-high heat, stirring constantly. Reduce the heat to low and simmer 5 minutes.

Remove from the heat and cool 5 minutes, stirring twice.

Pour into dessert bowls. Sprinkle with the cinnamon and nutmeg, and serve warm.

Makes 8 servings

Per serving: *215 calories, 7 g protein, 40 g carbohydrates, 4 g fat, 259 mg sodium, 0 g fibre*

Diet Exchanges: *½ milk, 0 vegetable, 0 fruit, 1 bread, 0 meat, 0 fat*

Banana Chocolate Chip Cake

Linda Ann Archie

"Bananas with cinnamon and chocolate with cinnamon are two of my favourite flavour combinations. In this recipe, all three flavours are combined into one sweet treat."

185 g/6½ oz plain flour
1½ tsp baking powder
½ tsp bicarbonate of soda
½ tsp salt
½ tsp ground cinnamon
115 g/4 oz sugar
2 egg whites
115 g/4 oz fat-free vanilla yogurt
30 g/1 oz butter, melted
3 large ripe bananas
85 g/3 oz mini semi-sweet chocolate chips

Preheat the oven to 180°C/350°F/gas 4. Coat a 20 × 10 cm/8 × 4 in. loaf tin with non-stick spray.

In a medium bowl, combine flour, baking powder, bicarbonate of soda, salt, and cinnamon.

In a large bowl, beat the sugar and egg whites with an electric mixer until light and fluffy. Blend in the yogurt and butter. Mash the bananas with a fork and stir into the yogurt mixture. Stir in the flour mixture, then fold in the chocolate chips. Pour into the prepared tin.

Bake for 50–55 minutes, or until a wooden cocktail stick inserted in centre comes out clean.

Remove from the oven. Cool for 10 minutes in the tin on a rack. Remove from the tin and cool completely.

Makes 1 loaf (10 slices)

Per slice: *220 calories, 4 g protein, 41 g carbohydrates, 6 g fat, 214 mg sodium, 1 g fibre*

Diet Exchanges: *0 milk, 0 vegetable, 1 fruit, 1½ bread, 0 meat, 1 fat*

Double Chocolate Chip Fudge Brownies

Don Mauer

"Everyone who tastes these brownies mistakes them for their high-fat cousins."

170 g/6 oz unsweetened apple sauce
125 g/4½ oz plain flour
65 g/2¼ oz unsweetened cocoa powder
½ tsp salt
1 large egg
2 large egg whites
450 g/1 lb sugar
1 tsp vanilla extract
15 g/½ oz mini semi-sweet chocolate chips

Place a sieve lined with muslin over a deep bowl. Spoon in the apple sauce and set aside to drain 15 minutes (makes about 115 g/4 oz drained apple sauce). Discard the liquid.

Preheat the oven to 180°C/350°F/gas 4. Coat a non-stick 28 × 18 cm/11 × 7 in. cake tin with non-stick spray. Set aside.

In a medium bowl, combine the flour, cocoa, and salt.

In a large bowl, beat the egg and egg whites until frothy. Add the sugar, drained apple sauce, and vanilla extract. Stir until the sugar dissolves. Add the flour mixture and the chocolate chips. Stir just until the dry ingredients are moistened.

Pour the batter into the cake tin and bake for 30 minutes. Cool in the tin on a rack.

Makes 15

Per brownie: *178 calories, 3 g protein, 40 g carbohydrates, 2 g fat, 111 mg sodium, 1 g fibre*

Diet Exchanges: *0 milk, 0 vegetable, 0 fruit, 2 bread, 0 meat, ½ fat*

Pumpkin-Ginger Rice Pudding

209 Calories

Erica Berman

"Arborio rice makes a very creamy rice pudding. You can dress this up with dates, raisins, or nuts."

115 g/4 oz sugar

1 vanilla pod, split lengthways, or
  1 tsp vanilla extract

1 tbsp grated fresh ginger

¾ tsp mixed spice

¾ tsp cinnamon

900 ml/1¾ pints skimmed milk

200 g/7 oz Arborio rice

225 g/8 oz pure pumpkin purée

In a large saucepan, combine sugar, vanilla pod (if using), ginger, mixed spice, cinnamon, and 225 ml/8 oz milk. (If using vanilla extract, add along with pumpkin purée at the end.) Heat to boiling over medium heat. Reduce heat to low and simmer 5 minutes. Remove and discard vanilla pod, if using. Stir in rice.

Add the remaining milk, 300 ml/½ pint at a time, and cook, stirring frequently, 30 minutes, or until the rice is tender and most of the milk is absorbed but still creamy. Stir in the pumpkin purée and vanilla extract, if using. Cook until the pudding is thick and heated through. Serve warm.

Makes 8 servings

Per serving: *209 calories, 7 g protein, 44 g carbohydrates, 0 g fat, 65 mg sodium, 1 g fibre*

Diet Exchanges: *1 milk, 0 vegetable, 0 fruit, 1 bread, 0 meat, 0 fat*

Chocolate Chunk Cookies

Jayne Tingley

"These aren't your everyday chocolate chip cookies. Oats keep them moist and flavourful. If you can find chocolate chunks or pieces, they make for a dramatic cookie. Traditional chips work just fine, too."

125 g/4½ oz plain flour

140 g/5 oz wholemeal flour

25 g/1 oz quick-cooking oats

1 tsp bicarbonate of soda

½ tsp salt

225 g/8 oz sugar

100 g/3½ oz brown sugar

85 g/3 oz butter or margarine

2 egg whites

2 tbsp skimmed milk

1 tsp vanilla extract

170 g/6 oz semi-sweet chocolate pieces
   or chips

Preheat the oven to 190°C/375°F/gas 5. Coat 2 baking trays with non-stick spray.

In a large bowl, combine the plain flour, whole-wheat flour, oats, bicarbonate of soda, and salt.

In another large bowl, combine the sugar, brown sugar, butter or margarine, egg whites, milk, and vanilla extract. Add the flour mixture and stir just until moistened. Stir in the chocolate pieces.

Drop by rounded teaspoonfuls, 5 cm/2 in. apart, on the baking trays. Bake for 10–12 minutes, or until lightly browned around the edges. Transfer cookies to racks to cool.

Makes 48

Per cookie: *52 calories, 1 g protein, 9 g carbohydrates, 2 g fat, 57 mg sodium, 1 g fibre*

Diet Exchanges: *0 milk, 0 vegetable, 0 fruit, ½ bread, 0 meat, ½ fat*

Chocolate-Pecan Meringues

36 Calories

Jane Imm

"When you need a sweet, crunchy biscuit, but almost no fat, try these. If you use a food processor to chop the pecans, be careful not to grind them so fine that they become pecan paste!"

3 egg whites

⅛ tsp cream of tartar

75 g/2¾ oz sugar

2 tbsp unsweetened cocoa powder

15 g/½ oz finely ground pecans

85 g/3 oz strawberry or raspberry jam

Preheat the oven to 120°C/250°F/gas ½. Line a baking tray with baking parchment or foil.

In a large bowl, beat the egg whites until frothy. Add the cream of tartar and beat until stiff.

In a small bowl, combine the sugar and cocoa. Gradually beat into the egg whites. Fold in the pecans.

Spoon the meringue into 3.5 cm/1½ in. mounds on the baking tray. Using the back of a spoon, depress the centres and build up the sides of each meringue to form a shallow cup.

Bake for 1 hour. Do not open the oven door. Turn off the oven and let the meringues cool in the oven. Store in an airtight container. When ready to serve, fill each meringue with jam.

Makes 16

Per biscuit: *36 calories, 1 g protein, 6 g carbohydrates, 1 g fat, 20 mg sodium, 0 g fibre*

Diet Exchanges: *0 milk, 0 vegetable, 0 fruit, ½ bread, 0 meat, 0 fat*

(Hamantaschen recipe on page 269)

FROM THE PROS

Dean Ornish, MD

Ahh … gingerbread. Sweet, spicy, and satisfying, whether it's warm from the oven or at room temperature. All that and calorie-savvy, too! Dr Dean Ornish, who proved that a healthy diet can reverse heart disease, wows us once again with this delightful quick bread from a friend.

JOHN'S GINGERBREAD

168 Calories

140 g/5 oz soured cream

115 g/4 oz unsweetened apple sauce

1 extra-large egg

3 tbsp brown sugar

2 tbsp molasses

100 g/3½ oz wholemeal flour

100 g/3½ oz plain flour

4 tsp ground ginger

1 tsp ground cinnamon

½ tsp ground cloves

1 tsp bicarbonate of soda

1 tsp baking powder

½ tsp salt

Preheat the oven to 180°C/350°F/ gas 4. Coat a 23 × 23 cm/9 × 9 in. or a 20 × 20 cm/8 × 8 in. cake tin with non-stick spray.

In a large bowl, combine the soured cream, apple sauce, egg, brown sugar, and molasses.

In a medium bowl, combine the whole-wheat flour, plain flour, ginger, cinnamon, cloves, bicarbonate of soda, baking powder, and salt. Sift on to a piece of greaseproof paper. Add to the soured cream mixture and stir just until moistened. Do not overmix. The batter may be lumpy.

Spread evenly in the cake tin. Bake for 25 minutes, or until the gingerbread rises to the top of the tin and a wooden cocktail stick inserted in centre comes out clean. Cool in the tin on a rack for 30 minutes before cutting.

Makes 8 servings

Per serving: *168 calories, 5 g protein, 28 g carbohydrates, 2 g fat, 304 mg sodium, 2 g fibre*

Diet Exchanges: *0 milk, 0 vegetable, 0 fruit, 2 bread, 0 meat, 0 fat*

Hamantaschen

74 Calories

Babette Miles

"These traditional Jewish biscuits are shaped like triangular hats filled with jam. Browning the butter intensifies its flavour, so you don't need as much."

100 g/ 3½ oz soft butter

1 egg

115 g/4 oz sugar

1 tsp vanilla extract

375 g/13 oz plain flour

1 tsp baking powder

⅛ tsp salt

85 g/3 oz apricot or raspberry jam

Preheat the oven to 180°C/350°F/gas 4. Coat a large baking tray with non-stick spray.

Melt the butter in a small saucepan over medium heat until nutty brown, constantly swirling the pan. Set aside.

In a large bowl, beat the egg and sugar with an electric mixer. Gradually beat in the butter and vanilla extract.

In a medium bowl, combine the flour, baking powder, and salt. Gradually stir into the egg mixture. Turn the dough out on to a lightly floured surface and knead until smooth, adding more flour if necessary. Roll into 36 balls and place on the baking tray. Press into 3.5 cm/1½ in. circles. Place a scant ½ teaspoon jam in the centre of each circle. Fold 3 sides of the dough over the filling to form a triangle.

Bake for 25 minutes, or until lightly browned.

Makes 36

Per biscuit: *74 calories, 1 g protein, 12 g carbohydrates, 1 g fat, 26 mg sodium, 0 g fibre*

Diet Exchanges: *0 milk, 0 vegetable, 0 fruit, 1 bread, 0 meat, 0 fat*

(Photograph on page 267)

Tapioca Pudding

121 Calories

Susan Jones

*"Cardamom and cinnamon give this pudding a sweet aroma.
Here's a bonus: it's a great source of calcium."*

900 ml/1¾ pints skimmed milk

3 tbsp quick-cooking tapioca

75 g/2¾ oz sugar

1 egg, beaten

1 egg white

¼ tsp ground cardamom or coriander

¼ tsp ground cinnamon

45 g/1½ oz raisins

1 tsp vanilla extract

In a large saucepan, combine the milk, tapioca, sugar, egg, egg white, cardamom or coriander, and cinnamon. Heat to boiling over medium heat. Reduce the heat to low and simmer, stirring constantly, for 5 minutes. Remove from the heat and stir in the raisins and vanilla extract. Pour into a serving bowl. Refrigerate until cold.

Makes 8 servings

Per serving: *121 calories, 5 g protein, 24 g carbohydrates, 1 g fat, 83 mg sodium, 0 g fibre*

Diet Exchanges: *½ milk, 0 vegetable, 0 fruit, 1 bread, 0 meat, 0 fat*

Rancho la Puerta

At Rancho la Puerta health and fitness spa, chef Bill Wavrin is a popular man. He has a friendly personality and a winning way with sweets. This one is among his most requested treats.

119 Calories

CORN CREPES WITH STRAWBERRY SAUCE

135 g/4½ oz wholemeal flour
50 g/1¾ oz cornmeal
¼ tsp ground cinnamon
¼ tsp ground cardamom
¼ tsp ground nutmeg
4 egg whites
450 ml/16 fl oz skimmed milk
1 tbsp honey
½ tsp vanilla extract
300 g/10 oz strawberries, hulled
    and sliced
120 ml/4 fl oz apple juice
3 tbsp lime juice

In a large bowl, combine flour, cornmeal, cinnamon, cardamom, and nutmeg.

In a medium bowl, beat the egg whites until frothy. Add the milk, honey, and vanilla extract. Pour into the flour mixture and mix until just combined. Do not overmix. Cover and refrigerate for at least 30 minutes.

Meanwhile, in a small saucepan over medium-low heat, combine the strawberries, apple juice, and lime juice. Simmer for 5 minutes, or until the berries soften.

Coat a non-stick griddle or frying pan with non-stick spray and warm over medium heat. Spoon about 3 tablespoons of batter onto the griddle or frying pan and cook for 1 minute, or until bubbles break on the top and the underside is golden. Turn and cook a few seconds, or until set. Transfer to a plate and keep warm. Repeat with the remaining batter. Serve the crepes with the strawberry sauce.

Makes 8 servings

Per serving: *119 calories, 6 g protein, 24 g carbohydrates, 1 g fat, 49 mg sodium, 2 g fibre*

Diet Exchanges: *0 milk, 0 vegetable, 1 fruit, 1 bread, 0 meat, 0 fat*

Black Cherry Baked Apples

157 Calories

Scott Coleman

"As simple as it is unusual. 'Nuf said."

4 baking apples

½ tsp cinnamon

45 g/1½ oz dried cherries or raisins

30 g/1 oz chopped walnuts

**225 ml/8 fl oz diet black cherry fizzy drink
(for example, Dr Pepper)**

Preheat the oven to 190°C/375°F/gas 5. Using an apple corer or small knife, remove the apple cores from the stem ends without cutting all the way through to the other end. Place the apples in a 23 × 23 cm/9 × 9 in. ovenproof dish.

Sprinkle the cinnamon inside and outside the apples. Spoon the cherries or raisins and walnuts into the apples. Drizzle a little fizzy drink into each apple. Pour the remaining fizzy drink into the dish. Bake for 20 minutes, or until tender.

Makes 4 servings

Per serving: *157 calories, 2 g protein, 27 g carbohydrates, 5 g fat, 9 mg sodium, 4 g fibre*

Diet Exchanges: *0 milk, 0 vegetable, 2 fruit, 0 bread, 0 meat, 0 fat*

FROM THE PROS

Golden Door

Chef Michel Stroot is a pioneer in health-resort cuisine. One of his many culinary contributions is being able to make healthy foods like fruits and vegetables as mouthwateringly appealing as the sticky, gooey fattening stuff. Here's a popular example from the Golden Door spa.

BAKED APPLE WITH PAPAYA SAUCE

111 Calories

4 Golden Delicious apples, cored
4 tsp raisins
4 tsp honey
½ tsp ground cinnamon
125 ml/4 fl oz unsweetened apple juice
1 papaya, peeled and seeded
1 tsp lime juice
1 tsp finely chopped crystallized ginger
4 fresh mint sprigs

Preheat the oven to 180°C/350°F/gas 4. Place the apples in a 23 × 23 cm/9 × 9 in. baking dish. Spoon 1 teaspoon raisins into each apple. Drizzle with honey and sprinkle with cinnamon. Pour the apple juice around the apples in the dish. Cover loosely with foil and bake for 50–60 minutes, or until fork-tender. Allow to cool in the dish.

In a blender, combine the papaya, lime juice, ginger, and juices from the baked apples. Blend until smooth. Place the apples on small plates and spoon some sauce over each. Garnish with mint.

Makes 4 servings

Per serving: *111 calories, 1 g protein, 28 g carbohydrates, 0 g fat, 14 mg sodium, 3 g fibre*

Diet Exchanges: *0 milk, 0 vegetable, 3 fruit, 0 bread, 0 meat, 0 fat*

Cranberry–Apple Crumble

Mary McMurtrey

215 Calories

"I like to put a cranberry twist on the basic yummy fruit crisp. Serve this with frozen yogurt if ice cream isn't in your calorie budget."

500 g/16 oz whole berry cranberry sauce
5 baking apples, peeled and sliced
1 tsp ground cinnamon
¼ tsp ground nutmeg
140 g/5 oz plain flour
200 g/7 oz brown sugar
50 g/ 1¾ oz quick-cooking oats
¼ tsp salt
30 g/1 oz butter or margarine, melted

Preheat the oven to 190°C/375°F/gas 5.

In a large bowl, combine the cranberry sauce, apples, cinnamon, nutmeg, and 2 tablespoons flour. Spoon into a 33 × 23 cm/ 13 × 9 in. ovenproof dish.

In another large bowl, combine the brown sugar, oats, salt, and remaining flour. Stir in the butter or margarine until well-distributed. Sprinkle evenly over the fruit. Bake for 35–40 minutes, or until hot and bubbly.

Makes 12 servings

Per serving: *215 calories, 2 g protein, 50 g carbohydrates, 3 g fat, 60 mg sodium, 2 g fibre*

Diet Exchanges: *0 milk, 0 vegetable, 2 fruit, 1½ bread, 0 meat, 1 fat*

Wonton Fruit Cups

46 Calories

Susan Burns

"My husband, who has diabetes, inspires me to create new recipes like this treat, which we both enjoy. Wonton wrappers are available in the refrigerated section of many supermarkets and Oriental food stores. If you can't find wonton wrappers, use filo pastry."

24 wonton wrappers

30 g/1 oz butter or margarine, melted

125 g/4 oz all-fruit strawberry jam

225 g/8 oz low-fat lemon yogurt

200 g/7oz fresh blueberries, blackberries, or raspberries

Preheat the oven to 180°C/350°F/gas 4.

Using a 12-cup muffin tin or two 6-cup muffin tins, line each cup with a wonton wrapper. Brush the wrappers with a little butter. Place a second wrapper diagonally on top of each of the first ones, making sure that the points of the wrappers make sides to the cup. Brush the second wrapper with a little butter. Bake for 10 minutes, or until golden brown. Cool, then remove from tin.

Spoon about 1 teaspoon of strawberry jam into each wonton shell.

Place the yogurt in a medium bowl. Fold in 150 g/5 oz berries. Spoon the mixture evenly into wonton shells and top with the remaining berries.

Makes 12

Per fruit cup: *46 calories, 2 g protein, 6 g carbohydrates, 2 g fat, 37 mg sodium, 1 g fibre*

Diet Exchanges: *0 milk, 0 vegetable, 1 fruit, ½ bread, 0 meat, 0 fat*

Guiltless Banana Split
Lynn Metzke

176 Calories

"Sweet, fruity, and creamy! This has all the best parts of the real thing without the caloric consequences."

1 banana, peeled and sliced lengthways
1 slice fresh pineapple
4 large strawberries, hulled
2 tbsp chocolate syrup
1 tbsp low-fat whipped topping

Place the banana on a plate. Cut wedges from the pineapple slice and arrange on half of the banana. Place the strawberries, point up, on the other half of banana. Drizzle with the chocolate syrup and top with the whipped topping.

Makes 1 serving

Per serving: *176 calories, 2 g protein, 32 g carbohydrates, 5 g fat, 7 mg sodium, 2 g fibre*

Diet Exchanges: *0 milk, 0 vegetable, 3 fruit, 1½ bread, 0 meat, 0 fat*

Roast Fruit Wraps with Dipping Sauce

261 Calories

Kurt Wait

"As a single dad, I do all the cooking for my son and me. This is a great way to include fruits in our daily diet. It's like a warm fruit pie without all the fat or fuss. And it keeps me light on my feet for tennis."

DIPPING SAUCE

225 g/8 oz low-fat vanilla yogurt

2 tsp finely chopped crystallized ginger

2 tbsp orange juice

FRUIT WRAPS

2 Golden Delicious apples, peeled and sliced

2 peaches or 1 mango, peeled and sliced

4 slices canned pineapple, halved

2 tbsp orange juice

4 tsp sugar

A pinch each of mixed spice, ginger, and cinnamon

4 flour tortillas

To make the dipping sauce:

In a small bowl, mix the yogurt, ginger, and orange juice. Cover and refrigerate.

To make the fruit wraps:

Preheat the oven to 220°C/425°F/gas 7. Coat a large non-stick baking sheet with non-stick spray. Add the apples, peaches or mango, pineapple, orange juice, sugar, and spices. Toss to coat and spread in a single layer. Bake for 10–15 minutes, or until the fruit is tender.

Place a quarter of the warm fruit down the centre of each tortilla. Roll up like an envelope and place, seam side down, on the non-stick baking sheet. Bake for 8–10 minutes, or until crisp and golden. Cut each wrap in half diagonally. Serve with sauce.

Make 4 servings

Per serving: *261 calories, 8 g protein, 58 g carbohydrates, 1 g fat, 205 mg sodium, 3 g fibre*

Diet Exchanges: *0 milk, 0 vegetable, 2 fruit, 2 bread, 0 meat, ½ fat*

GET A GRIP ON CHOCOLATE

What is the one thing that Dean Ornish, the high priest of low-fat cooking and healthy eating, is never willing to give up? You guessed it: chocolate. He loves to finish his meals with one small, exquisitely rich, mouth-coating, dense, dark piece of chocolate.

And who can blame him? For many people, especially those watching their weight, chocolate calls louder than any other flavour. And most nutritionists say: give in. When you eat around a food trying to avoid the one thing that you really want, you're apt to eat more calories than if you ate what you wanted in the first place.

That doesn't mean you should grab a huge piece of fudge at the first nudge of a craving. Have a little. Psychologically speaking, some is better than none.

One note of caution: don't waste your time on fat-free ersatz chocolate bars and fake chocolate coatings. They won't give you the satisfaction of real chocolate. Is this the voice of experience? You bet. Try one of these chocolatey, but saner, choices. They're listed from most calories to least.

Chocolate	Calories
225 ml/8 fl oz low-fat hot cocoa	157
2 tablespoons M & Ms or Smarties	125
30 g/1 oz chocolate crispy rice breakfast cereal	120
25 g/1 oz chocolate crispie cereal bar	110
45 g/1½ oz chocolate chips	100
1 scoop fat-free chocolate sorbet	100
3 chocolate wafer biscuits	78
2 chocolate wholemeal digestive biscuits	60
1 sachet low-calorie hot chocolate drink	50

Tiramisu

323 Calories

Larry Benson

"The classic Italian recipe has troppo *fat and calories. (That means a lot!) This version may have more calories than diet gelatin, but it's far more satisfying, too."*

2 sachets instant vanilla-flavoured whipped dessert mix

1 tsp instant coffee granules

225 g/8 oz ricotta cheese

225 g/8 oz reduced-fat cream cheese

50 g/1¾ oz icing sugar

1 tsp rum extract

85 g/3 oz mini semi-sweet chocolate chips

300 g/10 oz low-fat madeira cake, pound cake or lady fingers

225 ml/8 fl oz brewed strong black coffee

1 tbsp unsweeteened cocoa

chocolate curls (optional)

Prepare the whipped desssert according to the packet directions, using skimmed milk. Add the coffee granules. Cover and refrigerate until well-chilled.

In a medium bowl, combine the ricotta, cream cheese, icing sugar, and rum extract. Fold in the chocolate chips and dessert.

Cut the cake into thin slices or separate the lady fingers. Arrange a quarter of the slices in a single layer on the bottom of a large glass bowl. Set the remaining cake aside. Drizzle the cake in bowl with 55 ml/ 2 fl oz of the brewed coffee. Spread one-third of the ricotta mixture over the cake in the bowl. Top with another quarter of cake. Drizzle with another 55 ml/2 fl oz of coffee. Repeat layering 2 more times, ending with cake. Sprinkle the top with cocoa. Decorate with chocolate curls, if using.

Makes 8 servings

Per serving: *323 calories, 6 g protein, 36 g carbohydrates, 17 g fat, 236 mg sodium, 1 g fibre*

Diet Exchanges: *0 milk, 0 vegetable, 0 fruit, 3 bread, 0 meat, 2 fat*

Terrific Trifle

187 Calories

Barbara Pashkoff

*"This is one of those tastes-even-better-the-next-day kind of recipes,
Plus, it's easy to make and low in fat."*

2 sachets instant vanilla whipped
    dessert mix

300 g/10 oz Swiss roll, cut into 1-cm/
    ½-in. slices

60 ml/2 fl oz dry sherry or orange juice

3 ripe bananas, sliced

Prepare the whipped dessert according to packet directions, using skimmed milk.

Arrange a single layer of Swiss roll in the bottom of a deep glass bowl. Sprinkle with a generous tablespoon of sherry or orange juice. Top with one-third of the banana slices and one-third of the whipped dessert. Continue layering 2 more times, ending with the whipped dessert. Cover with cling film and refrigerate for a few hours before serving.

Makes 8 servings

Per serving: *187 calories, 4 g protein, 37 g carbohydrates, 3 g fat, 127 mg sodium, 1 g fibre*

Diet Exchanges: *0 milk, 0 vegetable, 2 fruit, 2 bread, 0 meat, 0 fat*

Two Weeks to a Slimmer You

Here's where it all comes together: 14 days of menus that really work. We took a wide range of recipes from the book and organized them into a variety of meals that balance flavours, textures, and colours (not to mention calories). You'll find everything from Blueberry-Pecan Pancakes to Grilled Pork Chops, from Broccoli Soup to Chocolate-Chunk Cookies. These menus prove that losing weight doesn't mean depriving yourself.

Each daily menu includes not three, but five 'meals'. Morning and afternoon snacks keep you from getting too hungry and overeating at main meals. You may want to save one of these snacks for later if your appetite alarm rings more loudly in the evening. For other snack ideas, see '50 Low-Calorie Snacks' on page 109.

Beverages aren't included here. That's up to you. Diet colas, water, and tea and coffee without sugar are virtually calorie-free. Standard colas contain about 250 calories. Wine and beer provide 100–150 calories per serving.

Notice that the menus are calculated for 1,500, 2,000, or 2,500 calories. To find the calorie level that's right for you, see 'How Many Calories Do You Eat Now?' on pages 18–19. Adjust the menus as needed for your calorie intake by omitting or adding foods.

Think of these menus as suggestions. And think seasonal. Corn on the cob, baby spinach, strawberries, and melons are short-lived treats that can be substituted for any of the fruit and vegetable ideas that follow without dramatically altering a day's total calories. When you make freshness a priority, you'll please your senses and your spirit. And that's the kind of soul-satisfying eating that leads to weight-loss success.

Day 1

MENU	CALORIE LEVELS		
	1,500	**2,000**	**2,500**
Breakfast			
Hot Banana-Wheat Cereal (page 64)	1 serving	1 serving	1 serving
Skimmed milk	200 ml/7 fl oz	200 ml/7 fl oz	200 ml/7 fl oz
Orange	1	1	1
Snack			
Peanuts	1 tbsp	2 tbsp	2 tbsp
Lunch			
Creamy Carrot-Potato Soup (page 88)	1 serving	1 serving	2 servings
Pitta Pizza (page 101)	1 serving	1 serving	2 servings
Snack			
125 g/4 oz pot low-fat yogurt	1	1	1
with digestive biscuit	1	2	2
Dinner			
Chicken Fiesta (page 117)	1 serving	1 serving	1½ servings
Baked tortilla chips	0	1 small packet	1 small packet
Brown rice	4½ tbsp	6½ tbsp	6½ tbsp
Chocolate-Pecan Meringues (page 266)	1	3	3
TOTAL CALORIES	**1,463**	**2,176**	**2,556**

MENU	CALORIE LEVELS		
	1,500	**2,000**	**2,500**
Breakfast			
Blueberry-Pecan Pancakes (page 60)	1 serving	1 serving	2 servings
Maple syrup	1 tbsp	1 tbsp	1 tbsp
Orange juice	200 ml/7 fl oz	200 ml/7 fl oz	400 ml/14 fl oz
Snack			
Wholemeal toast	1 slice	1 slice	1 slice
with peanut butter	1 heaped tsp	1 heaped tsp	1 heaped tsp
Lunch			
Wonderful Tuna Salad (page 236)	1 serving	1 serving	2 servings
with lettuce and shredded carrots	1 medium bowl	1 medium bowl	1 medium bowl
on wholemeal bread	1 slice	2 slices	2 slices
Chocolate Chunk Cookies (page 264)	1	2	2
Snack			
Broccoli soup (page 86)	1 serving	1 serving	1 serving
Wholemeal crackers	0	4	6
Dinner			
Beef and Macaroni (page 135)	1 serving	1 serving	1 serving
Steamed broccoli with lemon zest	4 tbsp	4 tbsp	4 tbsp
Wholemeal Italian bread	1 slice	2 slices	2 slices
Cantaloupe	¼	¼	¼
TOTAL CALORIES	**1,595**	**2,006**	**2,535**

MENU

	CALORIE LEVELS		
	1,500	**2,000**	**2,500**
Breakfast			
Chopra Cereal (page 65)	1 serving	1 serving	1 serving
Skimmed milk	200 ml/7 fl oz	200 ml/7 fl oz	200 ml/7 fl oz
Grapefruit juice	200 ml/7 fl oz	200 ml/7 fl oz	200 ml/7 fl oz
Snack			
Fig roll biscuit	1	2	2
Skimmed milk	100 ml/3½ fl oz	200 ml/7 fl oz	200 ml/7 fl oz
Lunch			
Kidney Bean and Corn Salad (page 246)	1 serving	1 serving	2 servings
on shredded romaine lettuce	1 handful	2 handfuls	2 handfuls
Home-Baked Chips (page 53)	1 serving	1 serving	2 servings
Salsa	1 tbsp	1 tbsp	1 tbsp
Snack			
Hard-boiled egg	1	1	1
Bread	1 slice	2 slices	2 slices
Dinner			
Orange-Almond Chicken (page 126)	1 serving	1 serving	2 servings
Italian bread	1 slice	2 slices	2 slices
dipped in olive oil	½ tsp	1 tsp	2 tsp
Chocolate-Raspberry Avalanche Cake (page 256)	0	1 serving	1 serving
TOTAL CALORIES	**1,424**	**1,921**	**2,664**

MENU	CALORIE LEVELS		
	1,500	**2,000**	**2,500**
Breakfast			
Good Morning Muffins (page 58)	1	1	2
Orange juice	200 ml/7 fl oz	200 ml/7 fl oz	200 ml/7 fl oz
125 g/4 oz pot low-fat fruit-flavoured yogurt	1	1	1
Snack			
Low-fat cottage cheese	2 tbsp	4 tbsp	4 tbsp
Rice cake	2	2	2
Lunch			
Quick Chicken Pasta Salad (page 82)	1 serving	2 servings	2$\frac{1}{2}$ servings
on shredded romaine lettuce	1 handful	1 handful	1 handful
Italian bread	1 slice	3 slices	3 slices
Pear	1	1	1
Snack			
Sliced turkey breast	1 slice	2 slices	4 slices
Wholemeal bread	2 slices	2 slices	3 slices
Dinner			
Crab Cakes (page 154)	1 serving	1 serving	1$\frac{1}{2}$ servings
Baked tomato halves	1	1	1
Steamed carrots	3 tbsp	3 tbsp	3 tbsp
Honeydew melon	$\frac{1}{8}$	$\frac{1}{8}$	$\frac{1}{8}$
TOTAL CALORIES	**1,538**	**2,037**	**2,499**

MENU	CALORIE LEVELS		
	1,500	**2,000**	**2,500**
Breakfast			
Jumbo Cinnamon-Raisin Muffins (page 51)	1	1	1
Orange juice	200 ml/7 fl oz	200 ml/7 fl oz	200 ml/7 fl oz
125 g/4 oz pot low-fat fruit-flavoured yogurt	1	1	1
Snack			
Pitta bread	½	½	1
stuffed with kidney beans	1 tbsp	1 tbsp	2 tbsp
and lettuce	1 handful	1 handful	1 handful
Lunch			
Broccoli Soup (page 86)	½ serving	1 serving	1 serving
Goat's cheese	30 g/1 oz	30 g/1 oz	60 g/2 oz
and sliced small tomato	1	1	1
and rocket	1 handful	1 handful	1 handful
and olive oil	½ tsp	½ tsp	½ tsp
on Italian bread	1 slice	1 slice	2 slices
Snack			
Frozen juice bar	1	1	1
Almonds	0	2 tbsp	2 tbsp
Dinner			
Grilled Pork Chops (page 180)	1 serving	1 serving	1 serving
Brown rice	2¼ tbsp	4½ tbsp	6½ tbsp
Steamed broccoli with lemon and garlic	4 tbsp	4 tbsp	4 tbsp
Chocolate-Raspberry Avalanche Cake (from Day 3, page 256)	0	1 serving	1 serving
TOTAL CALORIES	**1,512**	**2,021**	**2,509**

Day 6

MENU	CALORIE LEVELS		
	1,500	**2,000**	**2,500**
Breakfast			
Bran flakes	8 tbsp	8 tbsp	13 tbsp
Banana	1	1	1
Skimmed milk	200 ml/7 fl oz	200 ml/7 fl oz	200 ml/7 fl oz
Snack			
125 g/4 oz pot diet fruit-flavoured yogurt	1	1	1
Fig roll biscuit	1	1	2
Lunch			
Canyon Ranch Burger (page 92)	1	1	2
Carrot, shredded	1 large	1 large	1 large
and tossed with olive oil and fresh dill	1 tsp	2 tsp	2 tsp
Watermelon chunks	1 small bowl	1 medium bowl	1 medium bowl
Snack			
Cream crackers	2	4	4
with 20 g/²⁄₃ oz cheese portion	0	1	2
Dinner			
Vegetable Lasagne (page 192)	1 serving	2 servings	2 servings
40 g/ 1½ oz slice ciabatta	1	1	2
Green beans	4 tbsp	4 tbsp	4 tbsp
with sliced almonds	0	1 tbsp	1 tbsp
Tiramisu (page 281)	1 serving	1 serving	1 serving
TOTAL CALORIES	**1,527**	**2,004**	**2,568**

Day 7

MENU	CALORIE LEVELS		
	1,500	**2,000**	**2,500**
Breakfast			
Scrambled eggs	1	2	2
Wholemeal toast	1 slice	2 slices	3 slices
Back bacon	1 rasher	2 rashers	2 rashers
Orange juice	200 ml/7 fl oz	200 ml/7 fl oz	200 ml/7 fl oz
Snack			
Skimmed milk	100 ml/3½ fl oz	200 ml/7 fl oz	200 ml/7 fl oz
Chocolate Chunk Cookies (page 264)	1	1	1
Lunch			
Sweet Potato and Leek Soup (page 93)	1 serving	1 serving	2 servings
Tabbouleh Salad (page 251)	2 servings	2 servings	2 servings
Apple	1	1	1
Snack			
20 g/⅔ oz cheese sticks	1	2	2
Wholemeal digestive biscuits	2	2	3
Dinner			
Chicken Therese (page 123)	1 serving	1 serving	1½ servings
Brown rice with mint and tomato	2¼ tbsp	4½ tbsp	6½ tbsp
Steamed green beans	5 tbsp	5 tbsp	5 tbsp
Chocolate-Pecan Meringues (page 264)	2	2	2
TOTAL CALORIES	**1,496**	**1,961**	**2,347**

MENU	CALORIE LEVELS		
	1,500	**2,000**	**2,500**
Breakfast			
Peanut Butter and Banana Shake (page 112)	1 serving	1 serving	1 serving
Snack			
Sliced strawberries	5 tbsp	5 tbsp	5 tbsp
Aerosol cream	1 tbsp	1 tbsp	1 tbsp
Lunch			
Sliced avocado	⅛	¼	¼
Roast Vegetable Wraps (page 72)	1 serving	2 servings	2 servings
Salsa	1 tbsp	1 tbsp	1 tbsp
Orange	1	1	1
Snack			
Peanuts	1 tbsp	2 tbsp	3 tbsp
Dinner			
Lamb Chops with Herb and Apricot Sauce (page 145)	1 serving	1 serving	2 servings
Couscous	6 tbsp	6 tbsp	9 tbsp
Steamed green peas with mint	2 tbsp	4 tbsp	4 tbsp
Blueberries	5 tbsp	5 tbsp	5 tbsp
with 125 g/4 oz pot low-fat vanilla yogurt	½	1	1
TOTAL CALORIES	**1,504**	**2,012**	**2,435**

MENU	CALORIE LEVELS		
	1,500	**2,000**	**2,500**
Breakfast			
Orange-Raisin Tea Bread (page 69)	1 slice	2 slices	4 slices
125 g/4 oz pot low-fat vanilla yogurt	½	1	1
Banana	1	1	1
Snack			
Sesame bread stick	2	2	2
Cream cheese	1 tbsp	1 tbsp	2 tbsp
Lunch			
Tomato-Crab Bake (page 102)	1 serving	1 serving	2 servings
Cooked canned corn	2 tbsp	2 tbsp	2 tbsp
Italian bread	2 slices	3 slices	3 slices
Pear	1	1	1
Snack			
125 g/4 oz pot low-fat fruit-flavoured yogurt	1	1	2
Dinner			
Roast chicken	120 g/4 oz	120 g/4 oz	180 g/6 oz
Chicken Stuffing Casserole (page 222)	1 serving	1 serving	2 servings
Steamed broccoli with orange zest	4 tbsp	4 tbsp	4 tbsp
Roast butternut squash with rosemary	4 tbsp	4 tbsp	4 tbsp
Medium size baked jacket potato	0	1	2
John's Gingerbread (page 268)	1 serving	2 servings	2 servings
TOTAL CALORIES	**1,460**	**1,986**	**2,458**

Day 10

MENU	CALORIE LEVELS		
	1,500	**2,000**	**2,500**
Breakfast			
Lemon Wedges (page 62)	1	1	2
125 g/4 oz pot low-fat fruit-flavoured yogurt	1	1	1
Snack			
Apple	½	1	1
Lunch			
Tuscan Tuna Salad (page 239)	1 serving	2 serving	2 servings
Sliced small tomato with basil	1	1	1
Wholemeal bread	1 slice	2 slices	2 slices
Snack			
Baked tortilla chips	5	10	10
Smoked turkey breast	1 slice	2 slices	2 slices
Semi-skimmed milk	200 ml/ 7 fl oz	200 ml/ 7 fl oz	200 ml/ 7 fl oz
Dinner			
Red Chilli Steak Burritos (page 140)	1 serving	1 serving	1 serving
Brown rice	2¼ tbsp	4½ tbsp	4½ tbsp
Steamed courgette and yellow squash with red pepper	4 tbsp	4 tbsp	4 tbsp
Hamantaschen (page 269)	1	1	3
TOTAL CALORIES	**1,505**	**1,939**	**2,490**

Day 11

MENU	CALORIE LEVELS		
	1,500	**2,000**	**2,500**
Breakfast			
Porridge, made with water	8 tbsp	8 tbsp	8 tbsp
Skimmed milk	100 ml/3½ fl oz	100 ml/3½ fl oz	100 ml/3½ fl oz
Grapefruit juice	200 ml/7 fl oz	200 ml/7 fl oz	200 ml/7 fl oz
Snack			
30 g/1 oz snack-pack raisins	1	1	1
Lunch			
Kidney beans	3 tbsp	6 tbsp	6 tbsp
with fat-free Italian dressing	1 tbsp	1 tbsp	2 tbsp
Spinach Squares (page 97)	1 serving	1 serving	3 servings
Italian bread	1 slice	2 slices	2 slices
Snack			
Cantaloupe melon	¼	¼	¼
Low-fat cottage cheese	2 tbsp	4 tbsp	4 tbsp
Dinner			
Crunchy Baked Chicken (page 118)	1 serving	1½ servings	2 servings
Brown rice	3 tbsp	4½ tbsp	4½ tbsp
Sautéed Chinese cabbage with sprouts	2 heaped tbsp	2 heaped tbsp	2 heaped tbsp
Steamed green beans	4 tbsp	4 tbsp	4 tbsp
Banana Chocolate-Chip Cake (page 260)	1 serving	1 serving	1 serving
TOTAL CALORIES	**1,484**	**1,998**	**2,486**

Day 12

MENU	CALORIE LEVELS		
	1,500	**2,000**	**2,500**
Breakfast			
Fruit Smoothie (page 110)	1 serving	1 serving	2 servings
Snack			
Creamy Carrot–Potato Soup (page 88)	1 serving	1 serving	1 serving
Bread	1 slice	2 slices	2 slices
Lunch			
Sandwich on wholemeal bread	2 slices	2 slices	4 slices
with Herb Cheese Spread (page 107) and	2 tbsp	2 tbsp	3 tbsp
Mixed salad with 1 tbsp low-cal dressing	1 small bowl	1 medium bowl	1 medium bowl
Snack			
Skimmed milk	200 ml/7 fl oz	200 ml/7 fl oz	200 ml/7 fl oz
Digestive biscuits	2	3	3
Dinner			
Tomatoes and Courgettes with Meatballs (page 136)	1 serving	2 servings	2 servings
Romaine lettuce	1 handful	1 handful	1 handful
with low-calorie vinaigrette	1 tbsp	1 tbsp	1 tbsp
Wholemeal Italian bread	1 slice	3 slices	2 slices
125 g/4 oz pot low-fat vanilla yogurt	1	1	1
TOTAL CALORIES	**1,520**	**1,916**	**2,470**

Day 13

MENU	CALORIE LEVELS		
	1,500	**2,000**	**2,500**
Breakfast			
Scrambled eggs	1	2	2
Home Baked Chips (page 53)	1 serving	1 serving	1 serving
Back bacon	1 rasher	2 rashers	2 rashers
Wholemeal toast	1 slice	2 slices	3 slices
Snack			
Frozen juice bar	1	1	1
Skimmed milk	200 ml/7 fl oz	200 ml/7 fl oz	200 ml/7 fl oz
Digestive biscuits	2	3	3
Lunch			
Tofu Burger (page 78)	1 serving	1 serving	2 servings
Carrot, cut into sticks	1	2	2
Snack			
Air-popped popcorn with	3 cups	3 cups	3 cups
Parmesan cheese	1 tbsp	1 tbsp	1 tbsp
Dinner			
Lemon Red Snapper with Jalapeños (page 169)	1 serving	1 serving	2 servings
Baked sweet potato	1	2	2
Steamed green beans	5 tbsp	5 tbsp	5 tbsp
with pistachios	20	20	20
Pear	1	1	1
TOTAL CALORIES	**1,597**	**1,952**	**2,444**

MENU

MENU	CALORIE LEVELS		
	1,500	**2,000**	**2,500**
Breakfast			
Easy Ham and Cheese 'Soufflé' (page 50)	1 serving	1 serving	1 serving
Cantaloupe melon	¼	¼	¼
Snack			
Wholemeal digestive biscuits	2	4	4
Peanut butter	1 heaped tsp	1 heaped tsp	1 heaped tsp
Lunch			
Baked Black Beans with Orzo (page 79)	1 serving	1½ servings	2 servings
Wholemeal bread roll	1	1	2
Mandarin orange sections	4 tbsp	4 tbsp	4 tbsp
Snack			
Wholemeal toast	1 slice	1 slice	2 slices
Sliced turkey breast	1 slice	2 slices	3 slices
Dinner			
Prawn Risotto (page 187)	1 serving	1½ servings	2 servings
Steamed broccoli with lemon and garlic	4 tbsp	4 tbsp	4 tbsp
Double Chocolate Chip Fudge Brownie (page 262)	1 serving	1 serving	2 servings
TOTAL CALORIES	**1,512**	**1,936**	**2,479**

eat up
slim down

Index

Page numbers in *italics* indicate text in a box.

C

$\mathcal{E}$

Credits

Photography

Interior photographs by Mitch Mandel/ Rodale Images, except photos on pages 68, 152, and 172 © by Lisa Koenig, and 'After' photos on the following pages:

Page 2: Alan Wychuck/Liaison Agency

Page 27: Layne Kennedy

Page 37: Will Yurman/Liaison Agency

Page 45: Phil Matt/Liaison Agency

Page 84: © Lemay Design and Photography

Page 100: © Alan Levenson/Corbis

Page 104: © Jimmy Williams

Page 124: Bruce Kluckhohn/Liaison Agency

Page 174: 1996 © Capital Cities/ABC, Inc.

Page 196: © Robert Neumann

Page 214: © Don Chambers/Pelosi & Chambers

Photography Props

We would like to thank the following companies that generously donated props for the photography in this book.

Emile Henry
(Visit their web site at www.emilehenry.com)

- Portobellos and Goat Cheese (page 99): baking dish
- Taco Bake (page 139): baking dish and bowls
- Confetti Meat Loaf (page 177): baking dish
- El Dorado Casserole (page 179): baking dish
- Seafood Chowder (page 185): baking dish
- Vegetable Lasagne (page 193): baking dish

Mesa International

- Vegetable Quesadillas (page 77): jug
- Salmon Chowder (page 91): salad plate
- Mediterranean Pasta (page 151): bowl
- White Chicken Chilli (page 171): bowl
- Seafood Chowder (page 185): soup bowl

Pfaltzgraff
(Visti their web site at www.pfaltzgraff.com)

- Blueberry Brunch Cake (page 67): large bowl
- Hot Bean Dip (page 109): bowl
- Crunchy Baked Chicken (page 118): plate
- Fettuccine with Chicken Sauce (page 144): cutlery
- Veggie Cassoulet (page 199): baking dish and plates

Wedgwood
(Available in shops and by visiting their web site at www.wedgwood.co.uk)

- Lemon Wedges (page 63): small plate
- Breakfast in a Cup (page 67): small plate
- Tomato-Crab Bake (page 103): small plate
- Tomatoes and Courgettes with Meatballs (page 137): soup plate
- Warm Pepper and Pork Salad (page 243): white plate, salt and pepper shakers
- Chocolate-Raspberry Avalanche Cake (page 257): plate, jug, and bowl
- Hamantaschen and Chocolate-Pecan Meringues (page 267): plates, cups, and saucers

Recipes

The recipes for Chopra Cereal (page 65) and Tofu Burgers (page 78) are adapted from *Perfect Weight* by Deepak Chopra, MD. Copyright © 1994 Deepak Chopra, MD. Reprinted by permission of Harmony Books, a division of Random House, Inc.

The recipe for Canyon Ranch Burgers (page 92) is adapted from *Canyon Ranch Cooking – Bringing the Spa Home* by Jeanne Jones. Copyright © 1998 Jeanne Jones. Reprinted by permission of HarperCollins Publishers, Inc.

The recipe for Corn Crepes with Strawberry Sauce (page 271) is adapted from *Rancho la Puerta Cookbook* by Bill Wavrin. Copyright © 1998 Golden Door. Used by permission of Broadway Books, a division of Random House, Inc.

The recipes for Lamb Chops with Herb Apricot Sauce (page 145) and Chinese Chicken in a Bag (page 168) are adapted from *Healthy Cooking for People Who Don't Have Time to Cook* by Jeanne Jones. Copyright © 1997 Jeanne Jones. Reprinted by permission of Rodale Inc.

The recipes for Linguine Montecatini (page 148) and Sweet Potato Mash (page 212) are adapted from Jackie Abreu, chef, the Spa at Doral, Miami.

The recipe for Cod Dijon (page 153) is adapted from *7 Steps to Wellness: Control Your Weight, Control Your Life!!* by Howard J. Rankin, PhD. Reprinted by permission of Howard J. Rankin, PhD, StepWise Press.

The recipe for Joan's Jewel of the Nile Chicken Kebabs (page 175) is adapted from *Healthy Cooking* by Joan Lunden. Copyright © 1996 New Life Entertainment, Inc. Reprinted by permission of Little, Brown and Company (Inc.).

The recipes for Aubergine Parmesan (page 202), Twice-Baked Potatoes (page 209), and Almond-Mushroom Rice Casserole (page 219) are adapted from Marsha Hudnall, MS, RD, nutrition director at Green Mountain at Fox Run, a women's centre for healthy living without dieting, located in Ludlow, Vermont.

The recipe for Persian Cucumber Salad (page 228) is from *Healing the Hungry Self: The Diet-Free Solution to Lifelong Weight Management* by Deirdra Price, PhD. Reprinted by permission of Plume Publishing.

The recipes for Creamy Ranch Dressing (page 233) and Baked Apple with Papaya Sauce (page 274) are adapted from *The Golden Door Cookbook* by Michel Stroot. Copyright © 1997 Golden Door. Used by permission of Broadway Books, a division of Random House, Inc.

The recipes for Old-Fashioned Potato Salad (page 250), Carrot Cake with Cream Cheese Icing (page 258), and John's Gingerbread (page 268) are adapted from *Everyday Cooking with Dr. Dean Ornish* by Dean Ornish, MD. Copyright © 1996 Dean Ornish, MD. Reprinted by permission of HarperCollins Publishers, Inc.

The recipes for Peanut Butter Cake with Chocolate Frosting (page 254) and Double Chocolate Chip Fudge Brownies (page 262) are adapted from *A Guy's Guide to Great Eating: Big-Flavored, Fat-Reduced Recipes for Men Who Love to Eat* by Don Mauer. Copyright © 1999 Don Mauer & Associates, Inc. Reprinted by permission of Houghton Mifflin Company. All rights reserved.

Notes

Notes